stolen women

stolen women

Reclaiming Our Sexuality,
Taking Back Our Lives

Dr. Gail Elizabeth Wyatt

John Wiley & Sons, Inc.
New York • Chichester • Weinheim • Brisbane • Singapore • Toronto

Copyright © 1997 by Gail Elizabeth Wyatt. All rights reserved.
Published by John Wiley & Sons, Inc.
Published simultaneously in Canada.

This publication is designed to provide accurate and authoritative
information in regard to the subject matter covered. It is sold with the
understanding that the publisher is not engaged in rendering professional services. If professional advice or other expert assistance is
required, the services of a competent professional person should be
sought.

Library of Congress Cataloging-in-Publication Data

Wyatt, Gail Elizabeth.
    Stolen women : reclaiming our sexuality, taking back our lives / Gail
    Elizabeth Wyatt.
        p.   cm.
    Includes bibliographical references and index.
    ISBN 0-471-29717-8 (cloth : alk. paper)
    1. Afro-American women—Sexual behavior.   I. Title.
HQ29.W856   1997
306.7'089'96073—dc21   97-7409

Printed in the United States of America

10 9 8 7 6 5 4 3 2 1

My life is a journey

My ancestors and others show me the way

Like my mother, I chose my own path

For Lauren and Darren, I finish my sister's dream

With Lance, Lacey, and Gavin, I leave behind more than I received

God protects me, and

Lewis lights my way home with his love

Contents

Introduction   ix

Acknowledgments   xix

Part One
Redefining Our Image

1   Stolen Woman   3
      Surviving Our History

2   The Price We Pay   27
      Captive to the Stereotypes

Part Two
Understanding Our Sexuality

3   Doctor–Nurse   47
      The Role of Childhood Sex Play

4   Childhood Messages   67
      Gaining Permission to Have
      Sexual Knowledge

5   Our Adolescent Development   89
      Learning to Be a Lady

6   Ready or Not   121
         Learning to Control Our Bodies

7   Becoming Women   149
         The Role of Relationships in
         Our Adult Sexuality

8   Giving Our Love   171
         Surviving Our Choices

Part Three
Taking Back Our Lives

9   How Are You Doing?   199
         Taking Sexual Responsibility

10   Putting It All Together   223
         Affirming Our Sexuality

         Appendix I   231
         About the Studies

         Appendix II   237
         Background and Statistics

         References   261

         Sources   272

         Index   281

Introduction

Why I Wrote This Book

I bring over twenty-two years of professional experience as a sex researcher and therapist—and a lifetime of experiences as a black woman—to the book you are about to read. *Stolen Women* is a portrait of African-American female sexuality, documenting not only what it is, but telling the story of how it came to be, and how it shapes our lives.

There are no other books like this one about our sexuality. The few that come closest are based on interviews with a small number of people whom the author either knows or met in private practice. It would have been fairly easy for me to select just a few interesting individuals and write about them, but too much of that kind of work has already been done. What we need is an objective framework of information that can help us gain perspective on our lives. This book attempts to fill that gap by representing our experiences across seven generations, based on my clinical research and in-depth interviews with hundreds of women from 18 to 80 years old.

In Part I, "Redefining Our Image," I trace sexual images of black women through nearly five centuries and show how stereotypes that are centuries old still threaten our modern sexuality.

In Part II, "Understanding Our Sexuality," I explore our

formative sexual experiences, report their actual outcomes across our lifespans, point out the cultural patterns expressed in our behaviors, and uncover the principles and knowledge that enable us to take responsibility for ourselves and our sexuality no matter what society expects or what has happened to us in the past.

You will encounter several exemplary lives in this section, but if you are looking for a single ideal notion of womanhood, you won't find one here. I believe we are too diverse and far too complicated to fit neatly into one image to which we all could or even would want to aspire. It's much more important to get at the reasons why so many of us, like the women I have come to know and care about, need healing and insight. You will meet many of them here, including:

- Confident and independent Peggy, coping with her friends, her new teenage body, and two loving parents trying to teach her to be a lady.
- Heather, contemplating suicide at age 25 because her memories of childhood sexual abuse will not subside.
- June, settling for romantic flings that sometimes last for years—until the guys fall out of love and go on to marry someone else.
- Mickey, a sensitive college student, hiding behind baggy jeans, workshirts, and combat boots to blend in better with her "homeboys."
- Sandra, small, shy, and pregnant at age 15, pausing when I ask here what it means to "have a baby for a guy" and replying, "It means that you care."
- Marte, sleeping with men to have something to talk about, but still in a genuine romantic relationship with her girlfriend, Jean.
- Maya, finally unlocking the secret of lasting love with her husband after almost losing what they had together.

Perhaps these lives sound familiar. I try to portray them factually, not leaving anything out. Women's experiences are diverse as well as sexual, and it's time we recognize it and acknowledge how that diversity and sexuality may be relevant to our own experiences. Some stories may disgust or surprise you; some will amuse and enlighten you. I try to make the lessons of our individual struggles available to you. When possible, I link them to cultural patterns in the distant past in order to show how similar our cultural beliefs and practices have remained or how different they have become as we've struggled as an African people to survive sexual slavery and its aftermath.

In Part III, "Taking Back Our Lives," I encourage your self-awareness. Take my Sexual Responsibility Test and identify your personal problems, challenges, and unexplored potential as you continue on your private path through life as a unique sexual being, affirming the best of us across generations.

About My Research

Even though many of my findings have been published in professional journals, cited hundreds of times by other sex researchers and writers, presented at international conferences, and reported in the *New York Times, Ebony, Essence, Emerge, Vanity Fair, USA Today*, the *Los Angeles Times*, and other national media, this is the first time I have attempted to share them with other African-American women, our girls, our families, the men and women who love us, and the many people who have important reasons to care about us.

I have been fascinated by the mystery of black sexuality all of my life. As the granddaughter of a Methodist minister, I grew up in a very conservative Southern family that sheltered my sister and me from the world, but encouraged us to create our own. As little girls, we spent hours in our backyard playing with dolls. Eventually, of course, I got to know the outside world; and when I did, I was especially curious about people who looked more or less like us.

What I found was extremely contradictory. On television, I saw the comedians like Rochester, the spineless valet on "The Jack Benny Show," in contrast to Sapphire, the domineering wife on "Amos 'n' Andy." Looking at movies such as *Gone with the Wind* and *Pinky*, I discovered sexless, saintly, confused, or victimized black women. Then as a teenager, I saw mostly the opposite: violent, sex-obsessed characters in the black exploitation films. In all those years, no matter what images I saw, I wondered, Who were these people? Where did they live? I didn't know anyone who acted the way they did, so I wondered, Was my world the world, or was I missing something? Today, I find myself asking similar questions when I see sex-saturated music videos such as "Baby Got Back."

Eventually I figured out that truth always defies oversimplification. At historically black Fisk University, I learned not to accept the media's version of black people, but to observe and document black life instead. By the time I had completed my doctoral work in psychology at the University of California at Los Angeles, I was on a mission. I knew just what I had to do. I would become an expert on the social and cultural issues that affect our mental health, including what I now understood were all those sexual stereotypes I had noticed as a child. I broadened my clinical training to include sex therapy and sex education. Yet once again, I was struck by the gap between the reality I knew and the way we were portrayed.

When I looked for useful information about healthy black female sexuality, I found only descriptions of the sexual practices of poor women that compared them to middle-class suburban whites. The comparisons made us seem almost tragic, unlike the many individuals I knew who enjoyed healthy, expressive sex lives. Clearly, the full range of our experiences had not been studied. Having learned that the roots of human sexuality lie in the survival needs of the past, I tried to gain some insight into the traumatic impact of slavery on our sexuality in America. I found virtually no information on that subject either.

So I decided to find out for myself and began to do the research, determined to replace the sketchy, distorted images of black sexuality with accurate information at last. Few researchers before or since have attempted to do what I did in conducting the research on which this book is based. I set out to:

- include middle-class and affluent women in my studies with poor women and not just compare them,
- take cultural differences between us into account, factoring in our diverse personal backgrounds and specific life experiences, and
- trace the early patterns of our sexuality across our lifespans.

Beginning in 1980, I studied my first representative sample of 126 African-American and, for perspective, 122 white women ages 18 to 36 in Los Angeles County using the Wyatt Sexual History Questionnaire (WSHQ). I asked literally hundreds of questions about what they had learned about sex throughout their lives and why they engaged in the sexual behaviors that they reported. We chose to be very thorough in our interviews rather than to ask fewer questions of more women. It was not my intent simply to describe sexual practices but to understand the circumstances in which they occurred. In that study, I began to see certain cultural patterns in my respondents' sexual behavior.

In 1994, a decade later, my colleagues and I asked many of the same questions to a second representative sample of 305 African-American, 300 white, and 300 Latina women ages 18 to 50 in Los Angeles County. Similar patterns appeared again and again, regardless of when the women were born.

Even more recently, along with another research team, I used the same approach with a third sample of 71 African-American and 77 white survivors of breast cancer ages 39 to 80 in Los Angeles and Washington, D.C. Even their traumatic bouts with cancer and surgery did not alter the cultural patterns that I first noted in much younger women in my first study. You might think that these patterns would be influenced by regional differences, but in fact we did not find any differences between patterns reported in Los Angeles and those reported in Washington.

I realize that the numbers of women I have studied may seem small to you at first glance. Nonetheless, my findings give us an accurate picture of the connection between our culture and our sexuality. Further, they provide unlimited insight into the strength of the resulting patterns of behavior. For example, as a group, our basic sexual patterns did not change radically between the 1980s and the mid 1990s despite our awareness of the life-threatening consequences of AIDS. The fact that these patterns are so ingrained adds to the urgency of understanding them.

In Appendix I you will find more detailed background information on exactly how, when, where, and with whom I conducted these studies. In Appendix II and the reference section, you'll find the statistics supporting each observation. In a few chapters, I have included numerical data along with my general observations because the numbers speak louder than words.

What Else to Expect

No book, regardless of how thorough, can answer every question about a topic as broad and important as sexuality—and this one is no exception. So there are a few points I would like to make clear before we begin.

1. This is not a book about sex-related racial differences. I have learned to focus on ethnic and cultural factors, not on racial differences in sexual experiences. When I refer to African-Americans, I mean the history and cultural values we share, not our race. People all over the world have engaged in various degrees of mixing, particularly in the United States over hundreds of years. There is no way to look at every person and determine their exact racial background. Even if you identify yourself as an African-American, it does not necessarily mean that you have no ancestors from other places. You carry the genes from all the nationalities on your family tree. Placing all blacks in one category is like mixing different vegetables in a soup and refusing to acknowledge the varied ingredients. Well, you may not care what's in it, but each ingredient adds to the flavor—some more, some less.

2. This is an in-depth analysis. You might expect research of this scope to ask women if they engaged in a variety of behaviors, and simply report them. By contrast, I chose to ask women why they did or did not engage in the behaviors they reported. While it's important to report their behaviors—and I do—it's even more important to understand the reasons behind them. An in-depth analysis also allows us to better identify cultural patterns that shape subsequent decisions. I feel that the only way to debunk stereotypes and truly understand our sexuality is to learn more about what influences our decisions to express it.

3. This is a book about the lifelong effects of our early sexual experiences, not a book about every sexual experience in our lives. Our adult sexuality is essentially defined by certain critical decisions we make during childhood, adolescence, and young adulthood, including:

- when to become sexually active
- how to express our sexuality
- whether and how we should control our reproductive abilities
- the people with whom we express our sexuality
- how we use sex in our relationships

These early decisions tend to set the template for our entire sexual lives. I look closely at our decision making. I also look at what's done to, said to, or forced upon us during these early years because our sexuality is ultimately influenced as much by what we are made to do as by what we choose to do.

I also contrast women who grew up in rural versus urban areas, women who grew up poor versus those who were affluent, and those with more versus less education. These descriptions will highlight the importance of the environment on women's sexual experiences. And I describe the sexual patterns of women who were born before World War II or since the '60s, comparing my findings with the best-known sex research conducted in the early twentieth century—the Kinsey study—in an attempt to explain how patterns have or have not changed.

No doubt, there are essential lessons and sexual patterns later in life, including becoming menopausal, physically disabled, or ill with chronic or terminal diseases, that I did not include. These life experiences involve both biological and physical changes that deserve to be discussed in a book of their own.

4. This is not a book about African-American men. I acknowledge that there is equally little known about their
sexuality and even fewer studies that include them. But I
chose to focus on women for two reasons. First, to obtain
funds from the federal government to study sexuality you
must present a convincing argument telling why you are
the person to conduct that research. I elected to limit my
first study to the group with which I had had the most
experience in research, and that was women. Second, I feel
that studies of African-American men should be conducted
as carefully as I believe mine have been conducted. That
study should include African-American men making important decisions about the questions that should be asked and
what the findings mean. No one knows more about men
than men themselves do. Men deserve a book of their own,
because their experience, while similar to women's in some
respects, is also very different. Their exclusion from this book
is not meant to suggest that they should not be studied or
that they are not as important as women. They are.

Finally, this book is as much about me as it is about you.

No women are more devalued in our society than women
of color. It's been said that every woman bears the burden
of sexual stereotyping at some point during her lifetime. That
may be true; white women are often depersonalized, labeled
as less than intelligent or incompetent. But the
depersonalization of black women focuses on our sexuality
first. In our homes, in our neighborhoods, and around the
world, powerful stereotypes rooted in slavery perpetuate
myths about who we are. Society's message is that to be
black and female is to be without sexual control, to be irresponsible about our sexuality. Regardless of the circumstances, our age or our appearance, someone may assume
that we are sexually available or for sale at some price.

One day I learned this the hard way. Even though several years have passed since the incident, I still remember my shock and pain. I know I am not alone in this. The problem is that too many people, perhaps some very close to you, have the illusion that our culture condones these things:

- having sexual knowledge at a young age
- having an unusual interest in sex
- having first intercourse outside of marriage
- having a high number of sexual partners
- engaging frequently in unconventional sexual practices.

There are few books written about sex by an African-American expert, and I have written this one because I want my findings to make a difference, not because I want to harm or exploit anyone. Most important, I want to show that not everyone is a victim. You will meet women in this book who have many problems, and others who are doing just fine. This book is designed to expose myths and destroy negative stereotypes about who we are. But it does not pretend that we are perfect. Who is?

I want you to sit in my circle and let me tell you our story. Like the griots of old, I tell a story that began many centuries ago, and you must become familiar with the story in order to understand how we've survived. In telling it, I, too, am surviving. This is more than a book—it is a part of our lives, so get comfortable and experience it with me.

I'd like to think that Granddaddy Morgan is looking down from his heavenly pulpit and saying "Amen to that!"

Acknowledgments

I am standing on the shoulders of so many individuals who have helped and encouraged me to conduct my studies of African-American women's sexuality and to write this book. Early in my education, I had some powerful role models in Drs. Shirley Roberts, Henry Tomes, Reginald Jones, and Edwin Nichols, who were my first psychology professors at Fisk University. My experiences at Fisk set the template as I learned what had to be accomplished in conducting my research.

Years ago, Drs. Robert Staples and Wade Nobles were instrumental in helping me to place my work within the context of what they had begun to achieve in the areas of black sexuality and family life.

Drs. Leonard Lash and Stanley Schneider guided me through the application process of the National Institute of Mental Health Research Scientist Program and in doing so helped to shape my career as a sex researcher. The research grants that I received from NIMH, initially from the Center for Control and Prevention of Rape and currently through the Office on AIDS, would have been unattainable without the support of so many project administrators, specifically Dr. Ann Maney, who taught me so much about grant writing. Dr. Ellen Stover, director of the Office on AIDS, along with Drs. Willo Pequegnat and Leonard Midnick, as associate directors, have made it possible for me to focus on difficult research questions and to conduct work for the first time with African-American women in a scientifically rigorous manner. They have also included me in conferences where the research findings could be heard by audiences all over the world. It was this kind of support that made it possible for me to begin to both challenge traditional notions and influence research and policies relating to African-American women's sexuality and health. Dr. Delores Perron, associate director for Special Populations at NIMH, has been a tremendous advocate, working in conjunction with my funding sources to provide me with the information and support needed to continue my work. I am also indebted to Edna Hardy Hill for her advice and guidance in conducting research and negotiating through the federal funding process.

The Department of Psychiatry at UCLA, with Drs. L. J. West, Fawzy Fawzy, and Marvin Karno, provided me with a supportive research environment that was fundamental to conducting this work.

I have had the privilege of working with some outstanding research team members who have helped me to interview the women in this book and to publish my findings. None were more competent and compassionate than Drs. Stefanie Peters, Barbara Schochet, Cynthia Powell Hicks, and Ernestine Campbell, M.A. The Institute for Social Science Research, directed by Dr. Eve Fielder, with Tanya Hays, has helped with the research designs, interviewer training, and coordination in the 1994 research project.

I am deeply indebted to Madelyn Morel and Barbara Lowenstein for sharing my vision for this book and representing me so well in the publication process, and to Norman Kurtz for legal representation. Linda Villarosa did a masterful job of helping to present a convincing synopsis of the book.

Acknowledgments

Christopher Bailey worked tirelessly to prepare the manuscript, and Taneka Shehee, M.A., coordinated the data citations and library research. She found some marvelous literature that has been included here. Dr. Donald Guthrie provided expert statistical consultation and Gwen Gordon managed the data with her usual precision. Understanding its potential contribution, this team was uniformly enthusiastic about completing this project.

Debbie Jerkowitz taught me so much about the editorial process and challenged me to shape the book into the manuscript that I wanted it to be. Thanks, Debbie, for making this effort so pleasant and informative.

I have benefited enormously from the guidance and expert assistance of Carole Hall, associate publisher and editor in chief at John Wiley & Sons. Her commitment, unlimited knowledge, wisdom, and interest provided me with the technical and emotional support necessary to complete this project. From our first meeting, she shared my vision and never ceased to encourage me to translate the research findings into a book that everyone could understand. I am also grateful to the entire team at Wiley for their competent management of all aspects of the publishing and marketing process. Paula Woods and Felix Liddell, authors themselves, skillfully and enthusiastically helped to make the public aware of my book.

A small league of friends, namely Dr. Gloria Powell, Barbara Bass, M.S.W., and the noted author Bebe Moore Campbell, never doubted for a minute that I could write this book, work full-time, and live to tell my story. They encouraged me throughout the evolution of what you are about to read. Mr. Saunders Thompson provided the expertise needed to find biblical passages and citations.

Finally, I want to express my sincere appreciation to the women who allowed me to tell their stories. I hope that I have represented them well. While many of the experiences they shared were humorous and joyful, some were extremely painful. Yet these women had the courage to persevere because they wanted to better inform us about the past and current sexual experiences of women, particularly African-American women. In doing so, we hope that there will be more joy and respect, and less pain, for others in the future as we take back our lives.

I believe that so many wonderful people would not have allowed me to stand on their shoulders if they did not believe that I would put my heart and soul into this project. I'm very proud to say that I have.

"You can't know where you're going until you know where you've been."

An African Proverb

part one

Redefining Our Image

chapter 1

Stolen Woman

Surviving Our History

Her Story

She tried to close her mind to all the sights and sounds. It was hot and noisy. Men and women dressed in strange clothes and speaking a language she did not understand surrounded her coolly. This was auction day, and they weren't going home empty-handed.

Even chained to the others, she felt lonely. Where was her village? Where were her parents? She longed for things to be the way they had been—familiar and safe. But her life would never be the same. She had been stolen. Strangers now looked at her eyes, teeth, and breasts. Someone would come and feel the most private parts of her body to make sure that she was worth her price. Soon she would be owned by one of the strangers.

What happened on that auction block centuries ago is still unfinished business for African-American women today. In a society increasingly obsessed with sex, too many people— white and black—still hold this dangerous view: that black women must either ignore their sexuality altogether or be perpetually sexually available.

As an African-American woman, I know that this almost inevitably leads to being devalued and denied respect and information. As a sex researcher, I know that the average African-American woman lives with highly personal consequences, because throughout her childhood, adolescence, and young adulthood, her sexual development takes place either in sometimes deafening silence about her sexuality or in the midst of negative messages and expectations about

3

her ability to control it. That is the main reason I have written this book—to locate the distortions, negative messages, and cultural conflicts that have an impact on us, put them in perspective, and provide a broad understanding of how they influence our formative sexual experiences. I intend to help you look at your own sexual development more objectively and to show you the way to chart a freer, healthier course through our race- and sex-charged society.

To the degree that we allow our sexual self-image to be defined by others, we will remain, as our ancestors were, stolen women, captives not of strangers but of the past, and of our own unexamined experiences. The challenge we face is to see ourselves not as others see us or want us to be seen, but as we are, as we were, and as we want to be.

Our ancestors were probably different from the twenty Africans who were brought to America in 1617 as indentured slaves who could earn their freedom after working for a limited period of time. They were also unlike other immigrants, who came of their own accord to discover a better life. Sometime after 1619, they were captured, shipped across the Atlantic, and sold for their ability to tolerate the hot Southern climate, to work the fields, and to breed children who would, in turn, be enslaved to farm the lands and do skilled work that yielded enormous profits. Needless to say, their self-esteem had to be radically altered to make the system work. And that was not all.

Slavery ripped into the hearts and souls of African women, altering their culture, their families, and most intimately, their sexuality. It would be naive to think that time has healed those wounds or to believe that they are no longer relevant to the sexual experience of African-American women today. It is a central fact of our sexuality that we are the descendants of African girls, teenagers, and young women who stared out from the auction blocks so long ago. But something is missing from this picture—the image of our ancestors as a free people, without chains, before slavery changed their destinies. That is the image we need to recover as a first step toward seeing our history, our culture, and finally, ourselves through our own eyes instead of through the eyes of others who are less informed.

Africa—The World She Remembered

Our story begins in Africa, in the sixteenth century. Sex was an essential and sacred part of life's plan. Timing and respect were everything. Self-pleasuring, or self-arousal, was not condoned. In some societies, mutual sexual exploration was allowed, but there were strict rules governing the person with whom you could experiment. In other societies childhood sex play was not allowed, and punishment for breaking the rules was severe. It was all right to have sex before marriage if your partner was someone who met your parents' approval, someone you intended to marry, or your mate in a ritual ceremony. Societies like the Hausa and the Nupe of Nigeria forbade sexual contact before marriage. A man who had sex with you before the appointed time and spoiled the ceremonies that marked a turning point in your life was viewed as a thief who had stolen something precious from you.

If sex without marriage was sometimes tolerated, having a child out of wedlock generally was not. In fact, tribal law often branded it morally wrong. Such a pregnancy brought shame on the girl and her family, even though society held the father financially responsible when the child was born.

Modesty and privacy were respected in African societies, even though beliefs about specific parts of the human body suggested otherwise to Western missionaries. For example, breasts were not regarded as sexual objects but as symbols of life. Therefore it was not unusual for mothers to nurse their babies in public or for women to be seen bare-

chested. The buttocks and genitals, however, were covered.
If they weren't, a woman was considered to be naked. Protocol was both important and pervasive. The Nyakyusa
society considered it offensive to look at, discuss, or joke
about your parents' genitals. For Africans, then, the body
was sacred.

"I Am Because We Are"

Group solidarity was deeply important. It might even be said
that group identity determined individual identity. The African proverb "I am because we are, and since we are, therefore I am" is revealing. It illustrates how group membership defined and nurtured personal identity. For example,
a woman's identity was enhanced by her marriage to a man
who, with his family, had the respect of the tribe. Similarly,
tribal membership could enhance self-pride. Individuals
assumed responsibilities and made sacrifices for the good
of the group. Children were often cared for not only by their
mother and extended family members but by other women
as well.

The older women in the tribe taught girls their responsibilities as wives and mothers. They also taught them when
to have sex and when to refrain from it (while nursing a
baby or until the child began to walk), and in this way young
married women learned how to plan and space their children. When girls became women, they knew what was expected of them, for their elders had prepared them well for
the roles they would assume.

Although they were instructed not to have sex except
under the right circumstances, children were curious about
sex nonetheless. Older women frequently told young girls
tales to discourage sexual curiosity and experimentation,
and used misinformation to frighten the girls into retaining
their virginity. Fear was supposed to override curiosity. For
example, according to Ifi Amaduime, a noted author: "The

sight of a penis was said to be enough to make a girl pregnant—it did not have to enter the vagina to land her in trouble."

The Rites of Passage

From the sixteenth to the nineteenth century, Africa was composed of many societies with diverse practices, but some customs were shared by all. The following principles of African sexuality illustrate the attitudes and practices that were prevalent in some West African societies before Africans were abducted and brought to the New World. Numerous ceremonies prepared girls for their adult responsibilities and roles as women, though some of the ways in which they were prepared were unbelievably harmful and dangerous to their health. The specific customs, which varied widely from one society to another, ranged from the Krobo society in Ghana, which primarily educated girls in the duties they would assume as adults, to societies in which female circumcision (also known as female genital mutilation) was the principal ritual. Among the Nandi and several other tribes, traditional rituals of circumcision may not have occurred until girls reached the ages of 14 to 16, when they were ready for marriage. In some West African societies, these rituals occurred mainly in infancy. But the majority of them took place when a girl was between the ages of 4 and 8.

Female circumcision could range from clitoridectomy, or removal of part of the clitoris, to excision, in which the clitoris and part of the labia minora are removed. In infibulation, the most extreme form of circumcision, the clitoris was removed, the labia were cut, and the vulva was sewn together. A small hole was left for draining urine and menstrual blood.

Little has been written about how girls and women,

circumcised or infibulated in Africa and as captured slaves, were first treated in America. According to Soroya Mire, the Somalian filmmaker who produced *Fire Eyes,* a film that depicts this practice in Africa and other parts of the world, there is evidence that, somehow, either female circumcision or knowledge of it was passed down among the slaves. Alice Walker, in an interview with Pratibha Parmer, her coauthor of *Warrior Marks,* wondered what happened to pregnant infibulated women on slave ships during the middle passage from Africa to America. Without someone on board who had knowledge of how to reopen the vaginal canal, the babies, and certainly their mothers, died a horrible death.

This practice of female circumcision is a controversial issue today, as Alice Walker's recent book, *Possessing the Secret of Joy,* so vividly illustrates. Many denounce circumcision as a form of female genital mutilation because it can increase the risk of infection, create problems in childbearing, and alter or decrease a woman's capacity for sexual pleasure. It is mentioned here solely to describe how girls were prepared for womanhood in some of the regions from which Africans came before the early nineteenth century. Some were simply taught their roles as women, but others were physically altered.

Why would any society do this to its girls? Some tribes were concerned with hygiene, and they believed that the external genitalia made a woman "unclean." Others wanted girls to remain virgins until the proper time and thought that circumcision would control their sexual urges. Some thought circumcision would protect females from sexually aggressive men, making them more difficult to penetrate and therefore less desirable. Today we deplore these practices, but for African women who grew up in societies where circumcision was condoned, it was often viewed as an inevitable, predictable rite of passage that underscored the value of their sexuality.

These rites also marked a girl's passage from childhood

to adulthood and represented a legacy shared with other girls, their mothers, and their female ancestors. Though the specific traditions varied from one African society to another and some practices were undoubtedly harmful to the girls' physical and emotional well-being, each girl took pride in being a part of this legacy.

Treasured, Protected, and Prepared

African women were accustomed to living within strict sexual boundaries. Sexual contact between certain people was prohibited. Sexual relations were not permitted between a man and his mother-in-law, for instance; between a woman and her father-in-law, or between teenage brothers and sisters. In some tribes, such as the Masai, when a man was infertile, had been absent for long periods of time, or had died, his brother or a family friend performed sexual functions with his wife. But these were sacred and respectable relationships with a purpose—mainly procreation and the continuity of life. The rules regarding father-child and mother-child relationships were equally explicit, and sexual boundaries were clearly drawn.

There were sexual practices that were not condoned, such as adultery, rape, incest, or homosexual relationships. Intimacy with a forbidden relative or sex with domestic animals was also taboo. These practices resulted in severe punishment.

The family unit was solidified by marriage. Ultimately, sexual pleasure was considered an obligation between young men and women, and children were the expected result. Parents helped choose an eligible mate, usually by the mutual agreement of both families, and prepared their children for the responsibilities of married life. Each marriage ceremony signaled the end of immaturity and celebrated the beginning of a prized young person's adulthood and productivity.

Many people do not condone all of the sexual practices that took place long ago and continue today because we are familiar with the deleterious effects of these practices. We know that altering a woman's genitalia can result in severe problems in her bodily functions, make sexual intercourse painful if not impossible, increase the risks of childbirth, and multiply her chances of contracting life-threatening infections. There is no denying that some of the traditional rules and customs of these African societies resulted in harmful practices, but there were some very positive benefits that shouldn't be overlooked. The point to be learned from this part of our history is that an African woman not only knew what to do and to expect but that she understood the ritual purposes and social consequences of these rules as well. Moreover, she knew that she was treasured and protected.

White missionaries in sixteenth-century Africa failed to recognize this. Based on their own values, they looked at the sexual practices and rituals established by African communities and assumed that they were sinful. Because sex in African societies was practiced outside of religious control, the missionaries assumed that the "heathens" could not control their sexual urges. Trusted and respected members of American society confirmed the missionaries' impressions. In the sixteenth century, a noted Western physician described African women as "hot, unconstitutioned ladies." The literature of this time was full of such observations, which were used to help justify and institutionalize slavery.

The New World—The New Sexual Order

The institution of slavery irrevocably altered the sexuality of the stolen Africans and their descendants. Over the next several hundred years, a new sexual order emerged for black women in the New World that sabotaged the old in six ways:

1. Sex Became a Negative Experience

Taken out of its cultural and natural context, sex became
something to be dreaded. It was no longer an experience
marked by family approval, sanctioned as a function of marriage, or celebrated by rituals. As a slave, you had no rights
over your body. Your first sexual experience was likely to be
a rape. As a result, virginity was desired but not expected of
women. Regardless of the circumstance, it was assumed that
you wanted to have sex with white men:

> Sexual intercourse between blacks and whites seems to
> have begun as soon as the former were introduced into
> America. Many white men and women came to think of
> black women as basically immoral "loose and easy," [and]
> deliberately enticed white men.

In reality, however, in order to avoid being severely
punished, black women had to submit to any white man
who made sexual demands on them. If some were given a
choice, Cynthia's decision was typical. She could either accept or reject her master's proposal to accompany him to
another state and become his mistress and housekeeper. If
she rejected him, however, he threatened to sell her as a
field hand to the worst plantation. Fear of reprisals made
these choices a no-win situation. Yet in spite of the consequences, many women did resist sexual advances:

> This particular girl [in Kentucky] however, could not be
> coerced or forced, and consequently, she was violently at-
> tacked and beaten. In the struggle, she grabbed a knife
> "and with it sterilized him, and from that injury he died
> the next day.". . . The girl was put to death.

Darlene Hine, the author of *Black Women in America: A
Historical Encyclopedia,* recounts the story of Celia, a young
black girl in Missouri:

Celia was fourteen years old in 1850, when she was bought by Robert Newsome, a 70-year-old farmer. On the way home from the slave auction, he raped her. He raped her repeatedly after that until the night of June 23, 1855, when she resisted him with force. At that time, Celia, 19 years old, was pregnant for the third time and had been ill for at least four months. According to court testimony, Celia had told Newsome that she would hurt him if he raped her while she was still sick. Despite her warning, he came to her cabin that night to force sexual intercourse upon her. Celia, who armed herself with a stick, struck him twice. He died immediately thereafter, and Celia was charged with first-degree murder.

In Missouri, at this time, the law stated that it was unlawful for a man to force sex upon any woman. The law also provided that if a woman killed a man who was trying to rape her, it could be considered a legitimate act of self-defense, not a crime. Celia's lawyer appealed to this, arguing that because the law protected "any woman" in this situation, the legislators must protect slave women, too. The judge disagreed. Celia was sentenced to death and hanged.

If you did not resist, sex became a means to an end: special living quarters, better food, or small gifts from men who sought your favors. Still, submitting to a white man was risky. If these women began to "think too much of themselves" and demonstrated that they saw themselves as being more than slaves, they were often sold to other plantations by the wives and mothers of the men who had sexual relationships with them.

Captive women could not necessarily control the men with whom they had children, but there is evidence that they made difficult decisions about whether to give birth to children who would themselves be slaves. While some women were described as "honored to have the marsa," there are also numerous accounts of others who used a variety of devices (such as a roll of rags and sticks inserted into the vagina, or herbs and roots) or exercised excessively to terminate unwanted pregnancies. A black mother in 1863 reported: "I used to have one [baby] every Christmas . . . but when I had six, I put a stop to it, and had only one every other year."

In her novel *Beloved,* Toni Morrison explored this issue, contradicting the myth that enslaved women did not resist the loss of control of their sexuality and their reproductive rights. Their decisions may have been limited, but some women assumed as much control as they could when faced with the possibility of bearing or raising children only to have them abused or sold away.

This pressure increased after 1808, when legislation against importing slaves created increased demand. Masters who specialized in trading slaves became slave breeders. Concentrated heavily in states along the Atlantic coast and in border states, breeding was not simply a matter of slaves impregnating slaves. James Roberts, a freed African, described how breeding was accomplished on the plantation where he lived: "[Fifty] to 60 slave women were kept solely for Whites to impregnate them. From these women, 20 to 25 children were born and sold away when they were ready for market." A higher price could be demanded for children who were fathered by whites than for those who were fathered by slaves. So it was actually better business to mix the genes of Africans and whites.

Deborah White, the author of *Ain't I a Woman,* described how white Southerners bragged about their "breeding wenches" the way they bragged about their horses, cows, and mules. In her writings there are slaves' recollections of black women being valued like prize animals.

James Madison, the former president of the United States, did not conceal his pride in his slave women. One-third of his slaves were under 5 years of age, which indicates that breeding took place on his plantation as well.

2. Privacy and Modesty Were Not Respected

According to one eyewitness, "The clothing of slaves is in many cases comfortable, and in many cases it was far from being so. I have very often seen slaves, whose tattered rags were neither comfortable or decent." Children sometimes went naked until they were big enough to work.

Because they received constant beatings, many blacks had scars and unhealed wounds on their bodies:

> Mrs. Barr . . . saw a Negro girl about 13 years old, waiting around the table, with a single garment—and that in cold weather; arms and bare feet wretchedly swollen, arms burnt, and full of sores from exposure. All the Negroes under [Puryear's] care made a wretched appearance.

Being naked became commonplace. It was not unusual to see a woman who had been "stripped naked, tied to a stake and whipped with a hard saw or club, which was eventually broken over her body." Respect for your body was no longer determined by moral and social protocol. Deborah White describes how the bodies of women were handled at auction. Their stomachs and breasts were often kneaded to determine their fertility. Auctioneers invited potential owners to feel their ribs, look inside their mouths, and examine their teeth to determine their fitness for work.

For Africans, privacy and modesty had no place in this new world. Women in the fields often had to lift their skirts in order to bend and work effectively—an act that was frequently taken as an indication of their willingness to exhibit themselves. Similarly, it was difficult to maintain much privacy within the small, crowded slave quarters or dormitories that held from ten to one hundred men. The buildings resembled a tenement; the rooms were small, unlighted, unheated, and poorly constructed. Families were usually housed together. Young children sometimes slept in a different area from young men and women—an indication that, when possible, the black captives attempted to provide at least some degree of privacy for themselves.

Other incidents made it clear that our bodies were not regarded with the same respect that was accorded other women. Female slaves were used as human guinea pigs for physicians who were attempting to perfect gynecological surgeries during the slave era. For example, between 1845 and 1849, Anarcha, a slave, endured three hundred gynecological surgeries in a private hospital in the backyard of a physician who ultimately applied his techniques to wealthy white women. While these surgeries were performed on the slaves free of charge, the effect they had on the women and their bodies must have been endured at a tremendous cost to their health.

3. Group Solidarity Was Difficult to Maintain

Africans and their descendants had to use indirect methods to protect one another. They even relied on musical lyrics as a means of communication. For example, the words of Negro spirituals relayed information unbeknownst to whites who heard them, focusing on impending danger or plans to escape slavery through the underground railroad to "safe havens" in the North. A direct expression of concern from or for the group was rarely successful, as this story points out:

> Maria was a thirteen-year-old house servant. One day, receiving no response to her call, the mistress began searching the house for her. Finally, she opened the parlor door, and there was the child with her master. . . . The mistress beat the child and locked her in the smokehouse. For two weeks the girl was constantly whipped. . . . Some of the elderly servants attempted to plead with the mistress on Maria's behalf. . . . The mistress' reply was typical: "She'll know better in the future. After I've done with her, she'll never do the like again, through ignorance."

One of the greatest obstacles to maintaining a solid group identity resulted from the division of labor between the slave owner's house and the fields. If you worked in the house, you were more likely to be better clothed and fed, and you could develop special skills. Your children sometimes had opportunities to learn to read and write, and they had less strenuous housework.

There were consequences, however, for the privilege of being a house slave. The closer your proximity to the big house, the more likely it was that you were involved in a sexual liaison with a white family member on a routine basis. These unions created children whose skin color, features, and hair texture confirmed that sex was part of the bargain for being a house slave. This fair-skinned population was encouraged by their masters to regard themselves as better than those who toiled in the fields. In reality, their mothers suffered "privileged abusive or coerced relationships." Nevertheless, the schism that resulted from alleged class differences based on skin color grew both within and outside of the slave quarters.

In essence, group solidarity, particularly the historical pattern of drawing on group membership for individual identity ("I am because we are . . ."), became more precarious. Self-preservation was sometimes maintained at the expense of someone else. And frequently the group was powerless to protect the individual from the master.

Needless to say, there was little group solidarity among black and white women, either. The image of the childlike and fragile white woman who could not endure hard labor slowly replaced expectations that white women could labor in the fields, even sustain a passionate sexual relationship with their husbands. What they either could not or would not do, black women were called upon to do. Both women— black and white—became important pieces of the fabric of life in the growing agricultural South, but always in contrast to each other.

4. Women Were Often Unprepared for Their Roles

By 1850, the rituals of preparing girls for their roles as African women had been outlawed in America. With the passing of time, new training replaced the traditional socialization of girls by women. Many of the old customs were not tolerated by slave owners, and slaves risked severe punishment if they practiced African rituals, which some of them did.

In spite of all the hardships the women knew their daughters would encounter, they generally did not inform them about normal sexual development or about their own emerging sexuality. In Herbert Gutman's *The Black Family from Slavery to Freedom—1750 to 1925*, one woman, remembering her discovery of menstruation, recalled: "When it first came on, I ran . . . trying to make it stop. . . . I was trying to stop it for I didn't know whether I was going to get a killing for it or not. I didn't know what it was." Mothers might explain that babies come from "hollow logs." Real information, however, was withheld until it was felt to be necessary. Because of the impending trauma that slave mothers knew their daughters would encounter, theirs was not a normal human existence. As a result, the descendants of Africa's stolen women did not know what to expect of their bodies as they matured and entered puberty. But in America there was no proper time to be initiated into sex. Instruction occurred whenever a random and often traumatic event took place; it usually conveyed what a girl should try to avoid rather than what she might look forward to experiencing.

Older men and women did teach the young about courtship rituals. The dream of establishing lasting relationships remained a weapon against despair. Through oral history, this aspect of African socialization managed to survive. In Africa, the slaves remembered, families had a lot of say in selecting their children's mates. If your parents did not raise you, who could give you permission to marry? Who could find a suitable partner for you? The answer was simple. The available elders could.

5. Sexual Contact between Family Members Was Inevitable

As a consequence of abuse and forced breeding, family ties and relationships were severely disrupted during slavery. The results were often devastating and confusing. John Blassingame, the editor of *Slave Testimony: Two Centuries of Letters, Speeches, Interviews and Autobiographies,* included this slave's comment: "My grandmother was her master's daughter, and my mother was her master's daughter; and I was my master's son."

Because families were so often separated, the inevitable sometimes occurred. Isaac D. Williams, a former slave, told of a young mother who was sold by her master to a distant plantation.

> She was forced to leave her infant son who was just beginning to walk. Nineteen years later, all ties between the two having been broken her child was sold to the same plantation. Working near each other in the field, the two strangers became attached and, after a time, were married. Some time thereafter, the mother noticed a peculiar scar on her husband's head and asked him how he got it. He told her that as a child he fell out of his mother's arms into a fire and got badly burned. "Why," screamed the poor woman, "you are my own son!"

From all accounts, these were not infrequent episodes.

Enslaved African families and their descendants were highly dependent upon the extended family to raise and care for children and one another. The extended family frequently included friends and other relations who served as surrogates for the biological parents. In their own societies, Africans were accustomed to raising one another's children. This fact no doubt helped them to endure the separation of their families and to incorporate children born of other parents into a family unit as well as they did. This is the village concept of child rearing, and it is as important today as it was hundreds of years ago.

6. Marriage Was No Longer Protected by the Family

The courts did not recognize marriage between slaves. However, that did not prevent slaves from forming commitments to each other, behaving as if they were married, and using the terms *husband* and *wife*. For slaves who wished to live together or have a public ceremony celebrating their marriage, permission had to be obtained from the slave owner(s). Husbands and wives often belonged to different owners and might live apart on different plantations or elsewhere if one of them was free.

Given that slaves were not allowed to marry legally, the bonds that did form were based primarily on the level of emotional commitment two people had for each other and for their children. All the same, a husband's authority over his family was severely limited. He could not even protect his wife or children from sexual abuse:

> I knew a man by the name of Ben Kidd—a desperate mean man to his slaves who had three or four slave women, and some of them he had children by. . . . He made one of his women tend [a] stallion and used to meet her at that barn. She had a husband, too; but that made no difference; he used her whenever he saw fit.

Nor could a slave husband protect his wife from physical abuse:

> I was compelled to stand and see my wife shamefully scourged and abused by her master; and the manner in which this was done, was so violently and inhumanly com-

mitted upon the person of a female, that I despair in finding decent language to describe the bloody act of cruelty.

If a male slave attempted to protect his wife from abuse,
he faced severe retribution. Some slaves pretended that
they did not know how their wives were treated in order to
avoid having to decide whether to attempt to protect them
and face harsh punishment. Other slave men purposely
formed relationships with women on other plantations so
that they did not have to helplessly witness the daily mistreatment of their mates. Today we would call this denial
and lack of involvement. I believe that it was at this point
in our history as African-Americans that black men first
began to be viewed by black women as unavailable men,
lacking compassion as mates, who were unwilling to fight
for them. This, of course, is not true. But there is no doubt
that being in a relationship with a black woman extracted
a toll from a black man. It was risky, dangerous, and sometimes, life-threatening.

One more factor took its toll. Contrary to traditional
family constellations, slave children by law belonged to the
slave mother alone rather than to both parents. Whether
slave or master, men who fathered the children of slave
women no longer had to support them. Eventually, for slave
women, sex for procreation with an anonymous partner
became more common, though less acceptable, than sex
within the context of family life.

The Psychological Burden

Very little has been written about how the captive Africans
coped with the treatment they experienced at the hands
of slave owners or others, who could be cruel one moment
and kind the next. We know just as little about how they
coped with the sudden changes that resulted when their way
of life was supplanted by a totally foreign set of rules.

There is mention of how some of the slaves' spirits were broken or how their "mood changed from that day forth," after a severe beating, the mutilation of a limb, being sold away from family and friends, or the death of a loved one. And though they were often described as lazy, some slaves apparently became so depressed and hopeless that they were rendered dysfunctional, un-able to work or to care for themselves or anyone else properly.

What about women during slavery, many of whom not only continued to function but to have families and relationships of their own choosing? For these women, survival required several adaptations:

1. You Had to Learn to Behave One Way, Even If You Felt Another

Women who survived had to learn how to feign submission, happiness, and complacency in spite of whatever emotions they may actually have been feeling. It was this behavior, in part, that contributed to the common assumptions that slaves were happy and weren't interested in escaping to freedom. While some of them may have accepted their fate, there were just as many, if not more, who learned to appear submissive while manipulating their masters and wielding their power and influence over decisions made about themselves, members of the white household, and other slaves.

2. You Didn't Discuss the Kind of Abuse You Were Experiencing

Slaves were not allowed to discuss the sexual abuse of female slaves by their masters or other whites—the consequence was flogging. Secrecy was a necessary requirement for survival. Silence about the abuse was a sign of strength and a determination not to allow these experiences to dominate your mind even if your body was being assaulted.

Other slaves knew what was happening, anyway, since these incidents were hardly unique. While the silence made it easier to separate feelings from behaviors, it is likely that some women were haunted by a terror that they fought to suppress. Experiencing trauma of this kind sometimes results in sleeplessness, fears of impending doom, and flashbacks of frightening scenes that just won't go away.

3. You Had to Live with A Sense of Dignity in Spite of the Abuse

Given that abuse was so common, some women were taught to maintain a certain dignity, a kind of calm resignation, when possible. For example, one slave said: "I had a pretty sister; she was whiter than I am, for she took more after her father. When she was 16 years old, her master sent for her. When he sent for her again, she cried and didn't want to go. She told mother her troubles, and she [her mother] tried to encourage her to be decent, and hold her head above such things, if she could. . . ."

These three methods of coping include elements of "splitting," or dissociation. When used, they helped slave women maintain an emotional distance from the more abusive and discordant parts of their lives. Slaves tried to minimize the negative aspects of their oppression and focused instead on meaningful personal relationships and the satisfaction that could be derived from the people they cared about.

Freedom—A Different Captivity

Imagine how frightening and exhilarating freedom must have been if you survived to see January 1, 1863, when the

Emancipation Proclamation was signed, or December 1865, when the Thirteenth Amendment abolished slavery.

What was truly astonishing, however, was how little actually changed. In the process of freeing the slaves during the Civil War, in 1862, Union soldiers were said to have raped slave women as they plundered towns and plantations. It was obvious that although slavery had been confined to the South, stereotypes about the sexuality of slaves and the availability of slave women were persistent and far-reaching.

William Thomas, the author of *The American Negro: What He Is and What He Has Become*, wrote in 1910: "The Negro is so craven and sensuous in every fiber of its being . . . so deeply rooted in immorality are our Negro people that they turn in aversion from any sexual relation which does not invite sensuous embraces."

With emancipation, black families made a conscious effort to regain control of their children's sexuality and protect their women from the relentless sexual harassment that did not end with slavery. Strengthened by their adopted Christian principles, they tried to exert control over sexual information and the practices of females in order to raise the status of African-American women. Sexual conservatism was the order of the day.

The very last thing a decent, self-respecting black family wanted was to have their daughter do the things that had kept the stereotype alive for so long: become sexually active early in life, have sex and have children before marriage, engage in multiple sexual relationships, catch diseases, or infect other people and develop a bad reputation. They believed that too much sexual information, exposure to the world, and knowledge of street language or carnal behavior would be a direct indication that black women were as sexually immoral and impulse-ridden as whites claimed they were.

For at least fifty years after emancipation, most blacks stayed in the South and became sharecroppers on land owned by whites in order to feed their families. Women who had no skills began the long legacy of serving as domestic helpers in the homes of white families. Those who went North worked in factories as well. In these capacities, the women had no job security. The sexual abuse and harassment continued, and these women feared that they would lose their jobs if they dared to report the abuse or complain.

One woman told me the story, passed down in her family, of her great-grandmother, who worked as a housekeeper for a white family that had two sons. The father abused her regularly and threatened to have her fired if she told his wife. As the sons grew, each of them abused her as well. For her tolerance and her silence, she was given a ham and a half day off at Christmas, which she took. Her husband had been laid off, and it was her salary that supported their family. (The same scenario was played out on the factory floor in later years, with white supervisors threatening to fire black women if they did not "put out.")

Most African-Americans emerged from slavery with limited skills to prepare them for independence. More than 90 percent of slaves were illiterate. There were no national, regional, or other large-scale plans for dealing with the ex-slaves. As a result, sex was still a factor in the survival of the fittest. Whatever you had learned in captivity, you used to survive.

Nevertheless, the joy of freedom consisted in being able to marry legally, live as a family, worship in your own church, and work for wages. After emancipation, African-Americans rushed to legitimize their unions and reconstruct their families, which often meant finding their children and reclaiming them. Herbert Gutman, the noted sociologist and author, found that by the year 1917, 90 percent of black children were born within a married partnership. Obviously marriage and family were still desired among African-American families after emancipation. Many men and women, now free, were able to formalize the bonds they had established during slavery.

What This Means to You

Perhaps this healthy struggle to return to some kind of family life gave the impression that the New World had changed and African-Americans had rebounded virtually overnight from more than three hundred years of systematic assaults on their sexuality. Time would prove otherwise.

Given the passage of time, you might assume, African-American women should be very different from their ancestors in their vulnerability as members of society. But a group simply cannot walk away from such a systematic assault unscathed, particularly if the assault continues in new ways, as you will see as we turn to our modern struggle and the question of what it means to be stolen women today.

chapter 2

The Price We Pay

Captive to the Stereotypes

My Story

I was alone in a hotel lobby in Cleveland, Ohio. My husband and children had just returned to our room to retrieve something that somebody had to have before we left for my sister-in-law's wedding. I had been looking forward to this day for a long time. It wasn't often that we visited my husband's hometown, and I wanted to look my best for curious family members, his old girlfriends, and the inquisitive friends of my in-laws. I knew they'd all be giving me the once-over and I wanted to make a good impression.

I had gone to a lot of trouble, shopping first for the children and then for myself. My tailored emerald-green silk dress was made from fabric my husband had brought from Thailand, and my shoes were dyed to match. My nails and hair were done, and my outfit was topped off with a brand-new mink jacket that my husband had worked hard to buy for me. I was sharp.

As I waited for the elevator to return my family to me, two young white men came out of the hotel bar and headed my way. When they got within earshot, one loudly exclaimed, "She must cost at least $100!" His companion laughed as they walked past what was left me. I looked down at my clothes, trying for a minute to determine what it was about me that had given them the impression I looked like a hotel hooker and not simply a well-dressed wife and mother. My tears gleamed on the fur as I stood there with my head bowed. I knew that I had to pull myself together. I knew that my husband would be furious if he heard my story and would want to confront the men who had left me feeling so devastated. My young children would be upset if I was upset. Our day of celebration would be spoiled. When the elevator finally arrived I looked shaken, but I man-

aged to blame it on my excitement. It wasn't until the end of the day that I told my husband about my experience, and he was as angry as I'd anticipated. I never wore those shoes or that dress again.

For a moment, before those men came along, I felt like a beautiful lady. I wasn't thinking about color. Silly of me to forget. Dangerous of me to leave myself exposed to being hurt by a comment that was meant to belittle and humiliate me. I'm ashamed to admit that it did. Their words and laughter took their toll. For a while, I didn't feel that I deserved to have all those pretty things or to define myself by attributes other than my color. In fact, it was a long time before I would stand alone in a hotel lobby.

It's tempting to simply dismiss those men as insensitive jerks, a bigoted minority. Similarly, you could point out that I was in a conservative suburb or that this could happen to any woman standing alone in a hotel lobby. But these incidents are far too common to dismiss, and they don't happen only in hotels in Cleveland, or only in America.

My husband and I were in Hong Kong walking down the street when an Asian man pointed at me and asked my husband where he could "buy one like that." A few choice words made the man turn and run in fear and embarrassment, but the incident left me stunned and my husband, once again, enraged. Why didn't I look respectable even on the arm of a black man, *my* man?

Why My Story Matters

In our own neighborhoods and around the world, powerful stereotypes perpetuate the image of black women as sexually permissive. Society's message is that to be black and female is to be without sexual control, to be irresponsible about our sexuality. Regardless of the circumstance or our appearance, we may be presumed to be sexually available or for sale at some price. For so many years during slavery, we were bought and sold. It's hard for some people to believe that we can be anything else. Every other stereotype of the black woman springs from this one. My mission in this chapter is to explore the meaning of these stereotypes with you. You will begin to realize that they have extraordinary staying power and are at the heart of many longstanding, unresolved issues in our lives and relationships.

The Permissive Stereotype

The stereotype of the promiscuous black woman persists whether we are standing at a bus stop with our children, on our way to church dressed in our Sunday best, studying in the library for a class, sitting in a business suit testifying before a congressional committee, or standing in a hotel lobby. Age, dress, appearance, and even economic status have much less to do with our image than do race and gender.

Not long ago, I read an article about a handsome (white) actor on one of the hottest television series. He was quoted as saying that his black girlfriend was "the sexiest woman that I've ever met." For a brief moment, I hoped that sister would be described as intelligent, witty, charming, interesting, or even warm and personable—anything but sexy. He may indeed have described her other attributes, but these were the only words that found their way into the article.

Similarly, when I read that Hugh Grant had been arrested with Divine Brown for sexual misconduct on a side street in Hollywood, something told me that she was black—and she was. The media just loved the story of the curious English "gentleman" with the tempting she-devil, and labeled him a bad boy. While they wondered why he would cheat on his beautiful white girlfriend, no one questioned why Divine Brown was engaging in prostitution. It seemed more understandable that she should have chosen that profession than that he should have chosen her over his mate.

I was shocked at how blatantly the blockbuster movie *Independence Day* confirmed these stereotypes. The black heroine who was sleeping with the character played by Will Smith was a striptease dancer—a profession that discouraged Will Smith from marrying her. He was trying to get into flight school, and a white buddy warned that he would never be accepted with a stripper as a wife. It was only the threat of world annihilation that made him "do the right thing" and marry her. Why couldn't this female character have been a teacher or a doctor who was married to Smith? What purpose was served by having her writhe and gyrate half-naked in a scene or two except to make a subtle statement about the sexuality and acceptability of a black woman?

It's little wonder that some black women become righteously indignant at even the slightest suggestion that their desirability stems from their alleged sexual willingness and availability. It's *not* a compliment to be thought of as promiscuous and impulsive. You can take only so many demeaning incidents before you become like "Sapphire," a black female character on the infamous television program *Amos 'n' Andy* (telecast from 1951 to 1953). Sapphire was known for her ability to dominate poor, defenseless men, a head-gyratin' sister who "gets people told" in the wink of an eye and believes she has a good defense. If you respond in a vulnerable way, people might hurt you more.

Countering this negative stereotype is also hard on our partners. If we always have to be defended or protected against the tide of assumptions, the underlying message is that we shouldn't be left alone and we can't be taken anywhere. Who knows when you might lose control of yourself and start seducing innocent bystanders? If you have no one to protect and stand up for you, if you're always fighting for yourself, your self-esteem can be eroded very quickly. But self-reliance was and is the key to survival.

Just as the permissive stereotype has refused to die, so have the stereotypical personality styles that the slaves and their descendants adopted to help them cope with the pressures they faced. These behaviors have become well established for several centuries mainly because women have rarely had the opportunity to behave in ways other than what was expected of them, at least in public. To the larger society, these personality styles typify the black woman, and, unfortunately, some black women concur, confusing stereotypes with role models to emulate.

The Mammy

Al Jolson sang about her, and her smiling face has been on the pancake box for generations. In *The Myth of the Superwoman*, Michelle Wallace described her as "the personification of the ideal slave and the ideal woman." Mammy was characterized as an obese, domesticated, asexual house slave with a world of wisdom, the patience of Job, a heart of gold, and the willingness to breastfeed the world. Carolyn West, a psychologist and researcher who studies the effects of stereotypes on black women, described the mammy as "a dark complexioned woman with African features. . . ." The mammy characterized the moral black slave who had a staunch sense of right and wrong. She was a good woman because she was self-sacrificing when it came to the well-being of white families, especially the children, whom she often raised. Because of her good behavior, she had little reason to feel bad about her role as caretaker.

There were advantages and disadvantages to taking on the mammy role. The mammy had greater mobility and access to travel because she was considered to be trustworthy and mature. She often chaperoned white women and children in their journeys to other cities and plantations. Most important, the mammy was invested in her role as a slave and was not interested in freedom. Consequently, because she had access to the house, she was not a threat and could often gain inside information about the business or decisions of the slave owners regarding other slaves. Given her wisdom, she was often asked to make decisions about the lives of others. And because she was considered asexual and was usually overweight, she was not at risk of sexual abuse to the same extent as were other slave women.

On the other hand, a mammy had no life or other commitments to a family of her own, or so it had to appear. Her priority had to be the family that she served. She was a caregiver whose own needs were often overlooked. Her physical appearance and demeanor usually suggested that she had no vanity and was unconcerned about her body image or her health. The mammy was such an acceptable part of American culture that Hattie McDaniels was awarded an Academy Award for her performance as a mammy in the movie epic *Gone with the Wind*. Apparently this was an image that America could embrace. You can still see the remnants of those mammies in popular television personalities who are characterized by their largess and friendly personality. They, too, emulate the stereotype of the selfless caregiver. Women who characterize the mammy may, however, have an unhealthy lifestyle of overeating, along with little exercise, as a method of coping with the stress of poverty and the feeling of being unloved.

The She-Devil

The she-devil is the black woman who is basically evil. Walter Mosley referred to her dangerous aura in the title of his novel *Devil in a Blue Dress*, and Bebe Moore Campbell described her perfectly in an article that she wrote for *Essence* magazine on some of my research on sexual stereotypes:

> Black women know the sister very well. Skin-tight red dress, thigh high, back out, cleavage showing. Blond wig

all askew. "Hey, sugar! Come on and party with me." High, round fanny. Gum-chewing. Streetwise. "Hey, baby. You wanna party with me?" We know her too well. She haunts us. We move far away from where she struts, and breathe a sigh of relief. Then we turn on our television sets, and there she is again.

The she-devil typifies all of the most negative characteristics attributed to African women before and during slavery—the immoral, conniving seductress who loves sex anytime, anywhere, and will do anything to corrupt a man, disrupt his family, and take his money. If she can't find her man, she'll take another woman's man in a heartbeat and feel no remorse. This is one of the most pervasive images in American history. The assumption is that these women don't mind being sexual pets, exhibiting their bodies, or using provocative body language to communicate their readiness for sex. Given their corrupt behavior, they deserved whatever they got. The she-devil still lives in the multitudes of prostitutes and loose black women who are portrayed on television, in the movies, in rap music, and in political rhetoric about pregnant black teens.

While the mammy's image romanticized the caretaking skills and trustworthiness of black women, the she-devil was her polar opposite. Just as she was the best rationale for slavery—the sexual urges of Africans and their descendants had to be controlled—so, too, did she become the best revenge. There are few advantages to emulating the she-devil image. To some women, being seen in a sexual light was preferable to not being seen at all. Being sexy can be empowering.

The disadvantage of this image is that it depersonalizes a woman and overemphasizes her sexuality. It is also difficult to care about what happens to evil people, or what makes them that way. The woman who models herself on the she-devil image might attract men's attention, but she inspires little empathy, tenderness, or desirability beyond the purely physical pleasures of the moment.

Some black men have believed the myth of the lustful black woman. For example, here is an interview between an obviously curious white man and a freed black man in 1863:

Q: Have not colored women a good deal of passion?
A: Yes, sir.
Q: Are they carried away by their passion to have inter-
course with men?
A: Yes sir; but very few lawful married women are car-
ried away if their husbands can take care of them.
Q: How is it with the young women?
A: They are very wild and run around a great deal.

The most graphic illustration of the pervasiveness of this stereotype is found in pornographic writings, where fantasies of the she-devil are stoked like coals on a fire. In her book *Against Pornography: The Evidence of Harm*, Diana Russell quotes the following passage from the book *Soul Slave* by Rita Cochran:

Rance [a white man] looked down at me and said, "Get naked, Nigger!" And those words were like the greatest poetry in the world to me. . . . It was like that man had dug down there in the deepest part of me and found something that was ultimate nigger, ultimate bitch, ultimate pain-loving whore. "I am going to give you the fucking of your worthless, nigger life." . . . I had never felt more alive in my life, my worthless nigger life. . . . One of them [white boys] told me that I was a special nigger, that I could take more cock . . . than any dozen Southern belles. I thought about that and it gave me pride. There was little else that I could be proud of.

Stereotypes of black women continue to romanticize slavery and oppression. To accept this image, a woman would have to have the self-esteem or self-worth of a sex slave.

The Workhorse

Finally, there's the image of the workhorse. She is the woman who through hard, backbreaking work developed useful skills. She excels. Her work ethic contradicts stereotypes that she is lazy. The workhorse was thought to be so strong that she could tolerate rape or physical abuse. Because she could rebound, people assumed that nothing bothered her. Women who embody this stereotype represent what Zora Neale Hurston described as "the mules of the world."

Many women have aspired to this image in order to avoid feeling vulnerable and powerless or dependent on men who could not always protect them. While the advantage of this image is that a woman might be accepted for her ability rather than for her caretaking or sexual skills, the disadvantage is that she is perceived as hard, unfeminine, and masculine. A woman sometimes had to overlook her own feelings in the process of appearing strong. In part, she is also represented in the more contemporary image of Sapphire. Picture her rocking back on her heels with her hands on her hips. Nobody messed with her, but of course nobody wanted her, either. That's okay—she didn't need a man; she didn't need anybody.

The image of the workhorse also lives on in the new stereotype of the well-dressed executive black woman, who, though educated, well-spoken, -salaried, and -housed, presumably goes home childless and alone. Another hybrid is found in the image of today's girls who dress as "gangstas" or "hip-hoppers" in baggy, masculine clothing that does not reveal their female curves. They've presumably rejected their femininity in favor of being tough, streetwise women who can kick ass as well as any guy. That is the price of respectability—sacrificing their sexuality to behave the way people who matter to them expect them to behave.

Society's expectations can be powerful, controlling forces, particularly if we come to accept them, and to an astonishing degree, we do.

What Do Others Think of Us?
What Do We Think of Ourselves?

Like all stereotypes, the ones I've just described are based partly on incomplete information but mostly on prejudicial notions about a group. They are passed along through various means—by casual conversation, random observations, poorly conducted research, or the media in both subtle and not so subtle ways. When repeated, seen, or heard frequently, they become increasingly credible and receive additional confirmation. Soon, if enough people give voice to these beliefs, others assume that they must be true.

Years ago, people began asking me questions about black women's sexuality to determine whether the information they had was consistent with my research. Some of their perceptions and statements were so astounding and so stereotypical that I began to collect them. For ten years, I kept a list, adding similarly outrageous statements that I found in the scientific literature. Then I developed a survey to see whether black and white women were familiar with these statements and to find out which ethnic group they thought they best described.

If there was as much stereotyping of black sexuality as I thought there was, I expected many of the statements to be applied to us. I also expected the women to exhibit some of the negative sexual stereotypes as well. I asked all of the women interviewed to respond to the following statements. Each statement corresponds to a dominant stereotype that has characterized black women for hundreds of years.

In describing a workhorse, a woman who values performance and achievement and defers her sexual needs, and who might have a very limited notion of what sex should be like, statements like these were made:

1. Some women think that sex is to have babies and not for enjoyment.
2. Some women should be virgins before marriage.

3. Some women don't believe in partner swapping.
4. Some women don't engage in group sex (orgies).
5. Some women use complaints like headaches to avoid sex.
6. Some women think oral sex is unacceptable and degrading.

For the she-devil, the highly sexualized woman who has no morals and deserves what she gets, these statements were typical:

7. Some women have babies to receive financial support, like welfare.
8. Some women prefer their man to have a large penis.
9. Some women are more sexually responsive than others.
10. Some women are more promiscuous than others.
11. Some women are better lovers than others.
12. Some women use sex to get what they want.
13. Some women are more frequent victims of rape than others.

For the mammy, the asexual women who places others before herself and uses weight to mask her sexuality, the following statement was considered appropriate:

14. Some women have large buttocks and big legs.

An overwhelming majority—85 percent of the women I asked—had heard these statements before. When I asked where they had heard them, they said from parents, school, loved ones, the church, and, less surprisingly, the media. Friends were the most likely source of these sexual stereotypes, with one exception. As expected, the most common sources of the she-devil stereotypes were television, movies, books, and magazines.

I asked the African-American women which ethnic group they felt best fit the fourteen stereotypical statements. Their answers were even more consistent than I had expected. The majority believed that all of these statements applied to African-American women. In contrast, the white women interviewed felt that these statements could have applied to an ethnic group other than blacks or whites, or to women in general. There was, however, one exception: They were in agreement with their black peers that the statement about having large buttocks and big legs applied only to African-Americans.

These findings highlighted the degree to which African-American women have internalized and accepted statements that depict them as stereotypical characters. It seemed that these black women agreed with any statements about themselves, even if the statements themselves are contradictory. Some of them depict black women as deferring sex, and others depict them as highly sexualized. Obviously these women found both the black workhorse and the she-devil to be credible images.

Who was more likely to accept these statements? Women who were younger (born after 1960) were slightly more likely to have heard them, but age did not influence whether they agreed with them. I anticipated that women with more education and higher incomes would reject these statements for what they are—assumptions that are based on incomplete information and prejudicial attitudes. That was not the case, however. Women who were educated or more affluent were just as likely as less educated, poorer women to accept these statements as true of black women. It appears that regardless of age, education, and income, black women endorse these statements as characteristic of black women.

In essence, we do believe what people say about us, and white men are not the only culprits. Other women, our parents, our friends, and, of course, the media all play a part in making these stereotypes seem credible.

Younger women or adults who have not yet developed a sense of themselves that is strong enough to withstand the influences of negative stereotypes frequently attempt to emulate them.

These women might dress and behave like the images they see, or like those that are marked to appeal to subgroups in the black community, including the hip-hop girls, the gangsta rappers, female gang members, groupies who hang with entertainers or sports figures, or starlets who want to be discovered by the entertainment industry. Or they may stay at home watching the soaps or talk shows, living vicariously through others and functioning in caretaking capacities in their families, assuming such responsibilities as cooking or caring for children or ailing family members. They may be marginal students and have very little social life outside of home and church.

More than twenty years ago, I had a client who expressed an interest in sex therapy so that she could learn how to emulate the she-devil stereotype. This woman had heard from family members and friends that black women were, above all, sensuous and sexy, and she wanted me to teach her how to act that way in order to improve her sex life with her partner. Her boyfriend, who also came to therapy, agreed that she should act in this fashion and wanted to learn how to be a "stud." She was the first of many women I have encountered who had the impression that the stereotype of sexual impulsivity is culturally condoned. With therapy and parental involvement, these women learned to move beyond these images and adopt more responsible practices by discovering themselves and setting goals, many of which had to do with learning to excel in some endeavor and getting enough education to make them independent.

The good news is that there were several African-American women who agreed that all of the statements characterized black women but who did not allow them to rule their lives. They managed to deal with these stereotypes and prejudicial statements and keep them from affecting their self-esteem and sexual behavior by using one of the same strategies that their ancestors used to survive slavery: by

splitting, or distancing themselves, from these kinds of statements and not allowing them to influence individual decisions. In order to use this strategy, a contemporary woman
has to have adequate self-esteem and confidence in her
ability to control her sex life. She also needs a support
network of individuals who question the images that are
commonly promoted and encourage her to be her own
person.

Adopting this strategy is difficult for young adolescents
who are in the process of self-development or vulnerable to
suggestions from others and prefer to conform to expectations. Women with less self-esteem may also have trouble
distancing themselves from stereotypes that are firmly entrenched.

Invisible Chains

Think of the many ways in which sexual stereotypes are still
dramatized in the media. My favorite example is the movie
Colors. It depicts the lives of two policemen, played by Robert Duvall and Sean Penn, trying to contain gang involvement in the black and Latino communities. The movie
caused quite a stir in the black community, but the contro-
versy focused on how gangs and violence were portrayed
rather than on how sexually stereotyped behavior was being promoted.

This film has one of the most racist sexual scenes that
I can recall in several decades. It showed a black woman
and man engaging in very loud, animated, and continuous
sex, even while the police watched. These two people—the
"buck" and the "she-devil"—were heavily engrossed in their
animalistic methods of sexual pleasure in the middle of the
day. The scene says it all: Neither had the sense to lock the
door of their very messy, rundown home, and both were
obviously not working and were too distracted by sex to
notice several men standing in the doorway. The couple

doesn't seem very intelligent, and no morals or priorities interfered with their sexual pleasure.

This scene brings to mind the blaxploitation era of the 1970s and its volume of movies that continually portrayed men and women as sexually impulsive, aggressive, and violent. Dr. Alvin Poussaint, the noted Harvard psychiatrist who has been a consultant on many media projects that promote positive images of African-American family life, wrote about the changes in the roles assigned to blacks from the 1920s to the 1970s. According to Poussaint, "the same insidious message is there: Blacks are violent, criminal, sexy savages who imitate the white man's ways as best they can from their disadvantaged sanctuary in the ghetto." These same negative images have simply been reborn in contemporary images in the media.

A few years ago, I was on *Our Voices* on Black Entertainment Television, where I engaged in a lively discussion with Shahrazad Ali, who had written a book that was meant to teach black men how to treat black women. Her book was filled with stereotypical characteristics of the she-devil and suggested coercive methods such as slapping to manage or control women's supposedly crafty and manipulative tendencies. Obviously, some black women share the responsibility for promoting stereotypes. They are entitled to their opinions, but the problem is that they endorse physical abuse, perpetuate the idea that black men cannot trust black women, and breathe new life into the old stereotypes. Writer Joan Morgan delineated another example of this phenomenon in a 1997 article in *Essence* magazine, quoting the lyrics of a song by the hip-hop rapper DaBrat:

"With 50 grand in my hand, steady puffin' on a blunt, sippin' Hennessy and Coke, give ya what ya want." It is obvious that the relentless pursuit of status, power and ducats is not gender-specific, as evidenced by the willing complicity of not only these rappers but also umpteen scantily clad "video hoes," . . . sistas who are going to get theirs by any scandalous means necessary. Rather than grant them victim status, I suggest we start holding them accountable.

What are the consequences of these negative messages over time? Little, if any, research has been done on the subject, but I believe one recent study on another negative stereotype sheds light on the problem. Claude Steele and Joshua Aronson of Stanford University studied the effect of stereotyped threat, or being at risk of confirming a negative stereotype about yourself or your group. They used black female college students and evoked stereotypical threat in the students prior to administering a standardized test. They described the test as difficult, and noted that there was little likelihood that black students would answer many of the items correctly. The black students who were given this spiel performed worse than both of the white participants and the other black participants. The researchers concluded that the awareness of negative expectations lowered test results by lowering the students' expectations of their own performance.

It is quite possible that stereotypical threat operates in a fashion similar to sexual practices. If images of sexually irresponsible and impulsive women are presented consistently for many decades, we might indeed anticipate that a "stereotyped acceptance" would result. That is, one's sexual behavior might be altered to fit the stereotype. If this is plausible, does it mean that the media and others are invested in further distorting African-American female sexuality? The media I described certainly offer credible evidence of this possibility. But we cannot expect other people to reject these images if we don't actively protest the media's persistent focus on the worst rather than the best of us. More important, we have to take some responsibility for the worst.

According to an African proverb, if you know your history you will know your future. The racist descriptions of Africans in the sixteenth century are strikingly familiar. The negative stereotypes of the past are the negative stereotypes of today. Some of us manage to ignore them. But the most disturbing fact in this chapter is that the average black woman believes them, and may even think that they provide a standard for her sexual behavior. My research demonstrates the discrepancies between stereotypes and reality, and attempts to correct assumptions that have become deeply entrenched in this society, but it also reveals that stereotypes exert a continuous and insidious force on our sexual self-image.

True images of the African-American woman are ill-defined partly because our sexuality has been so distorted by our history and so poorly understood and partly because some of us are actually satisfied with these stereotypes and want to mold ourselves and everyone else to fit these images. But the woman who exaggerates or avoids her sexuality and allows others to simplify or stigmatize it eventually finds herself paying the unnecessary price of continued sexual slavery as one more stolen woman. What do I mean by that characterization?

Stolen women today:

1. Are still captive to stereotypes and don't understand that African-Americans have a culture that does not endorse everything acceptable or promoted in mainstream America;
2. Believe that what other people think of them is true;
3. Do what other people want them to do, regardless of the consequences to themselves;
4. Let their bodies define who they are; and
5. Defend and excuse others who reduce them to stereotypes. They reject the right to be free.

I have talked to hundreds of "stolen women" during my career. From time to time, I have felt as if I had been stolen, too. Analyzing my professional and personal experiences has led me to the conclusion that if we sincerely want to be free from the invisible chains of history and stereotypes, we have to be willing to free ourselves. That process begins with the fundamental recognition that we could even *be* stolen women today. No one has ever described this concept more pointedly than Harriet Tubman when she said, "I freed thousands of slaves. I could have freed thousands more, if they had known they were slaves."

I believe that every African-American woman can benefit from stretching her mind and patiently examining the critical years of her sexual development for evidence of invisible chains that could be binding her to distorting stereotypes, images, messages, and experiences. Those were the years when she was setting the template for her adult sexuality. What she did (her behaviors and decisions), what was communicated to her by others (their messages), and what she was forced to do all converged to shape her sexual being.

That means we need to know which of our behaviors were healthy, and which were not. We need to re-evaluate the messages we heard as we were coming of age. We need to consider how factors such as our economic status, our parents' involvement, exposure to abuse, and other social and psychological issues may have made a difference. We also need to see our experiences in a broad cultural context. Discovering the patterns of sexual development that we share as African-American women will give each of us a wealth of specific clues to the role that cultural values and expectations played in our personal development. It will also help us locate the line where our culture may have stopped condoning our actions and where destructive stereotypes started to determine our ideas about the way black women were supposed to either be or be perceived.

Let's begin that journey to understanding.

part two

Understanding Our Sexuality

chapter 3

Doctor-Nurse

The Role of Childhood Sex Play

Erin's Story

Erin, a 34-year-old dog trainer, remembers growing up in the South, the oldest of four sisters and three brothers—a close family by her description. Her father was a farmer, and her mother was a house-keeper and cook. Both parents worked hard to raise their children properly. They felt that they had set reasonable standards for their children: They wanted them to attend the Baptist church at least once a month and to graduate from high school, something neither of them had been able to do.

Sex education, at least learning the basic differences between boys and girls, came naturally. Erin grew up with young boys and used to change her brothers' and sisters' diapers. Nothing else was said about sex, except that when Erin was in a bad mood her mother would tell her that she needed a man. This statement hurt Erin's feelings, because it implied that there was something that a man could do to assuage her moody behavior that she couldn't do for herself. However, by no means did Erin take it to mean that her parents endorsed premarital sex. They were rather formal with each other, rarely kissing or hugging in front of the kids. Erin did recall playing doctor-patient with her siblings and friends, and remembered touching her body when she began to develop breasts. But that was the extent of her early sexual exploration.

Erin had intercourse for the first time at age 19, with a guy she later married. Looking back over her sexual development, she prided herself on controlling her sexuality. She wasn't supposed to have sex until she was ready to marry, and she didn't. Her personal experience did not cause her to feel that her daughter would require any more information than that.

Why Erin's Story Matters

Erin's childhood sex play happened naturally in the course of her sexual development, which, even without much information, was strongly influenced by a relatively safe environment and a protective family. This, of course, contradicts all the stereotypes about "promiscuous" African-American girls, who are supposed to be little she-devils in the making.

Once, at a conference of world-renowned sex researchers, a white colleague exclaimed, to my disbelief, that in order to conduct studies of first intercourse among black adolescents he had to go to the fourth grade to find virgins! I wasted no time in pointing out that his remark was based on stereotypes and limited exposure to a true cross section of black children. If he had bothered to ask the young girls he talked to why and with whom they were sexually active, he might have discovered that many of them were being sexually exploited, abused, and reared in troubled families in which there was inadequate supervision.

Contrary to stereotypes about the early sexual activity of black girls, most African-American girls under the age of 13 are not sexually active and have little or no sexual experience beyond the normal sex play that occurs in early childhood. Erin's story is typical of the black women in my research. Her childhood sex play—including self-touching, masturbation, sexual arousal, and exploration with other children—was kept to a minimum and accompanied by enough specific factual, age-appropriate information.

What does Erin's story tell us about other African-American women? Why does it matter to you? I believe it gives you a clear picture of the predictable childhood sexual behaviors that help set the stage for her adult sexuality. I have seen many women who have never taken the measure of their youthful behavior because they never considered it to be particularly important. My research findings prove that to the contrary, these behaviors remain a critical dimension of our sexuality long after memory fades.

In this chapter, I will guide you through a simple review of your own childhood sexuality by asking a set of basic questions. I will also provide background information and more stories to expand your understanding of the connection between your life and the typical range of experiences that African-American women have reported to me.

Playing Doctor-Nurse Games—Was It Innocent and Exploratory?

Like most parents, yours probably assumed that prior to adolescence and puberty you were not yet a sexual being. But parents who watched and listened discovered otherwise.

Kids are born with the capacity to be sexually aroused. Through sex play, they express their sexuality. They use whatever they know about sex, however limited, to gain familiarity with their bodies by having some initial sexual contact. Children participate in sex play for pleasure, to satisfy their natural curiosity about parts of the body that are hidden and rarely discussed, and to rehearse things they may do again as they grow older. Through play, they show how much they understand about the roles men and women assume. In trying on these roles, children also reveal their familiarity with sexual language and practices.

Typically, early-childhood sexual activities are innocent and often accidental. Young infants and children naturally explore or touch their bodies; they enjoy the pleasant sexual sensations. School-age children may find similar pleasure in sliding down the monkey bars at the playground or riding a horse. Sooner or later, however, they will add more complex, deliberate, and self-conscious sexual behavior to their play.

A child's first sexual exploration with someone else usually takes the form of a game, like doctor-patient. Of her experience with this type of play, Carrie recalled, "We'd play house or doctor and nurse. We'd say 'Time to go to bed', and the doctor would say, 'You're sick. I've got to put you in the hospital—off with your clothes.' That was with my friends, my sisters, and me. We never were supposed to tell about our games, but if my sisters told on me I would tell on them. I only did it with the [kids] I liked."

Being the doctor gives a child the authority to examine someone, and the patient is allowed to submit to this. Within this framework, there is nothing wrong with looking and touching. In fact, exploring and probing is a necessary part of the role. When children explore each other's bodies they get to see or touch body parts that are the same as or different from their own. This can bring sexual pleasure or excitement, but if they have no information or only appropriate amounts and no one stimulates their interest in sex, these feelings are both minimal and harmless. If they have too much or conflicting information before they can understand how their bodies work and the consequences of sex, however, they are often increasingly motivated to initiate or participate in sex play in order to find out more about it.

Self-Touching and Masturbation—
Pleasure or Problem?

Young girls commonly touch their breasts and genitals either to examine them or to experience sexual pleasure, although their parents neither encourage nor accept this behavior. In fact, parents often begin discouraging self-touching with toilet training. When mothers discourage prolonged wiping between the legs to prevent chafing, girls learn to use toilet tissue only to dry themselves and to limit the amount of touching that takes place. As girls grow older, their parents may use biblical stories and religious beliefs to show that self-touching and masturba-

tion are sinful. Limited conversations about nudity and masturbation and explicit warnings against them reinforce this
negative message. Girls learn quite early that if they touch
themselves, they have to do it in private or risk being punished or embarrassed if they are discovered by a family
member.

Normally a girl's self-touching increases at puberty, when
her breasts begin to develop. Most girls first explore their
own bodies between the ages of 9 and 12. Cynthia, one of
the women we interviewed, remembered rubbing her breasts
nightly when she was 9 because they "itched" and had begun to grow. One in five African-American women in my
research reported that they never touched their breasts or
genitals before age 13.

Similarly, only one out of four reported that they masturbated before age 13. The rhythmic self-stimulation of
the genital area for sexual pleasure usually involves more
prolonged touching. For example, girls may explore their
labia and clitoris with their hands or fingers until tension
builds up to a warm rush throughout the body and breathing deepens and becomes more rapid as the rhythm of
movements sometimes culminates in orgasm. When children do begin masturbating early in life, the most common
method is also the most direct—the hand. Masturbating by
rubbing the genitals and the breasts or by repeatedly inserting an object like a comb, the handle of a brush, or a
finger into the vagina were equally popular methods in
childhood.

Very few children go to unusual lengths to touch their
bodies. Jessica, for instance, discovered a way to masturbate at age 10 by using her fingers and a hairpin on her
clitoris. She never reached orgasm, however, and always
wondered if she would get pregnant by doing this. Some
girls squeezed their thighs by crossing their legs and press-
ing them together repeatedly to orgasm. This method, the
most indirect, did not require them to touch their genitals.
A few girls tried rubbing themselves against the monkey bars

at the playground or against a bed to masturbate, but few were more creative than Jessica.

In sex research before the AIDS epidemic, 14 percent of college-educated black women in the study conducted by Kinsey and his associates reported masturbating before age 13. In my research, 33 percent of the women in this category reported masturbating. The difference between my findings and Kinsey's may reflect an increasing social and religious tolerance for masturbation, as well as a change in parental attitudes. There are fewer warnings these days about growing warts on your hand, going insane, or losing your eyesight! Ministers no longer preach as frequently about girls or women going to hell if they touch their bodies. And scenes from movies suggest that masturbation is sexy and erotic, and may give viewers the impression that touching one's body isn't all that bad.

We also know more about masturbation today than we did in the past. The reasons for engaging in masturbation are not always sexual. Studies by William Friedrich, Ph.D., have shown that excessive masturbation (more than once daily) has been associated with other psychological or emotional problems, such as depression, low self-esteem, anxiety, and sexual abuse. It is also a form of self-stimulation that children use to comfort themselves when they have no other source of affection or when they are being over-stimulated. Some of the women whose patterns of sexual activity escalated from one sexual practice to another may, in fact, have been trying to call attention to an emotional or family problem that they needed help with as children.

Sexual Arousal—A Crush, Curiosity, or Out of Control?

Sexual arousal involves pleasant sensations that can result in sexual excitement, including heavy breathing and vaginal lubrication, but not necessarily orgasm. Almost two out of every three black women interviewed in my research said that she experienced any kind of arousal before age 13. Those who did shared common scenarios that took place between the ages of 9 and 12. One woman said that she and a friend—male or female—took turns rubbing or lying on top of each other. Another woman was excited by the sight of a man's penis in public, and some of the women became sexually excited by having crushes on their teachers in school. First-time sexual feelings can be so powerful that you never forget the person who made you feel that way.

Irma's Story

Irma once wrote to me about a crush she had on her science teacher in junior high school. Irma wasn't a very good student, and her teacher often stayed after school with her to go over the lessons that she did not understand. Sitting next to him, she could smell his cologne, which she thought was heavenly. He had a broad smile, was well built, or so it seemed to her, and he was just out of college and single.

Irma's attraction grew to the point where she would find excuses to ask him questions so that she could be alone with him. Finally, her crush became so intense that it began to interfere with her ability to concentrate on her work. Her mother complained that she daydreamed a lot and didn't listen when she was spoken to. Puzzled by her daughter's behavior, the mother searched her room expecting to find drugs and found a collection of unmailed love letters that Irma had written to her teacher. Irma and her mother, armed with the love letters, met with the teacher. He was flattered but firm, explaining that sometimes kindness and special attention are confused with other feelings. What Irma was feeling would pass, he assured her, as she grew to understand these feelings better.

Although Irma was furious with her mother for exposing her love, she passed the course but could not get that teacher out of her mind, even years later when she was in college. She later returned to her old school to see him, only to realize that he was right. He did not look quite so fine, but he was still just as kind. Although he was delighted that he had helped her to overcome her fear of science, Irma was grateful that he had also helped her to realize that her feelings shouldn't be mistaken for sexual attraction.

Women have also written to me about the crushes they had on their female teachers, but their concern was whether this meant that they were lesbians. I advised them that one crush or even several do not necessarily indicate an exclusive preference for the same gender as a sexual partner. Sometimes crushes simply signal the need for love and attention from a woman. It's also important not to take feelings of comfort with the same sex as a sign that a girl is attracted only to females. These feelings are natural and quite common, particularly at the age when social skills are not yet fully developed. Sexual orientation can be more clearly discerned only after observing patterns of sexual attraction over time.

Sexual arousal or feelings of excitement, whether generated through self-touching or with someone else, remind a young girl that her body can and will respond sexually. These feelings, no matter how intense, should be accepted but not acted upon until girls are mature enough to understand their parents' expectations about delaying sexual activity or until they are able to make their own informed decisions about when, where, and with whom they will express their sexuality.

This pattern is confirmed by Harold Leitenberg and other researchers who have also studied sexual activity in childhood and adolescence. In essence, excessive genital contact in childhood, both alone and with others, is often followed by sexual activities in adolescence that can increase the risk of such unwanted outcomes as pregnancy and sexually transmitted diseases. These patterns are further influenced by other factors, particularly self-esteem—how girls feel about themselves and how much control they give to their sexual partners. Other factors may include immaturity, poor school performance, and inadequate social skills, along with limited time spent being supervised by or involved with parents.

Frequent mutual exploratory experiences seem to increase curiosity about sexual arousal and experimentation, and to put girls at greater risk for having sexual intercourse at an early age and multiple partners in adolescence. The more girls became aware of their sexuality—and that of others—the more interested they were in discovering more about sex, as Dianne's story illustrates.

Dianne's Story

When Dianne, a Southern Baptist from Tennessee, was 12 years old, she and a group of friends observed the couple next door having sex. This happened about four times when the couple forgot to pull down their window shades. On other occasions, Dianne and her girlfriend would explore each other's body. She knew it was wrong, but they both found the experiences to be pleasant, and they got a chance to practice what the neighbors were doing.

Given the taboos that surround mutual self-exploration, children sometimes select a best friend to explore with in order to ensure that the incidents are kept secret. In recalling these experiences, however, some women think that they are lesbians because their child sex play involved girls. The fact that Dianne engaged in sexual exploration with other girls does not necessarily suggest that she or other children who have these experiences are homosexual. According to the eminent sex researchers William Masters, Virginia Johnson, and Robert Kolodny, child sex play between the same and the opposite sex is normal and does not indicate sexual orientation.

The age at which sex play occurs is far more significant than the gender of the girl's partner, but the age of the partner is very important. When the African-American women in my research reported mutual sexual exploration with someone who was an adolescent between the ages of 9 and 12, one-third of these partners were males, one-third were females, and one-third were groups of boys and girls. Perhaps because the participants were older (they were between

13 and 17), the play was riskier, particularly when boys were involved. In other words, what started out as child's play often turned into something else. Cherie's story is an example of mutual exploration with an older male that eventually involved more than exploring each other's body.

Cherie's Story

Cherie, a part-time cosmetics salesperson, knew relatively little about sex until age 11, when she discovered a book that illustrated the positions men and women could assume during sex. Before that, she had never masturbated or spent time arousing herself. When she was 12, she began to play with her 17-year-old neighbor. He would wrestle her to the floor and she got excited while attempting to fight him off. Eventually they got tired and stopped. At least, that was the way it started. But these wrestling matches happened quite often, and they escalated into more intimate exploration and experimentation.

In that same year, Cherie recalled, her neighbor began to come over and ask for sex directly. This happened about twice a month for three and a half years while her mother was at work. If she refused, he would throw her down and sometimes tear off her panties. Then he would take his penis and rub it against her labia with his fingers, kiss her vagina, and kiss and fondle her breasts. Cherie felt responsible and did not tell anyone what was happening. She blamed herself for "always being in his face."

Early Nonconsensual Childhood Exploration

Cherie's story shows that early sex play with older persons can begin as a harmless game and turn into something else entirely. When force is used to guarantee a girl's cooperation, she becomes a victim. Under these circumstances, a girl's control of her body is taken from her. Some may argue that Cherie got what she deserved because she initially encouraged her neighbor's advances until he began to demand sex. However, interest in sex is not always a prerequisite for involvement in sexual activity. Children also learn about sex when sex play is initiated by someone else—an older and more experienced person who may be trying to exploit their innocence and vulnerability.

Roxanne's first experience of sexual stimulation, for example, resulted in sexual abuse. This experience is shared by far too many other African-American women. Indeed, one in five women in my study revealed that their childhood sexual experiences included having someone older fondle their bodies in an attempt to have intercourse with them. Thirteen percent of these women had sexual intercourse before age 13, usually with an adult who was at least five years older.

Roxanne's Story

Roxanne, a 22-year-old part-time manager at McDonald's, grew up in a small town in Florida. Her parents divorced when she was just 2 years old. She described her relationship with her five sisters, her mother, and her father as "fairly close, even with the divorce," but I got the impression from her tone of voice that they didn't get along that well.

Roxanne's parents never explained sex to their children, and references to anything sexual made it sound vulgar and dirty. For example, with regard to dating their stock comment was, "All men want to do is get into your pants." They made it clear that virginity was an absolute necessity before marriage, and that their daughters would be "ruined" if they had sex before marriage. However, when Roxanne was 11 years old, her older sister got pregnant. Roxanne would silently eavesdrop on conversations between her sister and her mother as they struggled to deal with her sister's condition. That's when Roxanne began to understand how babies were made.

Consequently, Roxanne had the idea that sex could be pretty troublesome, and she had little interest in expressing her own sexuality. She never masturbated or engaged in doctor-patient games with other children. But one day when Roxanne was 12 years old, everything changed. Her mother's boyfriend forcefully unbuttoned her pants and ran his hands over her genitals. This happened about four times a month over the next three years while her mother dated him. Fed up but scared, Roxanne became sick to her stomach when she finally told her mother about the incidents, only to become more upset when her mother told her that she had "brought it on herself." Needless to say, her relationship with her mother changed after that. Too many things had happened, and she had no one to talk to. She remembered not being allowed to date during this time. Her family changed from a Baptist church to the Christ Church, which did not allow dating.

At age 13, Roxanne recalled having a sexual experience with a girlfriend on two separate occasions. She and her friends were curious about each other's body, so they undressed and touched each other all over. Roxanne also secretly began seeing boys, kissing them and letting them touch her all over. At age 15, she had intercourse for the first time with a boy whom she liked. She felt that she could talk to him about everything. That relationship lasted just long enough for her to become pregnant at age 16. She did not use birth control at the time because her church did not condone it. Instead, she used the rhythm method after the birth of her first child.

Today Roxanne is a single mother of three. When she is asked what she thinks her parents could have done to help her gain sexual knowledge and develop healthy attitudes toward sex, she said, "They should have sat me down and talked to me about the facts of life. They should have prepared me for what was waiting for me out there. They should have inquired about what was going on in my head and straightened out my confusion." She was adamant in her conviction to teach her own children more than she had learned about sex at their age.

Coping with Trauma—Was Professional Help Needed?

Ironically, while Erin's childhood sexual experiences mirrored those of the majority of African-American women we interviewed, most people seem to think that Cherie's and Roxanne's experiences are the norm for African-American girls. Stories like theirs are recounted over and over again, particularly when the issues being explored center around the age of sexual intercourse, the use of birth control, or the number of unintended pregnancies for blacks in comparison with white women. Taken out of context—i.e., reported without a framework—the experiences these women relate tell only part of our story. But this makes them no less painful or important to recognize.

When girls have childhood experiences that involve sexual abuse, they may fall into an unhealthy cycle that requires professional intervention to help them cope with early sexual trauma. Although both Cherie and Roxanne reported their early sexual abuse, their self-esteem and sexuality were damaged either by their own interpretation of what occurred or by the response of significant others. Roxanne's experience clearly took place without her consent, yet she failed to gain the support of her mother, who blamed her for the incidents. On the other hand, Cherie willfully participated in what began as a game and escalated into an abusive relationship for which she assumed responsibility. My research indicates that both Roxanne and Cherie were at high risk for sexual and psychological problems later in life—not so much because one consented and the other didn't but because they accepted the blame for what had happened.

When girls blame themselves or accept responsibility for the abuse they have experienced, they are more likely to remain silent about later abusive incidents and to have difficulties in exerting control over future decisions about sex and relationships. Whether Cherie welcomed sexual advances or not, she was at an age where children do not always understand the outcome of their behavior. Even when girls *do* understand the consequences of their consensual behavior and allow themselves to enter into abusive relationships, it is usually for the wrong reasons. Many girls feel that there is no one else who will pay as much attention to them as the perpetrator of the abuse. In some ways, Roxanne's boyfriend seemed more available than her mother was.

In almost half of the incidents reported by African-American women in my studies, the women had not told anyone about the abuse. When they did, in two out of three cases, they were more likely to tell extended family members than their mother or dad, a sibling, or an authority figure like a police officer, a teacher, or a minister. In other words, they were less likely to tell their mother about being abused even if their father or stepfather or their mother's boyfriend abused them.

Rarely do children have someone with whom they can sort out experiences that they feel they have brought upon themselves. This is especially true of African-American girls. When we asked women their reasons for not telling, over one in three women cited fear of what might happen if they did. For example, women recalled that they feared that their families would suffer some financial hardship, or that their father or stepfather or their mother's boyfriend would leave the family. This is a very important finding because there are increasing numbers of single-parent households in the black community, and children who are abused may feel that their silence will in some way help to preserve the stability or economic status of their own family. That is too great a price to pay.

African-American women who report being sexually abused in childhood also describe problems sleeping at night and concentrating in school during the day. They claim that their friends ostracized them when they disclosed their abuse to them. Whether or not these incidents are reported, it seems that abusive experiences have the potential to distance black girls from their parents and their peers.

Sadly, this alienation can also make girls more likely to become victims again, as was the case with Roxanne, who gravitated toward someone who took advantage of her emotional vulnerability and low self-esteem. Like Roxanne, fewer than five percent of women received any kind of counseling for their early sexual trauma. In lieu of professional help, sometimes the message a girl received from her family was that she should be strong and get on with her life. For some girls, that was easier said than done.

The worst thing that can happen is to leave a child who has been exposed to sexual trauma to sort these experiences out alone. Children simply have no way of understanding what has happened, so they blame themselves. They often feel that something in their appearance triggered the abuse—large breasts, small breasts—things that have little, if anything, to do with their being victimized. As they grow older, girls may attempt to control these characteristics rather than learn how to protect themselves from being victimized again. For example, one woman claimed that she wore baggy clothes well into adulthood because she thought that these clothes hid the fact that she was large-breasted, which was what she believed "caused" her to be abused in childhood.

The irony of Roxanne's experience is that she repeated her sister's history of early unintended pregnancy. While we often read about families in which two or three generations of women have children during their early teens, there is very little written information explaining how these patterns emerge. Some people automatically assume that there is an implicit acceptance or even encouragement of early sexual activity in African-American families. Roxanne's story illustrates how negative expectations about sex, limited sex education, and emotional estrangement combine to increase a girl's chances of becoming involved in sex for the wrong reasons.

It is painful to imagine how many generations of women have been looking for love and acceptance, misreading cues from men that by having sex they will be loved or have someone to love. With more research to understand the effects of early sexual trauma, we could begin to identify the factors that lead to unintended pregnancies and other life choices that reflect a poor understanding of sexual responsibility. But it is clear that sexual trauma can be one of the most powerful predictors of later sexual and emotional problems for women if, as young girls, they do not receive the help they need to deal with it.

Did You Grow Up in a Risky Environment?

Of all other factors that can influence childhood sexual activity, poverty has been most strongly linked with abusive early-childhood experiences. Children who grow up amid poverty, often with families who are themselves disenfranchised, are at risk for a variety of social, health, emotional, and physical problems. When the quality of family life diminishes, the likelihood that the child will be protected from harmful experiences increases.

Growing up in large cities may also be conducive to sex play among black children. Women who grew up in this environment rather than in small towns or rural areas were more likely to engage in self-touching and masturbation. Those who grew up in urban areas were also slightly more likely to engage in "doctor" games before age 8.

We may speculate that having both parents at work and having more unsupervised time and greater exposure to more sex-related information are characteristics of urban families and city living that increased the chances that the black women in my research would become in-volved in sex-related activities. Still, their exposure occurred later in childhood than one might imagine for girls who are frequently labeled "fast" or sexually promiscuous.

It is not always the naive professor who misinterprets black children's sexual activities. If your parents failed to understand your sexual precocity or unusual interest in sex, they may have attempted to either ignore or punish the behavior away. But once aroused, sexual curiosity rarely disappears. Curiosity and subsequent sexual activities just become more secretive, more difficult to observe, and more deeply entrenched.

Lessons from the Distant Past

Some African societies seemed to acknowledge that a girl needed to rehearse sexual roles and behaviors. This led to a point in time when, with the right partner, it would be permissible for her to engage in sex. Childhood was the right time for rehearsal, because under the right circumstances there were apparently fewer negative sexual outcomes. Childhood is still the right time to start learning about sex, but in America today, permission to rehearse sexual roles and behavior is not given openly in childhood, and there is little to indicate that these societal rules will change. Given the many opportunities that exist for older adolescents and adults to take advantage of a child's curiosity about sex, it is unwise to assume that exploratory behavior among children is harmless. How can parents keep curiosity to a minimum?

Clearly, unlike traditional African culture, the old tales that were supposed to frighten children out of their sexual curiosity and delay sexual activity are no longer effective methods—not today, not in America. What can help ensure that sex play among children is kept to a minimum and remains innocent and exploratory? Having a close-knit family that keeps busy with child-related activities helps. Parents who do not rely on what they learned or were told as children help, because the world is changing and sexual knowledge must meet the reality of each child's world today. I believe that by the time they are 5 or 6, girls need some sexual knowledge. For example, girls who have had sexual feelings such as the pleasant sensations of touching or gently rubbing their labia, the external part of their genitals, should be taught what those feelings are, why these body parts are so sensitive, and who should or should not touch these areas.

Specific factual information that is age-appropriate, open communication, and an ongoing dialogue between children and responsible adults are crucial. When girls are taught how to control their sexuality and their bodies, they also gain the confidence they need to exert control in sexual and other relationships. Sometimes parents give their children mixed messages about their developing sexuality. Statements like the one Erin's mother made about her daughter's needing a man to improve her behavior can give a young girl the impression that learning to be responsible for her own behavior is less important than having someone else become responsible for her. These statements may be intended to be humorous, but the subtle message of sexual ownership is reminiscent of times past, when someone owned us. Parents need to make it clear to their daughters that in sexual matters girls are responsible for themselves.

What These Findings Mean to You

Contrary to stereotypes about the early sexual activity of black girls, for the average African-American woman, child sex play—including self-touching, masturbation, sexual arousal, and exploration with other children—was not a common experience. More specifically, childhood sex play does not appear to be an accepted aspect of African-American culture. When it does occur beyond appropriate limits, it seems to be more a by-product of city living and perhaps lack of supervision than a practice that black parents condone.

It is important to bear in mind that sexual "acting out," which is characterized by excessive masturbation and sex play, is often less an indication that a girl is fast or loose than a signal that she is crying out for help. It could be that she desperately needs a little attention, a responsible person to help or protect her from someone else's sexual aggression, more sex education, or professional help. Excessive sexual practices are also an indication that children need to develop other areas of competence in their lives. However, far too often when African-American girls engage in sexual behavior at an early age, it is assumed that they are simply more sexual. My findings do not support this notion.

In order to prepare you for your sexual role as an adult, your parents needed to teach you about sex and its consequences, supervise your activities, protect you from exploitation, surround you with friends who came from homes that offered the same messages, and help you to develop competence and self-confidence as an individual. Some of our parents did a better job of this than others. But if we are honest with ourselves, we will begin to see that there was almost always room for improvement.

That was certainly the case for Wanda, a 60-year-old widow who had begun dating again, much to her surprise, after the death of her husband three years ago.

Wanda's Story

She had met a nice man at church who was very kind and expressed interest in teaching her to play golf, something that she had always hoped her husband would teach her before he died.

Wanda had pretty much given up worrying about men, but Dan was determined to teach her, no matter how many excuses she gave to put him off. He really liked her; she blushed as she described how he complimented her on her dress, her coat, her hair. Anything to get her to smile.

Once she got into her lessons, she realized that he had a great sense of humor and that they had a lot in common. Time passed, and he asked her to have dinner at his home for their next date. Sensing that he wanted to be more intimate, she packed a suitcase and put it in her trunk, but returned it to the house because she did not want to seem that she was too eager.

Actually, they were both eager, but once they got into bed the problems started. When Dan tried to fondle her breasts, she explained that she was not accustomed to that kind of touching. She didn't do those things—they weren't right. Dan considered her to be a prude and told her so. Wanda, feeling hurt, hurriedly put on her clothes and left. She came to see me to determine if it was true. Was she a prude?

We traced her strict limits on touching back to things her parents had told her when she was a little girl in America's farm belt, and we discussed how they controlled her definition of being sexual even in adulthood. Without labeling, Wanda got the message. We discussed how to negotiate with partners about the things that you are uncomfortable with, those that you might consider, and some that you prefer.

Wanda used those guidelines to return to Dan with apologies for not discussing her feelings and ideas about what she would be willing to try, and explained how powerful her early sexual experiences were in shaping her adult practices. She decided that at age 60 she was ready to begin to broaden her definition of what it meant to be sexual and that he was a good partner with whom to begin that process inside a committed relationship.

Wanda was taught that body touching was not only culturally unacceptable but sinful, that sexual curiosity should not be a part of sexual experience, and that certain sexual feelings should be ignored rather than understood and enjoyed. These early lessons, however, were not hard to unlearn once she realized that she could look back on her childhood sexuality and redefine it for herself.

Typical African-American women don't have to search their memories very long to recall the prohibitions against sex play that they heard as children. But we rarely question whether or not those early lessons have any particular relevance now. I want you to know that they do. For example, if your parents did not allow you to have childhood sexual activity of any kind, it was for good reasons at the time. However, their messages about body touching and masturbation may have limited your curiosity about the body and how it works to the point that years later you are reluctant to check yourself for lumps or masses that may require medical attention. If that sounds familiar, it's time to learn new rules that could save your life.

Put the past behind you? Of course I realize that it's never entirely possible. But you can move on if you know where you've been. Let's look at another set of powerful childhood messages that have undoubtedly influenced your adult sexuality.

chapter 4

Childhood Messages

Gaining Permission to
Have Sexual Knowledge

Sonia's Story

Sonia grew up in California, in a working-class neighborhood, with her mother. Before she reached the age of 12, she had had three stepfathers. Even so, sex was a private matter that took place behind closed doors— nothing seen and nothing said, except a warning that sex before marriage would not be allowed. Sonia first became aware of sexual differences when she was 4 years old. While she was at a baby-sitter's house, she got a chance to see the nude body of a little boy of her own age. As Sonia grew older, her mother instructed her to come straight home from school and not talk to strangers, so nobody would "get her." She did as her mother told her, though she had no idea what it meant to be "gotten." She imagined that someone would beat her up, so she stayed clear of strangers.

Other sexual experiences were quite limited. Sonia's mother was a teacher, and she kept her daughter pretty busy. When Sonia was 9, she touched and explored her body on several occasions but did not masturbate or engage in exploratory games with other children. Finally, when she was 14, her mother sat her down and drew pictures of the male and female bodies. She explained intercourse and, said Sonia, "She told me flat out not to do that" before marriage.

Years later, Sonia could see that her mother had helped her set a pace in her life, placing career goals before her sexual development.

She felt that she had learned enough sexual information in childhood to sustain her, and she planned to teach her own children in the same fashion.

Our Reluctant Guides on Childhood's Path to Knowledge

Sonia grew up in typical circumstances. A majority of African-American children growing up today are raised by a single parent from early in their lives. Most of them learn very little about sex from their parents or parent figures. Sonia's mother eventually ensured that Sonia received some basic sexual information, and that she was the source of this information. Sonia's mother not only expressed very explicit opposition to sexual intercourse before marriage but explained its consequences.

Most parents, African-Americans included, dread discussing sex with their kids. Sonia was lucky in that her mother at least talked to her frankly, even though the conversation came late in her development. After all, it's better late than never. Few parents know exactly when, how, or what to tell their children. How could they? Most of them have been socialized to view sex education as basically unnecessary, and they themselves received little, if any, formal education in this area. Some forty years ago, Kinsey and his associates at the Kinsey Institute stated that American parents did not teach their children about sex. Little has changed today.

This chapter offers a set of questions to help you assess the quality of the guidance you received on your own path to sexual knowledge.

How Did You Learn about Sex?

When parents *do* attempt to educate their children about sex, it is often prompted by something catastrophic, like the early pregnancy of someone else's child or the news that someone has been sexually abused. So they cover only one specific topic or simply repeat their opposition to sex between unmarried people.

Did you learn about sex the way you learned about math or reading? Did your parents sit down to dinner and ask you after a day at school, "And what did you learn about sex today?" Did your mother even quiz you on your sexual knowledge, which includes an understanding of how the body functions and how to stay sexually healthy? Probably not. Sex just isn't something that we discuss openly. Despite epidemic numbers of pregnant, unmarried adolescents and increasing cases of STDs and AIDS, Americans continue to debate whether children need sexual knowledge when they are not supposed to be sexually active, as if lack of knowledge could prevent exposure to sex, prohibit sexual activity, or stop the flow of information—or misinformation—from other sources.

Perhaps you're beginning to see the specific dilemma that black parents face. No one reacts more nervously to questions about sex than parents who are attempting to socialize their children "properly." One black mother shared this story with me. Her daughter chose to confirm her understanding of a recent conversation about the differences between boys and girls while they were standing in the checkout line at the grocery store. The little girl pointed to a male cashier and said loudly, "Does he have a penis, too?"

The mother, shrinking into the floor and eager to end the discussion, tried unsuccessfully to distract her daughter. Assuming that her mother hadn't heard her, the little girl repeated the question in an even louder voice. She was determined to test her knowledge and gain her mother's approval. By now, other people were beginning to snicker. The mother, mortified that her child would be viewed as unsocialized or even uncivilized, quietly began to threaten the child, saying, "We do not discuss sex in public!"

If the child had read the headline of one of the tabloids next to the checkout stand aloud, her mother would have beamed with pride that she demonstrated such fine reading ability. Instead, she hurried through the line and avoided the cashier's glances, secure in the conviction that she had taught her daughter not to discuss sex in certain settings. I wondered whether she had not also taught her daughter that if she had questions about sex, she should avoid her mother.

This scenario could have happened in any family, regardless of its ethnicity. But for black families, it is more likely to be loaded with meaning and handled with alarm. Our girls receive the impression that asking or learning about sex is impolite, rude, or unladylike, and that sex should not be discussed with anyone, even with adults who can be trusted. The following story is a happy exception to the rule.

Shirley's Story

I learned where babies came from by noticing my baby-sitter's stomach. I was 7 years old when Shirley agreed to watch my sister and me for the day because we had colds and couldn't go to school. Shirley and Leonard were recently married, and they were expecting their first child. They were the first friends of my parents whose lives unfolded at a time when I could begin to understand the relationship between marriage, sex, and having children. I recognized that these events were supposed to occur in some order, and that sex and children belonged within the context of marriage. If you had sex, you could get a baby.

That particular day, something drew my attention to Shirley's growing midsection. I was one of those persistent children who, given the chance, would ask a million questions. My curiosity got the best of me. "What's wrong with your stomach?" I asked. Shirley continued to do whatever she was doing and calmly replied, "There is a baby growing in there."

My sister Sandra punched me teasingly. "Don't you know anything?" she said. Well no, I thought to myself. I was beginning to wonder how my sister knew so much about where babies came from and I didn't. Admitting my ignorance, I figured I needed to get at least as much information as she had, so I seized the moment.

I had taken a great risk in asking an adult a personal question about sex. Shirley was kind enough to answer with as much information as I could handle at that time. I hoped that my sister wouldn't tell on me and get me into trouble for asking. (She didn't.) Through that brief interaction, I also learned that all conversations about sex with adults did not have *adverse consequences, as I had feared. Shirley's explanation satisfied my curiosity and did not interrupt our activities or conversation. I saw that a question about sex was no different from one about any other matter.*

The fact that a cherished adult answered my questions made the information I gained far more credible than the sex gossip or jokes that I heard at school. Since then I have been very grateful to Shirley Walker for explaining where babies came from, and to my sister for not telling on me for being so curious. I was very fortunate that this experience gave me the confidence to ask more questions about sex.

When Did You Learn? From Whom?

Throughout our lives, we inhale information about sex the way we breathe air. We learn directly by being taught by others or through personal experience. We learn indirectly by overhearing conversations, openly watching people's sexual activities, sneaking peeks, or, like me, simply by putting pieces of information together. For most of us, this information comes from our homes, schools, churches, friends, and the media.

Each bit of sexual information we learn adds up, preparing us for the time we decide to become sexually active. Ideally, we make this decision when we marry or reach maturity—that is, emotional and physical maturity and financial stability. Although it is highly probable that we will make this decision for ourselves, our parents are crucial. They provide the moral and cultural values, as well as the factual information, that will enable us to become increasingly more sexually responsible.

Remarkably, African-American women receive almost *no* factual information about sex from their parents before age 13. White women also receive little information about sex during childhood, but the important difference is that the information they do receive is more likely to come from their parents. By contrast, the information that African-American women receive is more likely to come from movies, magazines, friends, or as a result of some personal experience or observation.

Was Talking about Sex Allowed?

African-American parents are reluctant to give their daughters factual information for fear that they won't be considered respectable, chaste, and sexually uninitiated—and behave accordingly. These parents don't want to raise promiscuous little she-devils and give further credence to unjust and inaccurate stereotypes. In a safe environment, if parents also assume enough responsibility for their daughter's sex education, they tend to get along despite random events. On the other hand, when no adult assumes responsibility for providing any information and a child's education results from unsafe experiences that she cannot understand, the results can be devastating. Eboni's story is not uncommon.

Eboni's Story

Twenty-seven-year-old Eboni recalled that the sex education she received as a child had been difficult and disturbing. She grew up in the housing projects in Texas with her parents until their divorce when she was 10. Her mother had been a custodian by day but decided to go on the road and seek her fame as an entertainer, leaving Eboni in the care of her father and his mother. As a result, Eboni did not get a chance to see how two adults could express their love and affection for each other in a romantic relationship. Hers was a strict Baptist family, and sex was never discussed. Eboni could recall only numerous rules about modesty and privacy. In fact, as a very young child she was whipped by her father if she didn't wear clothes in the house.

Eboni's basic education about sex came from what she saw and the direct experiences that she had. When she was 5, she and her brother were wrestling with their uncle. Suddenly her uncle locked her brother out of the room and began taking off Eboni's clothes. He held her down on the bed and began to penetrate her but stopped abruptly. Naturally, Eboni was frightened of him from then on. She didn't really understand what he intended to do or why he wanted to do it, but she knew that his behavior was unexpected and strange.

Although they were silent about other matters, Eboni's grandmother and father insisted that she not talk to strangers or take money from them. Eboni understood why—she knew that being molested meant being raped. But strangers were not the predators. When she was 8 years old, Eboni was at a neighbor's house watching their baby while the mother was away. The baby's older brother wrestled her down, claiming that he was playing with her. Then he got on top of her and fondled her body, touching her nipples and the area between her legs. She was beginning to get the idea that her body was something that everybody wanted. Her friends were always giggling and talking about kissing, hugging, and touching boys, anyway. She figured that she was just like everybody else.

By the time she was 10 years old, Eboni had begun to understand what her uncle and the others tried to do. She used to hide and watch her uncle having sex with other children—doing what he tried to do to her, doing what her father and grandmother told her that strangers would do if they could. But they did not mention that it could happen with someone you saw every day.

What Eboni did not learn at home, she learned from a variety of other sources with which she came into contact. It was the responsibility of Eboni's father and grandmother to ensure that the amount of sex-related information she received corresponded with her ability to understand what she was told. Even so, the family could not always monitor Eboni's sexual experiences. No family can. However, an ongoing dialogue with Eboni about sex could have helped her father and grandmother realize that some negative exposure had endangered her well-being.

Less traumatic events than those that Eboni experienced can be equally scarring if they are repeated throughout a girl's life. Feeling at risk of sexual exploitation is something that girls do not get over or outgrow. Eboni's value as a person was overshadowed by her value as a sexual object.

The Power of Five Strong Messages You Might Have Heard about Sex

The basic and strongest messages about sexual activities that should be communicated to girls by their parents concern nudity, masturbation, homosexuality, premarital intercourse, and being safe from sexual abuse. The first two involve attitudes about privacy and intimacy regarding our own bodies. Homosexuality and premarital intercourse involve expressing sexuality with someone else and represent the expectations parents have for their daughters as sexual beings. Messages about abuse indicate both parental and community concern about protecting girls from sexual assault. What girls are told—if anything—by their families about these five behaviors determines how prepared they will be to handle the basic sexual decisions and dilemmas of childhood.

1. Messages about Nudity

Sonia's and Eboni's early experiences of nudity as a form of sexual knowledge is typical of the African-American women in my research. Either they learned nothing at all or they learned something negative. One out of four of the women didn't remember their parents saying anything. Over half recalled that their parents warned them to put on a robe or cover their bodies. A few women, like Eboni, were punished if they were ever seen nude. Clearly, there were unspoken and sometimes spoken rules that conveyed the message that little black girls were not supposed to be naked around other people, including family members.

2. Messages about Masturbation

Like Eboni's and Sonia's families, most African-American parents also said little, if anything, about masturbation during their daughters' childhood. If they did, the message was usually quite clear: It is sinful and taboo—something that you just don't do. Interestingly, women who grew up in homes that had two rather than one parent or caretaker were more likely to remember being told not to masturbate. Having the message repeated by both adults in the home may make the prohibitions even more memorable.

One of the reasons parents may not say much about masturbation is that they do not anticipate that their children will be sexual at an early age. Masturbation is a behavior that parents usually react to negatively. If a child is caught, the parent might say or do something; otherwise this is a topic that is rarely discussed.

A girl's comfort with her own body is an important prerequisite to sexual knowledge and responsibility. At the very least, even if masturbation (and nudity) is not openly condoned, girls need to grow up in surroundings that allow for privacy but also offer them the chance to control and come to know their bodies. They need permission to become familiar with themselves, whether they choose to touch and explore their bodies or not. It's part of being sexually responsible.

3. Messages about Homosexuality

Open and honest discussions of homosexuality are rare among black adults, especially those who are older, more religious, conservative about sex, and Afrocentric in their cultural beliefs. It certainly follows that conversations with children are even less likely. For most women, homosexuality is not mentioned or discussed before they are 13, probably for some of the same reasons that their parents do not discuss masturbation. However, homosexuality is something that most parents feel strongly about, and black parents are usually especially vocal about their opposition. One in five women whose parents spoke out against homosexuality were told that it "was an abomination as far as the Bible was concerned" and that homosexuals should be locked up.

Women who were born in the 1950s and '60s are more likely to remember their parents having very negative views about homosexuality. This is not surprising, given the times and the attitudes about gays and lesbians, especially in the black community. It was assumed that black people were not "like that." Parents thought they could dissuade their children from becoming gay or engaging in the sexual practices known to be associated with gays or lesbians by talking about homosexuality in negative terms. Some women learned, as many have today, that parental attitudes do not necessarily discourage homosexuality. One woman who grew up in rural Alabama recalled that her father was very much against homosexuality. Her mother, however, was more understanding, because her brother was gay.

At best, there is a diversity of opinion about homosexuality as a sexual orientation or lifestyle choice, and the moral and religious teachings that many people absorb further complicate the issues. Yet children see a variety of lifestyles and may make choices for themselves that contradict what they learned were acceptable behaviors. Silence among family members about homosexuality can simply reinforce children's silence with their parents. In addition, the opportunity for parents to provide their children with sexual knowledge and support is missed.

4. Messages about Premarital Intercourse

Like Sonia's mother, most parents are far from silent about premarital intercourse. African-American parents or parental figures are more outspoken about their opposition to sex before marriage than about any of the other sexual practices I've listed. Again, this is especially true of women who were born in the 1950s and '60s, who grew up hearing about waiting for the right time or for the right man or "until you know what you're doing." But did the girls understand what it was that they were supposed to wait for?

Intercourse is the sexual act that children are most likely to hear about. Like Sonia, the majority of them discover the real meaning of *intercourse* after age 9. Of that percentage, almost half learn what the word means after age 13.

It is clear that most girls know what intercourse is and what they shouldn't do before marriage. However, the information comes toward the end of childhood and is rarely followed by an explanation about why girls shouldn't engage in sexual behavior. The result was that often girls did not understand that the consequences of not delaying sexual activity had repercussions that extended far beyond the trouble they would get into with their parents or the church. They failed to recognize that the negative consequences could affect their bodies and their lives. When children receive only fear-inducing information or warnings that they cannot understand, it may serve only to increase their fear and shame rather than prohibit them from engaging in forbidden behavior.

Once, when I spoke to a parents' organization, a black mother pulled me aside to tell me how her parents used the threat of "burning in hell" to discourage her from engaging in sexual activity. She grew up in Mississippi, and that summer it was so hot that she wondered how hell could be any hotter. Growing up with no sexual information, her curiosity was stronger than her fear of hell. Before adolescence, children are often unable to understand concepts that they cannot see and feel. The familiar heat of her home state was the worst consequence this woman could imagine. Hell could be no worse. So she became sexually active just to see what sex was all about.

Curious children need to be told the consequences of sex in words that they can comprehend. More than other girls, ours have to understand that natural curiosity may be misinterpreted as a desire to have sex and may inadvertently encourage someone to try to involve them in sexual activities.

5. Messages about Sexual Abuse

Rarely in the research or discussion of how girls learn about sex is there mention of what parents tell their children about sexual molestation or abuse. Most girls, like both Eboni and Sonia, are warned about strangers trying to get them into cars or trying to touch them, especially if they grow up in large cities. However, the majority of girls have no idea what being molested actually means. While the warnings proliferate, only one in ten girls are given specific explanations; those who grow up in large urban areas are more likely to know that molestation can involve being raped.

Few girls are told nothing at all about the dangers of being molested. Even if it wasn't a clear and present threat, it is generally alluded to in one way or another. For example, Cheryl grew up in a small town. There were no strangers, and she was told that she did not have to worry about being molested. She was relieved, because she had no idea what being molested meant.

Generally, it seems that even though girls do not have a specific idea of what to expect, their families do convey that being molested is harmful, something to be avoided. Almost all of these warnings involve strangers in cars or in open settings where children can run away. Very few girls are told about the possibility of family members or people known to them, such as neighbors or family friends, molesting them in their homes, where they cannot escape their advances.

It is possible that because of our history, parents have been looking outside their families for the perpetrators of abuse. But as Eboni's experiences illustrate, incidents involving someone who is known to the child are far more common than those involving strangers.

Did You Experience the Joy of Seeing Affectionate Parents?

One of the great expectations of childhood sexual development is that children will have a chance to observe healthy expressions of love, caring, and affection, and to learn when, how, and with whom to express those feelings. This is most often exemplified at home, where children can see how adults relate to each other.

Like Eboni, more than a third of the women in my research did not recall seeing their parents kiss, touch in an affectionate manner, or behave in a way that suggested that they had a sexual or affectionate relationship. Many parents were not even involved in any significant relationship that their children could observe. Some women, like Sonia, felt that their parents tried to hide their sexual attraction to each other. These parents stressed that there was a proper time and place for everything, including sex. Whatever they did sexually or affectionately was done in private. Their children rightly assumed that sex takes place when there is no one else around and behind closed doors.

Despite the fact that many women didn't actually see their parents behave in affectionate ways, many believed that their parents had positive feelings toward each other. One women figured that her parents must have enjoyed sex, because they had six children. There were a few who had memories of their mother rebuffing the advances of a father or boyfriend in front of the children. The impression, though, was that the mother was either not interested in having sex with that person or she was embarrassed by this overt display of affection.

It is possible, though, that these mothers were not sure how to handle affection in front of their children—

how much is too much or too little to display, for example. These same parents might be surprised to learn that their children assumed that because there was no display of affection, they did not love each other. Imagine children who never see anyone enjoying, making, or receiving loving remarks. Suppose they never hear adults say that they miss each other, want to be together, or need one another. Imagine further that these children are never allowed to know that their parents comfort each other and share each other's sadness, pain, or sorrow. Then it is perhaps easier to understand how some children might believe that a baby is the only tangible representation of love between adults.

Some of these parents may have been trying to defy stereotypes about the inability of black men and women to control their sexual impulses. Mothers may have preferred the stereotype of the workhorse to the she-devil and were very reserved in their displays of affection. They probably did not intend to appear cold and unloving, and did not realize that their behavior had been misinterpreted by their children.

Finally, at least one in five of the black women in my research recalled seeing their parents display actions or feelings that gave the impression that sex was negative. These parents argued, yelled, fought, or ignored each other. A typical description of a "loveless" relationship is one in which the parents did not talk directly to each other and used the children to communicate instead. No warm and tender demonstrations of caring were described in these relationships.

When children are repeatedly told that they should wait until they get married before having sex, yet the married adults they observe are constantly engaged in a private war, it is difficult to convince them that love, sex, and marriage go together. If, on the other hand, they do see tenderness and love between two adults, the message is reinforced that marriage, or at least love with the right person, is worth waiting for. Parents can be the most effective reminder that something good can come from a long-term commitment to one person, and that sex is better within the context of a loving relationship.

What Did Your Church Say?

When organized religion plays a part in childhood sex education, it is usually to emphasize the church's position on what is right and wrong, and to provide a convincing moral tone. At least half of the women in my research reported that their earliest memory of the church's message about sex stressed that it was a sacred act reserved only for marriage. Women born in the 1950s could even recall the exact biblical passages about the evils of sex before marriage. One such passage, the epistle of Paul to the Galatians, declared, "Now the works of the flesh are manifest, which are these; Adultery, fornication, uncleanliness, lasciviousness." They also remembered Leviticus 21:7: "They shall not take a woman that is a harlot or profane. . . ." The consequences of violating covenants about sex were grim—going to hell, being labeled a whore, being ostracized from the church and even from your family.

If many women do not recall anything being said in church about sex when they were children, this is probably because the ministers in their churches thought children were sexually inactive. When children reach adolescence, however, the congregation becomes concerned about them going "astray." Today sermons about reducing teen pregnancy and preventing early patterns of substance abuse are heard far more frequently than lectures about the importance of early sex education for children. The irony is that early education is also a form of prevention, and on that subject the church is usually silent.

School—Mostly Dancing Tampons?

School is often the only place children have left to gain some factual information about sex. However, sex-education programs are so varied that it is difficult to determine whether an extended course is any more valuable than a movie or a class discussion. Usually, if sex education is included in the curriculum, there is little continuity in what is taught from one year to the next. School systems often have antiquated notions about what children need to know, and they do not demand that teachers who present this information be qualified to teach it. Consequently, while schools touch on specific topics like abstinence, anatomy, AIDS education, or sexual-abuse prevention, comprehensive programs that cover all of these topics for children from primary through secondary school are rare, especially in the public schools.

Eboni and Sonia were among the third of the women in my research who did not receive any sex education in school before age 13. Of those who remembered seeing a film about menstruation and pregnancy, one woman recalled a Disney-like cartoon that featured dancing tampons and sanitary napkins that "talked" to the audience about how to use them. The film did not make what was happening to her body seem real, nor did it cover *how* females could get pregnant. It's important to make sex education interesting, especially if it is aimed at young girls. But however entertaining sperm dancing along the fallopian tubes may be, there is little else to learn from cartoons about sexual development. Only one in five women attended a sex-education class before adolescence.

For women who attended religious schools, discussions about sex followed biblical rules. The story of Onan (Genesis 38:9) "spilling his seed" was often used to discourage masturbation or excessively touching one's body. Specific information was often laced with morals about what children should not do rather than with facts. So, while it is true that girls today receive more formal sex education than they were given years ago, it still isn't adequate preparation for the sexually stimulating society in which we live.

Friends—Peer Pressure and Sexual Hype?

The pressure from friends to have the facts about sex (if not experience) begins to increase in preadolescence. By about age 10, youngsters can recall the proper names of body parts and understand how the male and female bodies function, and how pregnancy and sexually transmitted diseases occur. If parents are relatively silent, except on certain topics, friends can fill in the gaps, or at least stimulate curiosity and interest in sex.

Eboni's perceptions about sexual experimentation were clearly influenced by her friends. Apparently, girls want to live vicariously by encouraging others to do what they have been told not to do or what they know only little about. Few express any negative views about experimentation to their friends. Possessing sexual knowledge and sophistication seems to foster acceptance among pre-teens, because it can be fairly risky to obtain this knowledge firsthand. For this reason, friends may suggest or encourage sexual activity to each other. Some teens may even fabricate incidents in which they are involved with someone in order to appear sexually experienced and fearless among their friends.

Girls have to determine what is sexual hype, who is spreading it, and why their friends are encouraging others to get involved in sexual activity. At the same time, some claims of early sexual experience may not be fabricated. The pressure to get more sexual knowledge and experience can come from girls who feel somewhat stigmatized by their own early sexual activity. They may be trying to create a peer group composed of girls whose reputations are no better than theirs.

There is an antidote, however: parental involvement.

Women who identify their parents rather than friends as having the greatest influence on them from childhood to age 18 also tend to delay first-time intercourse until late adolescence. They perceive their parents to be im-portant sources of guidance, modeling, and inspiration. This dilutes the potent peer messages urging sexual experimentation.

Lessons from the Distant Past

In many respects, our ancestors in Africa were better pre-pared and educated for the life in their environment than we are, regardless of Western perceptions to the contrary. Today many girls learn about sex on their own, through what they observe rather than from what they are told by par-ents.

As young girls, we receive too little information from the right sources and too much information from the wrong ones. The information that we do receive focuses correctly on moral behavior and pregnancy prevention, with the expectation that sexual activity will begin with marriage. But warnings and threats about what *not* to do sexually do not appear to be enough to sustain us.

In Africa sex education, and even sexual experimenta-tion, if allowed, was an essential part of a girl's preparation for marriage and motherhood. I am not suggesting that African-American women today should adopt this pattern; I am simply saying that it was at least explained and ex-pected. These once well-defined expectations about how girls should learn about sex seem to have been replaced by a social fabric that has no realistic order, no meaning, and no purpose.

What These Findings Mean to You

Children need a comprehensive understanding of sex, and they should be able to get it from reputable sources, especially their parents. But no one gives most African-American girls this start in life. The average African-American girl receives little sexual information from her parents, and what she does learn often comes late in childhood.

What did it mean if your parents said little to you about sex? One possibility is that they did not think that you needed information, but another is that they did not want to think of you as a sexual being. Sexuality in childhood for some parents may be a painful reminder of their own vulnerability. They may also have felt that sex education undermined their efforts to keep you pure, untainted, and respectable. But chastity should not be confused with a lack of sexual knowledge, and appropriate sex education should not be confused with sexually exploiting children or rushing them into sex. Ignorance can result in more sexually exploitative experiences, particularly in the unsafe environments in which many African-American girls grow up. Sadly, parents as sex educators, the most potentially powerful influence on childhood sexual information, have been replaced by school lessons of varied quality, misinformation from friends, and television, newspapers, magazines, or sometimes traumatic personal experiences.

My findings suggest that while African-American parents certainly do not ignore their responsibility to cover the five basic messages about nudity, masturbation, homosexuality, premarital intercourse, and being safe from sexual abuse, they generally avoid giving their daughters enough factual information about the big picture to have a comprehensive understanding of their sexuality or a sense that sexual knowledge is fundamentally important.

For better or worse, children internalize whatever messages they are given about how to behave. Therefore, if you got the right messages at the right time, you probably learned to make decisions about what to do and what not to do that were well-reasoned and in your own best interest. You grew up prepared to take each new step toward womanhood, even though each one required more information about your body, yourself as a sexual being, and the consequences of your sexual activity. If you did not get the right childhood messages or got them too soon or too late, you probably continued to struggle with your sexual decisions and their consequences.

Some of the sexual messages we internalized as children did not stand the test of time. For example, messages implying "you don't need to know something that you aren't supposed to be doing" contradict our present-day realities. These days, most women grow older struggling with the question, "What do I need to know about sex at this point in my life?" It's a good question to be asking when doing what's good for your sexual health may be outside of the realm of your prior sexual experience. For the same reason, you may also find yourself wondering if the things you were told when you were young are still accurate and sufficient. After all, your parents were young then, too, and may not have known all that you need to know today.

Now we are the grown-ups (or soon to be!). As we mature and begin to develop committed relationships and start families, it is suddenly our turn to communicate our sexual knowledge to others. We, ourselves, have become the bearers of the vital messages about condoned sexual behavior. This raises a lot of important questions. For instance, "How do I communicate my knowledge to other people? How do I avoid perpetuating or unconsciously behaving like one of those outdated stereotypes?" Confidently coming up with good answers is bound to be easier for women who heard effective messages about their own childhood behaviors, but all of us can handle the challenge. The following story is one of my favorite examples of what happens when a woman empowers herself to send the right messages to others, regardless of the ones that defined her own childhood.

Faye's Story

Faye and her husband Charles, both blue-collar workers in their forties, had been raised in homes where there was little opportunity to see how married love should be expressed, especially when children were around. They also had never seen two adults successfully resolve an argument in front of children or finish their disagreements in their bedroom, behind closed doors.

It was only a note passed from their son to their daughter about being afraid when "Mommy and Daddy close the door to their room" that made them realize that they were frightening their children unnecessarily. The kids never got a chance to see them make up, hug and kiss, and compromise.

They had to make a concerted effort to model affection in ways that were appropriate for the children to observe and comfortable for them as adults. Their determination motivated them to learn new ways to communicate the value of being married, to fight fair, and to let their children observe how compromises are made on some issues in a marriage. While not exposing every expression of affection and everything they disagreed on, they shared more of their relationship. As a result, the children became less concerned with what they could not see and more willing to respect their parents' need for privacy.

chapter 5

Our Adolescent Development
Learning to Be a Lady

Allie's Story

Alexandria, a married 28-year-old mother of two, manages the snack bar at a local public school. She grew up in a close-knit working-class family of seven in a small Mississippi town. As a growing teen, she was aware of how romance could get a person into trouble. She remembered her father lecturing her older brother about using a condom when it was discovered that he was seeing two girls at the same time. Her father, the disciplinarian, explained that he did not want her brother to have babies all over town. Her older sister also got into trouble for making out with her boyfriend on the porch. Her father told her that her behavior could give the neighbors the impression that she was fast and that her family had no morals and no control over her.

The family was protective of their children's reputations—boys and girls alike. Allie's parents also warned that they should trust no one. This was the family motto when it came to being around strangers. What Allie learned about how to behave around boys was consistent at home and at school. Her mother's advice was typical: "If you let a boy go to bed with you the first time, that is all he will want." And "It is not nice to let a boy touch your body or kiss in public" or "If a boy likes you and wants to get married, he will want you to be a virgin."

In sex-education class at school the teacher said that kissing and touching boys would lead to other things, like sex. He also described how people could become infected with various sexually transmitted diseases. But the teacher really shocked the class by telling stories about how girls could get pregnant even when boys ejaculated outside of the vagina. He explained that the sperm can sometimes live long enough to enter the vagina and travel up the fallopian tubes to fertilize an egg.

The entire class was horrified. A new fear had been introduced—getting pregnant without even having intercourse! Allie's friends decided to ignore the teacher and continued to discuss what it would be like to have sex and marry some cute guy. They spent every available moment in and out of class eyeing guys and discussing strategies to get them to call on the phone.

Allie's parents wouldn't ever allow her to kiss a boy, because it might lead to something else. They warned, "If you ever get pregnant, you'll be in a lot of trouble." In more calm discussions, they talked about the consequences of "becoming a mother before it was time."

Finally, when Allie was 16 her mother let her wear lipstick. It had to be a "soft pink color" and not red or black, because "only loose girls wear dark lipstick." Allie wondered whether her mother had seen the latest magazines and movies, in which everybody wore dark lipstick and nail polish—the darker the better! But her mother insisted that even in the '90s black girls had to live by different rules to be considered respectable. Any makeup she was now able to wear had to "look like she didn't have any on."

Allie protested, but not too strongly. At least she could wear it, unlike some of her friends, whose parents never allowed them to wear makeup at all.

Allie, after having thought a great deal about it, imagined that intercourse would hurt but felt that after sex she would be a different woman. If she couldn't wait for marriage, she would perhaps feel a bit guilty about it. She knew, however, that whenever she had sex she would be in love, and that love would be worth the pain and the guilt. This love would definitely be for life.

Guiding Our Transformation— The Uphill Battle for Parents

As Allie's story shows, parents are especially outspoken and insistent about the behaviors that they expect from their daughters between the ages of 13 and 17. What most parents want to achieve by this is what I call teaching their daughters "to be ladies." Parents' opposition to sexual activity increases and the tone of the message becomes more exaggerated. Parents are likely to use warnings and threats, to yell or punish in conveying their opposition to nudity, masturbation, and homosexuality. Two out of three African-American women recall that their parents also voiced their opposition to premarital intercourse. Clearly, parents feel that speaking out and applying pressure is important to their daughters' reputations and to their own. To the neighbors, Allie's teen years seemed calm. They wouldn't have recognized her as a typically emotional teenager, but she was.

The typical teen finds her body changing, her hormones raging, and her emotions in a constant state of upheaval. She menstruates, her breasts grow larger, her waist gets smaller, and her hips widen. Her world turns around her peers. But she is quite capable of controlling her sexuality, which is now visible not only to herself but to others as well, if her parents instruct her in ways that she understands. If they succeed, she will contradict well-established negative images of sexually irresponsible black teenagers. Parents, however, face an uphill battle.

Adolescents normally yearn for and gain increasing autonomy from their families during these years. Anything their parents say has to compete with what their friends, love interests, and popular culture may say about sexual experimentation. Furthermore, even though their first intercourse and the majority of their other sexual experiences still lie ahead of them, already they know more about sex than their parents realize. They have learned from childhood sex play and for some girls, sexual exploitation has already begun, usually without their parents' knowledge and certainly without their consent. For some teens, the process of learning "to be a lady" will coincide with rather than precede sexual activity. And yet they need more guidance than ever from their families in order to manage their biological transformation and learn how to behave in their new bodies. Allie's parents were on the right track. But they failed to do one enormously important thing. Did you notice it? Like most African-American parents, they failed to give their maturing teen any concrete information about her growing sexuality, leaving the facts to others and her lively, romantic imagination.

This chapter will give you a more informed perspective on the critical periods in the life of young African-American women. Exactly what messages did you receive between the ages of 13 and 17 about sexual behavior? What sources of information did you have to help you in making decisions regarding your sexuality? What events ruled your life? What physical and biological changes were you going through? What were your reactions to your parents urging you to be a lady? These are all questions that you need to explore before jumping to conclusions about the meaning of your past decisions or those of any African-American girls currently going through this sensitive phase of their lives.

Coping with Your Biological Development— Was It Hard to Handle the Changes?

With puberty, the gradual or sometimes sudden transformation of a girl's body into a more adult appearance can lead others to make assumptions about her morality and availability. The more curvaceous and physically endowed we are, no matter what age we are, the more attention we will attract.

This attention may be flattering to an adolescent, but it's a nightmare for her parents. If she is still young when her body changes, a teenage girl may hear sexual comments:

"Ooh, your daughter is stacked!"
"She's fresh!"
"She is phat (well built)!"
"She's fine!"

These remarks can be overwhelming not only to a girl's parents but also to the girl herself, who is beginning to gain confidence in her appearance and her ability to control her sexuality. If she is not yet a teen but is physically mature, she may be mistakenly thought to be older and more experienced than she actually is. If she is older and has not yet developed, reminders that she has not yet measured up to certain physical standards can be equally painful.

African-American girls may begin to look more grown-up and potentially more sexual at an earlier age than do their white counterparts. Since they appear more "womanly," their emotional maturity is assumed to be equal to their physical maturity. More is expected of them as sexually mature teens, when in reality they may still be little girls.

The onset of breast development gives us a clue to this phenomenon. African-American women remember their breasts beginning to bud at age 7; many more first notice their breasts developing at age 11. Even though this is currently the national average for puberty, black girls have been reported to begin puberty earlier than white girls do. Scientists think some of the reasons for this discrepancy can be found in the differing rates of growth in height and body weight between the two groups.

Research with 9- and 10-year-old black and white girls was conducted by a research team led by Dr. John Morrison at Children's Hospital Medical Center in Cincinnati, Ohio. Their findings revealed that body weight, particularly obesity, was a factor that contributed to the onset of puberty or to the appearance of breast development. Girls who are overweight are more likely to begin puberty earlier, and black girls are more likely to be overweight in early adolescence than their white peers. Sometimes what appears to be breast development may be fatty tissue in the arm and breast area of the body.

There are several theories about why more black girls may be overweight. It is possible that they simply gain weight because of what or how they eat in childhood and fail to lose the weight to assume their natural body size in puberty.

It is also possible that their natural body size may be larger than that of their white peers. Some girls may also enter adolescence overweight in an attempt to minimize the amount of attention paid to their physical appearance because they are not yet ready to handle changes in their bodies and their sexuality at the same time.

In their book *Black Rage,* Price Cobbs and William Grier described weight gain as a reaction to the excess attention that black women's sexuality attracts. Some teens may inadvertently assume the image of the mammy in order to divert attention from their sexual maturity. Being obese may become a way of managing their sexuality instead of dealing with it more directly. You might expect, no matter what theory you subscribe to, that weight problems will have a negative impact on a girl's body image and self-esteem. In addition, you might assume that there will be health concerns. "Baby fat" is difficult to lose, particularly without a proper diet and regular exercise.

Choosing Your Confidants—Were They Sources of Vague Information?

As a girl's body develops and changes, support and confirmation from others becomes increasingly important. With whom do black girls share this phase of their lives?

More than half of African-American girls discuss the changes in their breasts with either their mother or a mother figure, in contrast with white girls, who, based on my study, are twice as likely to discuss breast development with a friend instead of a parent. At the onset of menstruation (ranging from ages 9 to 18, with the average age being 12), girls also turn to their mothers for advice and help with the necessary equipment the first time. But once again, there are significant differences between the black and the white experience. According to my research, black mothers are most likely to explain menstruation in vague terms that focus more on hygiene than on what is actually happening to a girl's body. For example, mothers admonish, "Now you're a woman, so you have to keep yourself clean" or "You can get pregnant now, so be careful."

Who receives factual information about ovulation and menstruation? In my findings, two out of three girls who did were white. Perhaps black girls get such vague explanations because their mothers do not know the facts about menstruation. It's easy to see why this might be the case. If black parents did not learn sexual facts while they were growing up, they would have limited sexual knowledge to pass along and little awareness that for adolescents, specific instruction about changes due to puberty are sorely needed.

Did You Like Your Body?

You might expect these physical changes to be burdensome, especially for African-American girls, who may not be ready to deal with all the ramifications of their visible sexuality. With this in mind, I tried to discover just how girls felt about their bodies and themselves. What I learned surprised me. Four out of five African-American teens were far more likely than their white peers to feel good about themselves. Compared with their white counterparts, more African-American adolescents reported that they liked their teenage bodies. Fewer than one in three claimed that she was unhappy with her body during adolescence.

What Were Your Expectations About Sex?

Are young black women really obsessed with sex? To find out what girls think about sex and whether there is a specific person or a specific reason that would stop them from being sexually active, I asked women in my research if they ever thought about having sex and decided against it. Almost half of them had never thought about intercourse prior to their first experience. However, about one in three gave fear as the reason they did not have sex after thinking about it. The sources of this fear included their parents' reactions, followed by the possibility of pregnancy, and, finally, the chances of contracting a sexually transmitted disease. A less common reason was that they had thought about having sex but believed they were still not ready.

Since most women cited fear as a reason for delaying sex, I asked what African-American teens expected intercourse to be like and whether they had any realistic idea about what they were getting into. Certainly, our expectations contribute to our decisions about whether, why, or when to have sex.

Because African-American girls had so little factual information about sex, I anticipated that they would expect sex to be romantic. In fact, most girls generally expect that sex will be wonderful or that it will transform them in some way. This was true of the women that I interviewed as well. However, of those who expected that first intercourse to be painful, three out of four were black. Among the white women, the most common expectation was that sex would be a pleasant experience. Smaller, equal numbers of women in both groups didn't know what to expect.

Girls who were older when they first had sex were perhaps better prepared for what to expect. Many of the younger women reported that they did not know about the hymen and the possibility of bleeding upon penetration. Consequently, the appearance of blood was frightening to them and sometimes to their partners. Nor did girls generally know that females, if sexually aroused, can become lubricated before penetration, which can minimize pain and discomfort. Apparently their partners did not know this, either, or they did not care.

While the African-American women in my research seemed to have more realistic expectations about intercourse, they had less formal sex education overall than their white peers. Apparently girls had more information about what to expect when a female has sex for the first time than they did about how their bodies work. It is possible that actual intercourse is discussed more frequently among girls than are other sexual topics, and information gets passed along informally.

One other topic is often discussed. Even the missionaries who visited Africa hundreds of years ago talked about the size of African men's penises. Rumors about African-American men's large penises may have contributed to black teens' discussions about the possible pain of first intercourse, and these rumors may have circulated much faster than less interesting information about the female body and how the reproductive system works. For example, Maria described her surprise and fear to her girlfriends when she saw her boyfriend's penis for the first time: "I wondered how that six- or seven-inch thing was going to fit inside of me." Seeing that penis discouraged her from having sex at that time, and there is no telling what her friends said about her experience.

Research on penis size has been so poorly conducted that it is difficult to say whether this rumor is based on fact or myth. While there is a universal but often publicly denied belief that a well endowed man has more sexual prowess, I suspect that we'll probably never know for sure.

Did You Have Personal Goals?

Do you remember having something to work toward? Something for which to defer immediate gratification is an essential part of adolescent growth and self-development. Setting goals requires a focus on something intangible. For teens, achieving the exact goal they state may not be as important to their sexuality as learning self-discipline and recognizing that their efforts can move them toward their goals.

The most common goal among the women I talked to

was to have a career that required at least a college education. Some specifically wanted an education or a career in
the creative arts. Those who said they only wished to have
a family were relatively few. Vague and general desires, such
as "to be happy" or "to get away from home," or, sadly "to
be safe and not have someone hurting me" were not uncommon.

The range of personal goals was striking, but it confirmed that many adolescents understood the importance
of achievement and economic independence for black
women. Some teens could react to the chaotic circumstances
of their family life only by simply wanting to escape what
they had endured thus far. The majority, however, reported
that they had set long-term goals even in adolescence.

This finding is in sharp contrast to the image of black
teens found on television documentaries or on talk shows.
In media representations, the aspirations of many black
teens center on having a baby, collecting welfare, or being
in a dysfunctional relationship.

What Were Your Messages From Home?

As we have seen, even parents who have convinced themselves that their preadolescent girls were too young to be
considered sexual find that it's difficult to deny that womanhood is approaching, given the visible evidence of puberty.
Most parents are determined to make sure that their daughters understand that both their behavior and the way they
present themselves during this period establish their reputations as young ladies.

Whether it is based on fact or fancy, a black girl's reputation is long-lasting and will confirm or defy stereotypes
that she is fast, loose, or a "ho." A daughter with a sterling
reputation is a source of great pride to her parents, siblings,
and even extended family members. I am often asked to
speak to African-American adolescents and their parents

about sex, because parents realize that they must provide some guidance for the behavior they expect, even if they have been silent in previous years. The parents understand, too, that they must be not only their daughters' guardians but the protectors of their reputations as well.

Although adolescents are frequently viewed as mini-adults, capable of making their own decisions, I have found that responsible adults are a potentially powerful force in most black girls' decision making processes.

In the course of twenty years of professional work, I had begun to think that I had heard all of the methods of teaching daughters about the importance of sexual abstinence—that is, until I met the Park family. Their approach was so revealing that I told them if I ever wrote a book about black sexuality I wanted to include their story, and here it is.

Peggy's Story

"I'll tell you, if you ask them to leave," 16-year-old Peggy Park whispered to me.

She had been brought to therapy by her parents. Her father was a school principal, and her mother was a teacher. They were obviously uncomfortable about coming to see a psychologist—everyone in their family had too much inner fortitude to have mental problems—but they were desperate for help, according to Mr. Park.

Peggy had stopped speaking to her parents and was becoming increasingly withdrawn both at school and at home. She no longer hung out with her friends on weekends or at church. When she came home from school she went directly to her room and would not come out except for dinner. When her parents asked her what was wrong she refused to answer. When I asked her why she had stopped speaking to her parents, she voiced the above request that she be allowed to speak to me alone.

I asked both parents if Peggy and I might talk privately and was surprised to find that once they had left she became perfectly articulate and intelligent. But she was a very angry adolescent. She was quite animated while describing why she had changed her behavior.

"I'm more in control of my life this way," she began. Peggy had basically stopped talking to her parents except to answer questions with one- and two-word responses. Her silence was driving her parents crazy, much to her delight. She felt that this was only fair, since they were driving her crazy, too.

She explained that her parents were overly paranoid about her having sex during adolescence. They were constantly monitoring her calls, questioning her about any boys whom she liked, and giving her an earlier curfew than her friends had.

"They lecture me daily about how important it is for me not to get involved with boys too soon," she said.

Her parents would not allow her to negotiate with them on the rules that they had established; their only explanation was that they were protecting her reputation. They also made sure that her friends weren't exposing her to more than they thought she should experience as a respectable young lady.

Things got worse when Mr. Park came home one day with the following slogan for Peggy to memorize. She was to recite it, he instructed, when she felt that she was tempted with the forbidden fruits of life. It went like this:

S—*Don't sneak kisses in movies and public places.*
L—*Don't look at men's crotches.*
U—*If you are unable to keep your hands to yourself, you're in trouble.*
T—*Don't touch a boy's penis or let him touch your breasts or genitals.*

Peggy refused to recite the slogan and at this point began to withdraw from her family. She also stopped associating with her friends because she felt that it was disrespectful to discuss her parents with other people. They were role models in the community and had warned her not to discuss family business with outsiders. She had tried to tell her parents that their concerns and methods were absurd and insulting, but she had had no success.

"They don't trust me to make any decisions about boys," she said. *"Why do I need a slogan to recite when I am tempted with forbidden fruits? Why is going on a date forbidden? What do they mean by 'forbidden fruit,' anyway?"*

*The questions made it obvious that she did not understand her par-
ents' actions any more than they understood hers.*

Later, I began to understand why Mr. and Mrs. Park were
so concerned about Peggy's reputation. Both had college-
educated parents who lived in the North and had raised
their children to seek education as a means of overcoming
racism. Their children were expected to marry well—
which meant that they had to marry someone who was
also a professional or had financial security—and to be
model citizens in the community. There were no shotgun
weddings in their families, and they did not want Peggy to
be the first who had to get married due to an unintended
pregnancy.

Peggy's reputation was more important to her parents
than it was to her, but not because she was interested in
becoming sexually active—she wasn't. It's just that she was
less concerned about upholding the family legacy. What she
did want was to date and make her own decisions about
life. I realized that this family had not yet discussed or
described the stereotypes of black hypersexuality to Peggy.
Neither had they explained why adolescence was such a
frightening time for black people during slavery and its
aftermath. It was a time when parents often could not protect their children from sexual exploitation and abuse. I
doubt that parents' fears have changed much today.

Because of that history, if black girls wear short or tight
clothes they are assumed to be "oversexed"; if they have too
much makeup on, it suggests that they have no class. If
their behavior is loud or boisterous, it shows a lack of
proper training. Adolescent girls seen kissing or "hugging
up under a boy" in public are presumed to be sexually active and to have no concern for their own or their family's
reputation.

Peggy did not fully understand how her behavior would
affect both her parents' reputations as administrators and
as black leaders in integrated school settings. Mr. and Mrs.
Park feared that they would be known as administrators

who could tell other people's children how to act but could not control their own child. Their concerns were that presumptions of sexual activity would not only ruin Peggy's reputation but that she would seek out or attract friends who had tarnished reputations, too.

On the other hand, Mr. and Mrs. Park did not realize how much pressure they were placing on their daughter to do nothing that could be interpreted as sexually immoral. With counseling, they began to realize how their failure to trust their daughter's judgment would affect her. As the Parks began to compromise on their rules and expectations, Peggy became more and more communicative in therapy and at home. Since we all agreed on the usefulness of slogans, we jointly came up with a new one for Peggy:

C—Consistency in behavior over time, maturity, communication, trust, and mutual respect are necessary in any relationship before sex is considered.
A—Always remember to evaluate if you are dating someone who can be a life partner.
R—Responsibility begins with you.
E—Each time you consider sex, think about the consequences to you and your future.

Peggy needed to develop good judgment, and her parents had to learn to support her efforts to make her own decisions while she was still living at home. Their role was to shepherd her through the process of setting guidelines, trust her ability to make decisions, and discuss the results of her decisions on an ongoing basis. Their efforts to protect her reputation were based more on their fears than on anything that she was actually doing. Peggy framed her slogan and put it beside her bed as a reminder of important steps to sexual responsibility.

We also came up with a slogan for Mr. and Mrs. Park, as a symbol of the mutual respect that they were developing for their daughter and for her growing need to be appreciated as a responsible young woman:

C—Communication with our children each day should include permission to discuss anything and solve it with our help.

A—All we want is a competent daughter and not a perfect one.

L—Letting go during adolescence shows us how ready she is to make decisions on her own.

M—Make sure to tell Peggy how great she is and how much we love her each day.

Suggestions for improvement should always be preceded by praise. Their slogan was hung on the refrigerator door as a daily reminder of their role as parents.

I still hear from Peggy about once a year. She is in college and is doing well. While her parents can still be a bit overbearing, she understands them better and accepts the legacy that she carries for her family. Peggy also knows how to handle their anxieties better. She's more concerned, however, with the personal and professional goals that she has set for herself. And so far, there has been no need for a shotgun wedding.

Standards and Strategies—What We Say to Our Girls

Why are many African-American parents so concerned? While most adolescents have to learn how to relate to others in a social context, our girls have an additional responsibility that may be unique. Given our history and the stereotypes that proliferate about our sexual promiscuity, specific instruction is crucial to their sexual development. They need to recognize that their behavior, body language, and dress can sometimes be misinterpreted and lead to assumptions about their sexuality and morality. In many ways, to be considered a respectable lady is far more important than to simply be called a woman. Anyone with the proper biological parts can be a woman. A lady is someone who knows how to act. She accepts and celebrates the responsibilities and privileges of womanhood and requires others to give her the respect she deserves. Some of our attempts to get that point across still have the capacity to hit home. Others are, at best, humorous reminders of by-gone days.

While fathers and mothers may warn their children about what not to do, it's the mother who usually sets the sexual standards. Mothers who rise to the challenge must convey information about how their daughters should act, how they should handle their femininity, and what they should do with the stereotypes about African-American sexuality. These mothers help to smooth our transition into womanhood.

This information is often passed along from woman to woman, often out of earshot of men. These are the strategies that women have used for years to motivate men's interest or win their respect. If properly followed, these strategies are also expected to ensure that a girl has a good reputation, and perhaps in time will attract a suitable husband.

Here is what most mothers passed on to their growing adolescents as basic instruction about how to be ladylike.

On Behavior

Do you recall being told to wear clean underpants so that if you were ever taken to an emergency room you wouldn't be embarrassed to remove your clothes? If a black adolescent had on dirty underwear or that golden conical-shaped bra that Madonna wore in some of her concerts, her appearance might confirm assumptions that blacks are lewd and sexually perverse.

Teens are warned to keep their legs crossed and their skirts down so that people cannot see under their dresses. Exposing one's thighs, like Marilyn Monroe in the movie *The Seven-Year Itch*, one's crotch like Sharon Stone in *Basic Instinct*, or being half dressed in countless music videos, might not be interpreted favorably for a black girl. White women, we are told, can use their seductiveness as a marketing device to increase movie, record, or concert-ticket sales without missing other opportunities to portray very different roles, or casting an indelible stamp on their personal reputation.

Few black women have been able to do the same. If they acted like women who had no morals, it would not be assumed that their behavior was merely a marketing strategy. Perhaps the morals of these white celebrities are also called into question, but a woman who has economic power can transcend daily contact with people who might be very judgmental about her moral behavior. There are fewer black women whose economic status can protect them from perceptions that they are sexually promiscuous.

On Sexual Protocol

Sexual protocol is how to pace a relationship in order to receive and maintain respect from boys. The following are some of the more common statements our girls hear from adults:

> "All boys want to do is get in your pants."
>
> "They only want one thing [sex], and if you give it to them they won't respect you."
>
> "Don't let them go too far [have sex with you]."
>
> "If you are fast you won't have any boyfriends, just men who will use you. Nobody will want you, because when the word gets around fast girls don't get husbands—nice girls do."
>
> "They will call you easy if you let a boy get too close to you."
>
> "If you let a boy pat you on the bottom, he will think that you will let him touch you anywhere on your body."
>
> "Don't have sex in the back of a car. A man won't think you're worth the price of a marriage license."

Some of the typical comments are confusing to teens, who have no frame of reference for those old-time sayings:

"Men don't like worn-out doormats. Respect yourself, and they will respect you."

"If you lie down with dogs, you'll get up with fleas."

"Why buy the cow when the milk is free?"

On Appearance

As for appearance, girls sometimes hear:

"Don't let a man see you with your hair uncombed. He will think you are wild and just got out of bed."

"If your appearance is not neat, men will think you are slovenly, which is what some people think of us, anyway."

"Don't ever let your husband see you naked. Keep the mystery about your body."

"Privacy is something that black women have never had enough of."

"Black women who wear ankle bracelets look like whores who belong to a man."

"Don't pierce your body, because you'll look like a black whore."

"Don't wear loud colors or big earrings. People will think you have no class."

"Don't let your butt shake, unless you are advertising it."

"Hair on your legs means you like sex."

"Hair on your legs means that you're from the country and you're not sophisticated."

Some parents, as we have seen, attempt to monitor their daughters' reputations by focusing on makeup. The average African-American woman was allowed to wear makeup at age 15. Among her white peers, twice as many were allowed to wear makeup before they were 15. Many women report that they had no desire to wear makeup, either because of religious beliefs that prohibited its use or because it was their personal choice.

On Pride and Respect

Regarding pride and self-respect, here's a memorable standard: "Walk with your head up. We have had to walk with our heads bowed for too long. Be proud of your black beauty, and demand respect. You've got to get respect for those who died so you could."

We remember with fondness some of the strategies that a grandmother or an older person had shared. Even if the ideas were somewhat dated they made a lasting impression. It was often not their advice, but their determination that *you* should gain self-respect that made listening to them worthwhile.

What We Are Not Saying to Our Girls

Here is a disturbing trend emerging in the black community that I see far too often—teens who are receiving no information at all about how to conduct themselves as women. Consequently, they are dressing more and more like boys, covering up their female attributes in order to hang with the homeboys. They believe that dressing like a woman makes them vulnerable to physical and sexual violence. Too much of the wrong kind of attention is paid to them as females, so they dress, act, and speak like the characters in the movie *Set It Off*. Mickey was a good example of this hardcore image that is being promoted among some young inner-city women today.

Mickey's Story

I met Mickey when she called out "Yo, Doc!" as I walked across campus, but she didn't look like a typical university student. She wore no make-up or earrings, walked with a "pimp," and gestured the way that rappers do when she spoke. She had on baggy jeans, a plaid shirt buttoned to the neck, combat boots, and an oversized baseball cap that hid her hair. Her lips were chapped, her hands were ashy, and her nails had dirt under them. She had found an article that I had written and wanted to meet me. When I first looked at her I wasn't sure whether she was a girl, and her name didn't help. She finally explained that her real name was Michelle, but she didn't want to use it. She blended in better using her nickname.

"Blended into what?" I asked.

"My homeboys—you know, the guys in the hood," she said.

I was intrigued with why Mickey had chosen this particular look although she was attending a large, mostly white university. I invited her to visit me at my office. She said, "That's dope," and pimped on to the library, where she was writing a paper for an honors English class she was taking.

One day Mickey showed up at my door and agreed to rap a bit before class. I finally got her to take off the hat covering her unclean hair, which was almost matted from not being combed. Mickey was very embarrassed about her hair, explaining that her funds were limited, but she was comfortable with her overall appearance. Guys were always trying to hit on her, she said, and bitches would try to fight her when she dressed like a girl. She was a straight-A student and just didn't fit in. School was easy—so many of the kids never came, fell asleep, or were zoned out that the teachers took a special liking to her because she was smart and wanted to learn. Getting good grades got her the attention that she didn't get anywhere else in her life. By the eleventh grade, she started dressing like the guys in the neighborhood gang and hanging out with them and their women. Mickey told me about her man, a gang member who dropped out of high school and was "making bank" as a businessman. The twinkle in her eye gave me ideas about the kind of business he was in.

Mickey had received a full scholarship to the university, and she jumped at the chance. However, she was the first person in her family to attend college and the only kid in her neighborhood to even try. She needed to talk. She went on to say that she and her man started rollin' before she finished high school and got together on weekends now that she was in college. She was a little worried about getting pregnant. "Rollin'?" I asked. "What does that mean?" "You know, Doc," Mickey said as she smiled and blushed. "No, I don't know, Mickey. Tell me." She explained that rollin' was having intercourse—unprotected, of course, because he was her man and she was his woman. "Yeah, right, Mickey," I growled in disbelief at how this intelligent but lonely young woman could fall for that sorry excuse to have unprotected sex. I quickly looked up the phone numbers of the student health clinic and counseling center to give her.

Now I knew why Mickey sought me out. This young woman was crying out for a lot of help:

- No matter how bright she was, she was poorly prepared for college and what is required to look, speak, and behave like a serious student.
- She needed guidance and support to reconsider the choices she had made about her appearance, her self-esteem, and how she wanted others to see and treat her. Her self-esteem was being affected by her choices.
- She was taking dangerous chances by trying to fit in with neighborhood youths. She was still living off campus and felt out of place when she tried to socialize with her university peers; and
- She was really caught between two worlds and was risking her sexual health and her future.

Mickey took me up on the referrals and seemed to be taking better care of herself. However, months later I received a beautifully written letter explaining that she had used her scholarship money to help her mother pay some bills and had to drop out for a quarter to make some money. One quarter stretched into two. Her phone was soon dis-

*connected, and my letters were returned with no forwarding address. Mickey
had vanished as suddenly as she had appeared.*

It is so sad to see someone with so much promise
become overwhelmed by the challenges of growing up
black, female, smart, and poor. Behaving like a woman
may seem too risky to some, but girls who act like guys
may still be used as sexual objects, and have to face all
of the consequences of behaving in sexually irresponsible
ways.

There are so many Mickeys out there, begging for some
guidance, some role models, and a chance to develop into
bright young leaders of tomorrow. Too few make it. How
can we expect teens to make all of the right choices in
adolescence unless their parents and others are willing
to show them the way? How can we impress upon them
that they do not need to deny their womanhood or use
their sexuality to survive their neighborhoods, schools, and
families?

There is a lot of work that needs to be done to address
this growing crisis in our communities and the consensus that it's too difficult to be a black woman who acts
like one.

Parents' Rules and Warnings

Parents who are involved with their teens have a lot to say
about the pace at which they grow up. On average, the age
at which black women are first allowed to go on a single
date with a guy unchaperoned is 16. A few women are never
allowed to date before they leave home because of religious
beliefs. These strict rules seem to be related to three concerns that parents have for their teens. First, they do not
want them to kiss boys, because kissing can lead to other
things. Once again, parents are expressing a fear that under
certain circumstances their girls will not be able to control

their sexuality. Perhaps it was fear that caused Allie's father to punish her sister so severely for kissing her boyfriend in public.

The second concern that parents have is with petting, which is mutual kissing and touching from the neck down. Most girls are told that boys will assume that they will go all the way if they engage in petting.

The third concern that black parents have is the possibility that their daughters will be sexually molested or raped. This is especially true of girls who grow up in urban areas, most of whom are told that they need to protect themselves from being raped. Their parents, especially their mothers, warn them about strangers. One woman described how her mother used the fear of someone molesting her to get her to wear less-revealing clothes when she was a teen. Her mother would always threaten her by saying, "A man will snatch that tight little dress off you one day and rape you." Another mother warned her daughter, "You are not Madonna. Someone is going to use you like a 'ho' if you wear all of that makeup and dress like one."

However, in spite of the childhood warnings about molestation, adolescents are not prepared for the possibility that someone known to them might attempt sexual assault, which is often the case. They are, however, much more likely to be given specific information about how to protect themselves from sexual assault than their white peers (such as walking in a group and in well-lit areas).

Bombarded with Information— Some Good, Some Not

Learning from Siblings

Girls learn a lot about sex from their siblings. When brothers are caught either having sex at home with someone or word gets back to their parents that they are sexually active, girls know that their parents discussed their son's behavior and mildly admonished him. Only once in a while are their brothers corporally punished for their behavior or denied privileges.

In families where a sister becomes pregnant out of wedlock or is caught kissing a boy, girls witness a different result. In contrast to the way brothers are disciplined, many sisters receive corporal punishment for their sexual behavior or a strong verbal reprimand by parents. The transgressions of sisters are dealt with much more severely than those of brothers. Still, observing any family member's sexual experience that has consequences discourages a girl from contemplating sex outside of marriage.

Learning from School

Teens are bombarded with information about sex during adolescence—some factual, some not. They are more likely to receive some formal sex education as teens than as children, and there is a greater focus on sexual intercourse. Almost half of the women I studied had at least one sex-education class. However, as in childhood, the quality and quantity of these classes varied considerably.

Sometimes their formal sex education consisted of viewing a single film or getting religious instruction in parochial schools (mostly warnings about what not to do and how to avoid becoming a "sinner"). Still, about one in five adolescents received no formal sex education between the ages of 13 and 17.

Learning from Religious Sources

The messages from religious sources grow more powerful during the teen years and are directly targeted to adolescents. Most women remember religious proscriptions against kissing, touching, and sexual intercourse. They also remember hearing admonitions against using birth control and "killing beautiful black babies." One of the clergy's methods of discouraging "immoral sexual behavior" is to use celebrities—black and white—as examples of good and bad behavior. Sometimes the ministers use members of the congregation as examples.

Cora's Story

Cora admitted that she became pregnant at age 14. She had been a good Christian—singing in the choir, devoting her time to volunteering for church activities, attending Sunday school, and receiving good grades— that is, before she got pregnant and found herself in trouble. When her parents heard the news, they were devastated.

Cora was extremely embarrassed to attend church once her body began to reveal her pregnancy. Her relatives felt that the best thing to do was to hold their heads high, stick together, and attend church as a family. To Cora's surprise and horror, the minister called on her family to stand up and be recognized in spite of the shame that their daughter had caused the family. She was asked to go before the congregation and apologize for her behavior and her pregnancy, which she did with tears streaming from her eyes. When the service ended, the congregation embraced the family, welcoming them back into the church.

Nothing more was said about Cora's pregnancy at church. When she had the baby, the church ladies made a point of exclaiming at how beautiful he was. However, no one ever asked her to identify the father. No one, not even her parents, ever knew that he was sitting in the choir, next to the empty seat that used to be hers.

This is an example of an extreme tactic used to discourage premarital sexual intercourse. Unfortunately, such shame and humiliation only distances adolescents from religious institutions that might be the source of positive reinforcement. This tragic story also illustrates a minister's attempt to teach morality through negative example. Public humiliation is an unacceptable form of social control because it attacks the girl and undermines her self-confidence in making sexually responsible decisions in the future.

Participation in church activities and religious school attendance alone do not meet all the needs of adolescents who are trying to understand new emotions. Too few churches in the black community offer adolescents a comprehensive program of sex education, including constructive activities that increase their skills and self-confidence.

Probably the saddest outcome for Cora was that she chose not to disclose the name of the father of the child and shielded him by accepting blame for the pregnancy. In doing so, she placed herself in a position of being held unduly responsible, as if she had created the situation alone. For his part, the father learned less about how to avoid unwanted sexual outcomes than he did about how to avoid responsibility for his behavior.

Learning from Friends

Much of the literature and research on adolescence focuses on the influence of friends, and the findings are fairly consistent: If an adolescent's friends are sexually active, then she is very likely to be sexually active as well. What friends do or claim that they do can be a barometer for what adolescents think they should be involved in, and that includes sex. Most friends either talk about their own sexual activities or provide words of encouragement for others who are on the verge of experimenting sexually. More than half of the black women I talked to claimed that their friends discussed their own sexual experiences or sex in general. Fewer white women reported this. When girls hear friends discussing their own sexual exploits or encouraging them to experiment sexually, they experience this as subtle pressure—almost a call to action.

Learning from Music

Music clearly communicates sexual values and morality. So when friends who share the same musical tastes listen to really good songs together and comment, as if they were testifying in church, they reinforce one another's values.

While African-American girls are listening to rap, jazz, the blues, rock and roll, gospel, and rhythm and blues, white girls are more likely to listen to pop, rock and roll, country and western, and classical music. Black music can be so suggestive and sexual in content that I often think that you can be educated about sex by listening to your favorite music, but I don't suggest it!

In fact, there is a political debate over censorship of music for adolescents and younger children. To some extent, this issue is not new. While each generation of parents complains about teenagers' music, there is no question that the sexual content of much of this music has escalated to disturbing new levels. Adults are justifiably concerned about the effects that sexualized music can have.

It's also shocking to see some of the music videos today because they all too often tell a story about a sexual situation—lost a love, need love, prove my love, or simply making love—that gets resolved or consummated in a matter of minutes. The characters are one-dimensional and have a fantasy quality about them. They are often placed in unreal surroundings while engaging in sexy, violent, or weird behavior. Themes of men or women, regardless of age, as predators and victims, expressing lust rather than love, impulsivity rather than patience, aggression rather than tenderness, and intrusiveness rather than respect, raise questions about how our youth can learn about healthy relationships when they are being fed steady diets of these messages.

In the black community there is growing intolerance for music in any form that condones stereotyped sexual or violent behavior. But without effective parental involvement and community activism, the music teenagers listen to today is likely to have a substantial, problematic impact on their sexual attitudes and behavior.

Lessons from the Distant Past

There are more similarities between the ways in which contemporary and traditional African societies prepared young teens for their roles as women than exist at any other time in their development. African mothers or mother figures were instrumental in discussing biological changes and imparting sexual standards to their developing daughters. Mothers were also more likely to assume the responsibility of warning their daughters about the threat of sexual assault than were other family members.

But while there are similarities, there are also two dramatic differences. First, information shared long ago was for the purpose of preparing young women for marriage and family life. Today information is shared in an effort to control sexual behavior and protect young women from abuse, with no guarantee that marriage and children will follow in any particular order, if at all.

Second, in the past, respect for a girl was based on the family's reputation and its ability to control a girl's behavior. Today it is more difficult to protect a girl's reputation if her parents do not have a positive influence on her or do not themselves act as role models. Strong forces like sexual stereotypes, peer influence, and the media can also undermine parental authority, imparting unwelcome sexual standards to adolescents. This makes it even more important that adolescents know the consequences of sexual activity and how to establish a good reputation through their behavior.

What These Findings Mean to You

Did the changes that accompany adolescence create a uniquely tense atmosphere in your home? Adolescence is more complicated and perhaps more difficult for African-American teens than for the teens of other ethnic groups primarily because black female sexuality has been stereotyped so persistently. Additional factors compound this problem.

First, black girls tend to have less than adequate knowledge about how their bodies are changing, the consequences of those changes, and the possibility that people known to them might attempt to abuse or exploit them. Further, they have little appreciation of how the stereotypes about black females threaten their health and self-image, even with the support of mothers or mother figures who are trying to guide and help them. For many black girls, Mom is the only close source of support or advice. In my research, black adolescents were almost twice as likely to live with a stepfather and eight times more likely to grow up with no father in the home compared with their white peers.

These changes in the traditional black family are reflected across the nation. According to the most recent U.S. census, black children are almost three times more likely than non-Hispanic whites to have an absent parent. As a result, parental supervision has to be redefined as responsible adult supervision. If quality adult-adolescent interaction is not lost, a missing parent is not necessarily a terrible thing.

But adult-teen relationships are harder to sustain these days. Half of African-American girls, for instance, decrease their church attendance or stop attending church completely during the teenage years. These changes in the traditional sources of support are leaving a void. The school may be a girl's only source of knowledge on this subject, despite the fact that it offers too little information too late to offset other, contradictory messages. As a result, a girl's friends and the media may become her primary sources of sexual information and socialization, particularly if her parents concede their role and trade parental supervision for warnings and threats.

There is no substitute for daily positive parental involvement as girls approach womanhood. Slogans and empty words are not enough and can end up encouraging the very behavior they are meant to discourage. Something far more powerful is needed to motivate adolescents to be sexually responsible when so many others are encouraging them to just be sexual—and that "something" is an actively involved family.

An adolescent learns to be her own person within the context of family life. She is a young woman, but in this society she is not yet an adult. Her body might give that impression, but her mind and her emotions need much more time and support to catch up with the biological and physical changes that herald the end of childhood. Effective parents understand this.

No matter how old you are today, your self-image as a teenager is probably still an important influence on your sexuality. The messages we hear about who we are and how we are supposed to behave as adolescents last a lifetime. This is a particularly important concept to grasp, because it is difficult to grow up and feel confident against a backdrop of negative expectations and confusing messages about being black and female. However, it is easy to mature into adulthood unaware that many other black teens *are* sexually responsible.

Perhaps you heard people describe black women who controlled their sexuality as being "frigid" or "asexual." How could you know if their partners and others used those undesirable terms for the simple reason that they found it difficult to manipulate or coerce those women into engaging in sex contrary to their principles—or that they refused to believe that black women could use restraint? After all, images and reputations are based on both facts and perceptions. For example, if a girl is likable and approachable as well as sexually responsible, she will develop a positive reputation and self-image. But if she is not liked for whatever reasons despite being sexually responsible, her reputation and self-image can be distorted by the envy and jealousy of others.

Women who were accurately considered "fast" as teenagers also have reputation and self-image issues to contend with as adults. If they decide to take control of their bodies, they can still have difficulty outliving their pasts and the consequences of poor and uninformed decisions. The unwanted or traumatic outcomes of their teenage years become harsh punishments for adolescent behavior—having no children, having them taken away, recovering from addictions or self-destructive behavior, living with a chronic or terminal disease. Life is the sum total of our experiences.

It is heartening, however, to realize that as you grow older, it is not ultimately your past experiences that define you, but what you learn from them that makes the difference in who you are and how you survive.

---

chapter 6

Ready or Not

Learning to Control Our Bodies

Jo-Jo's Story

Jo-Jo, a 21-year-old medical assistant, grew up in a family of four brothers and four sisters in a large city in Illinois. She learned little about sex, except that her parents were opposed to sex and pregnancy before marriage. Her mother was adamant that her older sister should practice feminine hygiene when she became sexually active; she believed this was a good precaution against pregnancy. Little did her mother know that douching can sometimes help sperm and other bacteria to travel farther up the vaginal canal.

Nevertheless, Jo-Jo watched as her mother taught her sister how to douche. Though her sister howled, Jo-Jo's mother flatly stated, "If you can handle intercourse, you can handle this," as she handed her the nozzle that would squirt warm vinegar-water into her vagina.

When Jo-Jo was 12, her mother explained how breasts grow and all about menstruation. She took time to explain how an egg would come down if there were no sperm to "bother it." This information, combined with what she learned from the films at school, gave Jo-Jo a pretty good idea of what was going on inside her body, but she had yet to learn much about boys, even with all her brothers around.

One summer day when Jo-Jo was 16, her 17-year-old boyfriend invited her over to his house to listen to music while the family was away. They started to play strip poker and both ended up nude. As they sat across from each other intently viewing the other's nakedness, Jo-Jo got an idea. She was very curious about what sex would be like—this was something she hadn't learned about—so they decided to try it. It was *every bit as painful as she had always thought it would be. When he broke her hymen she felt sick to her stomach and began to bleed. He came pretty fast after that.*

When it was over, she wondered if it would have been better if they had waited. Since they hadn't planned to have sex, neither of them had used any birth control. Although she did not marry this boyfriend, he was her only sexual partner for the next two years, and she dated him exclusively. They really tried to make the relationship work, but they finally realized that they were too young to settle down. They had no reason to stay together except that they liked each other and had sex; this wasn't enough to make a relationship work.

Exploding the Impulsivity Myth— Our First Sexual Choices

The most common reason for first intercourse among African-American teens has little to do with sexual impulses and much more to do with the need to finally find out what sex is all about. Jo-Jo's sexual knowledge and sexual experimentation began early in childhood. Adolescence provided her first opportunities to show what she had learned and to discover what she hadn't. How would she behave sexually when she chose to do so? Would she risk trying something that might have far-reaching consequences? What decisions would she make about contraceptives? The answers lay in patterns of behavior she had established during childhood that were likely to continue into adulthood. This chapter helps you to discern those patterns in your own life.

We can also look at African-American adolescents like Jo-Jo between ages 13 and 17 now that we understand our history and see the results of historical patterns we've identified. During slavery, the first time a black girl had sex was determined by whoever owned her. Society assumed that she was interested and ready, regardless of her age. Today society isn't concerned about who her first partner is as long as she doesn't cry rape. Our society still may not even care if she is raped when she first has sex unless her partner is a celebrity or comes from a highly visible family. Even then it is still assumed that her first intercourse occurs because of her insatiable appetite or lust for sex. This lust supposedly overshadows her concern for where or with whom sex takes place and what will happen in the future.

According to this view, if a pregnancy results the girl could easily get an abortion. But, of course, there is no overlooking the fact that she had sex outside of marriage or a committed relationship, with multiple partners, and that she made little effort to prevent pregnancy or sexually transmitted diseases, including HIV. She'd be presumed to be a she-devil. According to the myth, her lifelong sexual impulsivity or carelessness is only to be expected.

Obviously this is a stereotype. The real story is more complex.

The First Time—Five Critical Questions to Answer

It's important to avoid simple descriptions of sexual behaviors if you are doing behavioral research or want to learn from it. You also have to be specific about which behaviors you mean and you must be careful to place them within their proper context. For instance, when I wanted to know under what circumstances black girls first choose to have intercourse, I asked women the following critical questions:

1. What Was Your Age?

How old are kids when they first have intercourse? The average age of the women in my study was 16½, which is consistent with the national average for all women.

The earliest age at which a black woman reported having had voluntary intercourse was 10, and the oldest was 25. One woman was still a virgin at the time of the interview. Almost one in three had had intercourse by age 15, and two out of three had lost their virginity by age 18. Despite parental and religious opposition to premarital intercourse, by mid-adolescence half of these women had had sex for the first time.

Only one in five women (20 percent) married their first partner. For most of them, then, first-time intercourse did occur outside of marriage.

2. What Were Your Reasons?

Many adolescents fear only their parents' disapproval, but others are concerned about pregnancy and sexually transmitted diseases as well. So why do they decide to take the risk and have sex despite the consequences? Four reasons were most common.

- *Curiosity and the desire to find out what sex was all about.* This was the most typical reason.
- *Pressure from their partner.* I heard such comments as: "He said if I loved him I would do it." "He would find another girl who would satisfy his sexual needs if I didn't." "He just insisted every time we were together, so I finally gave in." They indicate that many boyfriends make intercourse a test of a girl's love or a requirement for staying in the relationship.
- *Love.* "I was so much in love, I wanted him to be first" or "We were in love" were typical romantic reasons that motivated first intercourse.
- *Lust or sexual excitement.* When I hear a woman say, "I was ready, turned on, wanted him" or "I wanted sex," I know she fits this category.

3. Where Were You?

Like Jo-Jo, nearly three out of four women reported that they had sex for the first time either in their own home or that of their partner. A few lost their virginity in the park or at the beach. For a few women, the place was a car, a motel, or school.

4. Who Was Your Partner?

Nearly 84 percent of the women interviewed had sex for the first time with steady boyfriends, and 14 percent had this experience with partners whom they knew but hadn't dated. Almost half maintained their relationship with their first partner for one to five years after first intercourse. Another 17 percent had relationships with their first partner that lasted five or more years. Even though my research in 1994 showed that African-American teens were more likely to have sex for the first time with someone they knew but hadn't dated, having sex with that person sometimes led to seeing each other regularly and going out on dates that didn't always include sex. Clearly, most black women have long-term relationships with their first partners.

Only a few of the women (9 percent) reported having had sex for the first time with a one-night stand. This is a far cry from the prevailing stereotypes.

5. Did You Use Birth Control?

Eighty percent reported that neither they nor their partner used any method of birth control when they had sex for the first time. These girls and their partners were unprepared for sex when they experienced it. We'll explore the enormous ramifications of not using contraceptives in depth later, but the following comparison to white teens hints at its significance.

First Intercourse for Black and White Teens

How does this data differ for the white women whom I studied? For these women, the youngest age for first-time intercourse was 12; the oldest age reported was 27. In contrast to black adolescents, among white teens the most common reason was pressure from a partner, followed by being in love and lust. "One thing leading to the other" and curiosity about sex tied for the least common motives.

Having sex with steady dates (62 percent) was most common for white women, and almost one out of three were at least with someone whom they had known. Only 17 percent of white women married their first partner.

While the location of first intercourse was similar for black and white women, the length of relationships with first partners differed. African-American women had longer-term relationships (68 percent, versus 32 percent for white women). Of the women who had sex with their first partner only once, more than half were white women. While white women tended to have more sexual relationships in adolescence, almost two out of three white adolescents (64 percent) used some form of birth control the first time they had sex.

What is striking about these comparative findings is the number of similarities between the two groups. Neither group tended to lose their virginity out of burning desire or because of sexual impulsivity. Both groups' motivations were external: They wanted to find out about sex, or they wanted to please their partners. There were few differences in their ages, first places, or their relationship with their first partners. The greatest differences were in the number of partners (white teens had more) and the use of contraceptives (the majority of black teens didn't use them). Ironically, despite all the similarities, this last fact—failure to protect themselves with contraceptives—left black girls more vulnerable to unwanted sexual outcomes. Depending on your criterion (use of contraceptives or number of partners), either group could be seen as sexually irresponsible.

First Sex with Female Partner—What's the Real Reason?

Although almost all of the women interviewed for my research had their first sexual experience with a man, about 9 percent also had a sexual experience with another female during adolescence. The earliest age at which women reported having had an adolescent sexual experience with another teen that went beyond childhood exploratory sex play was 10, and the latest was 16. Almost all of these events involved a friend, and only a few involved someone whom the girls had just met. Curiosity about sex with another woman and pressure from the partner were also the most common reasons for a first experience with another woman.

Jessica, who had the unique method of masturbating in childhood, cited curiosity as the reason for her first sexual experience with a woman.

Jessica's Story

At age 15, Jessica and a friend were playing on her bed at her house. There was lots of hugging, kissing, and mutual vaginal fondling. Jessica felt that this was more acceptable than having intercourse with a boy. The year before, she had been raped by an old boyfriend and became pregnant. She wanted to see what it would be like to be with another girl—with someone she could trust. And, best of all, no pregnancies could result from what they were doing.

Although Jessica was at first confused by this encounter, she also felt that she now had a truly close friend. She and her friend were involved sexually for the next six months.

By contrast, Gertrude's reason for having a sexual experience involved pressure from her female partner:

Gertrude's Story

Gertrude was a 22-year-old security guard and a very religious Baptist when she was interviewed. She had been taught that not only sex out of marriage but any other sexual experience was wrong. But when she was 15 a lesbian friend talked her into a sexual experiment in her bedroom. Her girlfriend jokingly bet Gertrude that she could make her have an orgasm, but Gertrude didn't believe her. Her friend kept insisting that she could, so Gertrude finally gave in. Gertrude's friend began to touch her all over, and she performed oral sex on her. It happened only once. She was surprised to find that this was a very pleasant experience, and her friend won the bet.

In fact, the majority of African-American women who had a sexual experience with a woman during adolescence had only one such encounter.

Sexual Behaviors beyond First Intercourse— What Are the Hidden Patterns?

Contrary to the myths about black adolescent sexuality, most teens adopt a pattern of sexual practices (beyond first intercourse) that is not excessive but very much in keeping with their earlier behaviors and practices.

Masturbation

As was true in childhood, most African-American adolescents (83 percent) do not masturbate. This pattern of avoiding masturbation was also noted in the research that I conducted in 1994 with African-American women 18 to 50 years of age. More than half (54 percent) of these women had never masturbated at any time in their lives. For those who did, hand manipulation of the genitals was the most common method. Some tried new techniques and equipment—vibrators, dildos, and water flowing from the bathtub faucet. Stimulation of the breasts and genitals was another method described, and, finally, thigh squeezing. Still, only about one in three women were orgasmic each time they attempted to masturbate.

Contraceptive Use

Almost three out of four women did not use any form of birth control when they had sex for the first time, although most used some form of birth control later. In fact, for those who had sex before age 16, just over half used birth control after having sex for the first time. More who had sex after age 16 were likely to use contraceptives closer to but still after first intercourse. The gap was smaller when girls were older than 16 at first sex. Any gap between intercourse and birth control use is risky, though, because not only can pregnancy occur but diseases can be transmitted sexually. We found that one poor decision about contraceptives often led to other decisions that were similarly misguided.

Pregnancy

Sandra was 15 years old, single, and seven months pregnant when she agreed to talk to me about herself and her pregnancy. What I learned illustrated again that behaviors, or even a pregnancy, in adolescence don't always tell the whole story. The important patterns lie deeper within the circumstances.

Sandra's Story

Sandra, small, slightly shy, and soft-spoken, started skipping school in the sixth grade to hang out in the mall with her older sister and her friends.

Her sister had dropped out of school in the seventh grade, and Sandra was following in her footsteps.

She'd had a probation officer since age 12 because she would get into fights in school if someone teased her—she'd fight even though she knew that she would get into trouble. Her mother, a single parent, couldn't control her fighting or her habit of skipping school. Sandra had an attitude. Her sister had one, too. In the sixth grade, Sandra was placed in a class for kids who had problems with their behavior but had begun to do better. There were fewer kids and more teachers, and she liked the field trips they took. But by the seventh grade, she had begun to act out again. In the eighth grade, because she had to go to juvenile court once a month with her probation officer, her grades improved a bit.

But the summer before the ninth grade, Sandra and a friend started running away. They either stayed out all night or disappeared for several days. Her mother tried to discipline her by whipping her with a belt or calling the probation officer. Neither worked. Sandra wasn't involved in drugs or crime, but she really didn't seem to have a good enough reason to stay at home. She and her friend would go to parties at night. Sometimes her friend's mother was there, so it seemed okay. Sandra insisted that she knew how a girl could get pregnant. She wasn't trying, but she knew it could happen. She had seen her two older sisters get pregnant—one at 20 and the other at 16. Her mom was also 20 when she had her first child.

"It's a pattern," Sandra told me as she reported the ages at which the women in her family had become pregnant, realizing that with her pregnancy this was happening earlier and earlier. Sandra and her friend had even discussed what would happen if they became pregnant and how they would try to finish high school and college anyway.

"So, if you knew, what happened?" I asked. Sandra explained that she had a boyfriend whom she had been with since she was 13 and he was 15. They would hang out together, going to the movies at the mall. They had sex for the first time when she was 15 and used a condom, but not the second time.

"I just didn't have it in mind to use one," she said.

This time she became pregnant. When I asked her why she had sex the first time, Sandra explained that she had heard a lot about sex and was really curious.

"What does it mean to have a baby for a guy?" I asked. Sandra paused for a moment and said, "It means that you care." Her boyfriend was happy when she told him that she was pregnant.

"Did you two discuss marriage?"

"Oh no, I don't want to get married. I had a friend who was married, and it didn't work out. Besides, my mother has never been married," she exclaimed.

She went on to tell me her plan—how she was going to finish high school and live with her sister and her two children. It wasn't that Sandra hadn't thought her future through; marriage just wasn't in her plan. It didn't seem to be a workable option for anyone that she knew, and she did not see it in her future, either.

"Are you in love?" I asked, still searching for any other reason Sandra might have decided to have sex with her boyfriend. She explained that she liked her boyfriend but had never been in love. She still keeps in touch with him, but they are no longer together and their contact is limited. Sandra has to get a ride over to his house to visit him—she doesn't drive yet.

"What advice would you give young girls today?" I asked.

"Wait 'til you're really ready to have sex. All the girls that I know weren't ready. Start talking to girls about sex when they are about 12. That's the age of my youngest sister. Tell them don't have sex."

Sandra's biggest concern now is the upcoming birth of her baby and what that will be like. As she munched on juice and cookies, she also wondered aloud what kind of mother she would be.

"I think that I will be a good one because I baby-sat my sister's children a lot."

Sex for Sandra seemed to be just another one of those field trips that she described—a new and different experience. She did not go to bed for pleasure, lust, or even real desire. In her case the image of the hypersexual youth couldn't be further from the truth.

Sandra was following the lead of others whom she admired and was continuing a family pattern of having children out of wedlock. It seemed that if she had had other models she would have followed them. Instead, Sandra was a child having a child and struggling to put a life together around this event—this pregnancy—which seemed to shape her identity before she had a chance to define herself.

Her story is a good example of what can happen when the message about differences between sexuality and self-development are not communicated consistently enough by the significant people in our lives. Sandra didn't see men or women who had successfully separated their self-development from their sexuality or had learned how to have a happy marriage in which to raise children. Pregnancy was her way of learning about sex. It became an aspect of her growth and development, taking the place of adult guidance and sufficient information.

Abortions

Unlike Sandra, more than one in four black girls who had pregnancies before their eighteenth birthday ended them with abortions. Ninety percent of the women who had abortions had first intercourse before age 16. Those who had intercourse earlier were most likely to have had an abortion before 17. Women who ended their education before high-school graduation were likely to have had an abortion between ages 15 and 17.

Women who were born before the 1960s were more likely to report having had an illegal abortion, primarily because abortions were illegal when they became pregnant. For example, one woman went to a male nurse who tried unsuccessfully to perform an abortion by pouring turpentine down her vagina and into her uterus. A few months later, the woman's nephew hit her stomach and she miscarried. Other women described attempting to give themselves abortions by sticking coat hangers into the uterus or falling down steps to end unwanted pregnancies. Some were willing to risk their own lives to terminate a pregnancy rather than tell their parents or be judged by others, even when the pregnancy was the result of a rape or abuse by a family member—including their own fathers.

Multiple Partners

The perception that black women have a high number of sexual partners is far from the reality. The women I studied had an average of three sexual partners in adolescence, with more than half having had only one partner between the time of their first intercourse and age 17. Only 8 percent reported having five or more partners.

This is markedly distinct from their white peers. On the average, white women had four sexual partners. More than one in three reported one partner, but one in four reported having had five or more sexual partners during adolescence. The fact that black teens tend not to have a high number of sexual partners is consistent with other studies, but it is not consistent with negative stereotypes and perceptions about them.

Length of Adolescent Sexual Relationship

The length of a relationship indicates the degree of emotional bonding that exists between two people and suggests that partners may be looking for something beyond sexual gratification.

More than half of the African-American women I studied were likely to have relationships that lasted for years with a single partner during their teens, while only 2 percent reported that all their sexual relationships during adolescence were brief—meaning that they were either one-night stands or lasted only a few weeks. In contrast, 22 percent of white women reported having brief relationships during their teens and only one in three described having had a long-term relationship during adolescence.

Sex for Sex Alone

Clearly, most initial sexual emotions were not motivated by a desire for sexual gratification. When I asked black women if they had ever had sex for the sake of sex alone during adolescence, 91 percent responded "no." Again, this finding is in sharp contrast to assumptions of their sexual impulsivity, and it differs from the responses of their white peers.

More than one in five white women reported that they had sex solely for sexual gratification during adolescence, which may help to explain the higher number of partners among whites. If sexual gratification is the primary goal, relationships may be shorter so that other partners can be sought.

Delayed Sexual Activity—The Three Major Factors

These findings are not consistent with the she-devil stereotype so prevalent for African-American women during adolescence. To the contrary, teens who do have patterns of high or early sexual activity shared several characteristics that I believe are often overlooked or misinterpreted as sexual impulsivity. In part, these misinterpretations may stem from failing to examine the reasons behind frequent sexual encounters and the circumstances in which they occur. That's why I wanted to isolate the patterns of the women who delayed sexual activity at least until their late teens or until marriage from those who became sexually active early in their teens or in childhood. In doing so, three major factors emerged that influenced sexual practices.

1. Wealth and Education

Women who grew up in homes that they described as poor, based on the education and occupations of their parents or the adults who raised them, were more likely to have had intercourse for the first time before age 15. Their families' estimated income was at or below the poverty level, which today is about $13,000 for a family of four. Middle- to upper-class women were more likely to begin intercourse at age 17 or older. Similarly, women who had less than a high-school education were more likely to have first intercourse at 15, and women who had a college education or more did not have sex for the first time until they were 17 or older.

In part, the age discrepancy results from the fact that poor and undereducated African-American adolescents do not have opportunities for building skills and self-confidence. By missing out on setting goals such as completing high school or aspiring to college, they lack the kind of experiences that helps many girls defer sexual activity.

Girls who go into the entertainment industry or the creative arts often report event-oriented incidents of first intercourse. The event may be a part in a movie, a chance to perform, to meet an important person, or to secure the training needed to pursue a job in fashion design or modeling. Any type of bartering for jobs or skills often results in prolonged sexual contacts that are coercive and extremely risky. Condoms are rarely part of the bargain.

However, poverty was not always as important as the amount of sexual exposure that girls growing up in urban environments were likely to have. Regardless of the financial resources of their families of origin, women who grew up in rural areas had first intercourse at age 17, on average, compared with women who grew up in urban areas, who were 16 when they had sex for the first time.

2. Number of Caring Adults

Girls who grew up in homes where there was only one parent were much more likely to have sexual intercourse before age 16 than those who were raised by two parents. This finding is fairly consistent with the studies conducted years ago by the noted researchers Marvin Kanter and John Zelnick at Johns Hopkins University, in which the importance of two parents sharing the responsibilities of raising their children is clearly identified.

I was interested in determining whether it was simply the presence of two adults that made the difference or the fact that the parents were married. In my study, I categorized women who grew up with one parent, women who grew up in a two-parent home, and women who grew up with two adults—perhaps a mother and a grandmother, a father and his mother, or even two friends of the same or opposite sex—and compared the average ages of first intercourse.

The findings were very relevant to black families, who are less likely to have both parents living in the same home. In fact, the age of first-time sex (16 or sooner) was earliest for women who had been raised in single-parent homes. However, the age of first intercourse (17 and older) for women from two-parent families was no different from that of women who came from homes in which two unmarried adults were responsible for the children.

A single parent not only needs a village to raise her child, but the active involvement and supervision of other responsible adults can help delay sex for the first time. And although the difference in the age of first intercourse may amount to only one year, it still gives a girl additional time to mature, target goals, and learn more about sexual responsibility.

3. Protection from Abuse in Childhood or Adolescence

Women who reported that they experienced at least one incident of sexual abuse were likely to have had sexual intercourse an average of fifteen months earlier than those who did not report such a history in childhood or adolescence. For these women, two out of three had incidents of child sexual abuse that preceded the age at which they experienced their first voluntary sexual intercourse.

This finding suggests that abuse increased girls' feelings of worthlessness and vulnerability and established a pattern in which someone else decided when they should have sex. Histories of abuse may have made it difficult for them to avoid other male partners who also used pressure or coercion to have sex.

The combination of low self-esteem and poor choice of partners can be very risky for black girls who exhibit this pattern of behavior. At least one incident of sexual abuse before age 18 was also associated with more masturbatory behavior, a higher number of sexual partners, more short-term relationships—including one-night stands—and failure to use any method of contraceptives—including condoms—during intercourse, resulting in more unintended and aborted pregnancies.

Research by Dr. Debra Boyer at the University of Washington also confirms the relationship between sexual abuse and adolescent pregnancy. In her work with more than 500 pregnant and parenting adolescents, she found that the average age of first intercourse was 13.8 years (compared with 16 for the nation) and only one in four used contraception for the first time. Further, 62 percent of the pregnant teens had experienced an attempted or completed rape or sexual molestation prior to their first pregnancy. A consensus is growing that sexual abuse before age 18 is one of the most powerful predictors of promiscuous, sexually impulsive, and sexually irresponsible activity. The chances of becoming infected with sexually transmitted disease, including HIV, increases when a teen has a history of sexual abuse.

Do you remember Cherie? Her early sexual experiences at 12 with her 17-year-old neighbor included exploratory sex that gradually became more coercive until it ended in rape if she resisted. Her adolescent experiences followed the same pattern.

Cherie's Story

During the time that Cherie's 17-year-old neighbor was arousing her sexually, a friend, who had tried for a long time to get her to have intercourse with him, got her high on wine and tried again. Cherie finally gave in and had voluntary sex at 13 because she was a bit curious about what sex with him would be like. She decided that if he would "put some grease on it" she would let him have sex with her. Yet even the grease did not dull the pain or prevent her from bleeding.

The following year Cherie's parents got a divorce, and her life changed. Her parents allowed her to move out of her upper-middle-class home into a crowded apartment with her friend. She stopped going to church and eventually dropped out of high school in the eleventh grade.

By the time Cherie was 18 she had had three sexual partners, two of those relationships simultaneously. At the time of our interview, she had had six sexual partners over the past three years. She reported masturbating frequently, always to orgasm. With her primary partner, she reported having oral sex, in which he stimulated her about ten times a month and she stimulated his genitals about five times a month. She calculated that they have vaginal intercourse about twenty times a month. Until her twenty-first birthday, she had never used any form of contraception. She began to use birth-control pills only after four unintended pregnancies, two of which she aborted. Although she never intended to become pregnant, her partners did not use condoms. She contacted me while she was anxiously awaiting the results of an HIV test.

Today Cherie is an unmarried mother of four, struggling to make ends meet. She has decided to teach her children more than she learned about sex so they won't be so curious. I hope that the result of her HIV test is negative and that she gets a chance to teach her children about sex in a more responsible way than she learned.

On the surface, Cherie's behavior presents a picture of a woman who is deliberately being sexually irresponsible. She went from being a curious, highly sexualized young girl to a sexually active teenager and adult. In reality, Cherie is a woman who as a girl had little of the following:

- Sexual knowledge or family involvement.
- Scrutiny of her behavior by someone who might have suspected that she was being sexually exploited.
- Support from outside sources like her church or school that could provide her with information about her sexual health.
- Encouragement to learn to control her own behavior.
- Opportunities to discover her other strengths and talents.

She had too much sexual involvement that resulted in abuse and too many opportunities to exploit her own sexuality. Her behavioral patterns are misleading, but understanding the reasons for her behavior places them in proper perspective.

To label Cherie as sexually promiscuous and assume that she knew how to change her behavior is to overlook the realities that shaped her life, as well as her present need for information and support. After all, it is never too late to learn how to make decisions that are in your own best interest.

While sexual abuse is perpetrated mostly by males, we have to remember that females can also abuse other females. Shana's story shows how unexpectedly this can happen.

Shana's Story

Shana was admitted to the hospital to have her tonsils removed when she was 16 years old, and she was delighted to get a private room. A nurse came in one night to give her a back rub, but it didn't stop there. The nurse rubbed her body lower and lower, and then turned her over. She performed oral sex on Shana, who was so frightened that she did not say a word.

Shana's feelings of guilt at being too afraid and too confused to pro-

test were compounded by the fact that she experienced pleasure when the nurse stimulated her. Shana had never told anyone about this incident until our interview. She did not consider this to be a case of abuse because she did not protest.

These experiences are difficult for young women to discuss, in part because of the powerful feelings that result when a trusted woman exploits another woman. Men are usually stereotyped as the perpetrators of sexual abuse, so it's deeply confusing to be unexpectedly abused by a woman.

When victims derive sexual pleasure from this abuse, they have more difficulty blaming the perpetrator. They often feel that they have contributed to the incident by failing to protest. They may even wonder about their own sexual orientation. However, experiencing sexual pleasure at the hands of someone who exploits you does not indicate that you are or will be attracted to someone like this again. It indicates only that your body will respond sexually, given that level of arousal, even if what goes on is against your will.

What Helps Girls Defer Sex—A Profile

By age 16, half of African-American girls have *not* yet had intercourse. Certain forces have helped them to defer the experience by emphasizing other aspects of their development. Directly or indirectly, these forces fostered skill development, self-confidence, and sexual control. Women whose parents or parent figures had the greatest influence on their adolescent sexuality were most likely to have had sexual intercourse in late adolescence, after age 17. As expected, those who identified a same-age peer as having the greatest influence on their sexual development as adolescents were most likely to have intercourse before age 16. Women from homes in which two adults assumed parenting responsibilities and those from more affluent homes delayed sex until late adolescence or young adulthood. And finally, women who reported that their parent(s), religious institutions, schools, and friends all opposed early sexual intercourse delayed their first experience until late adolescence and beyond. Women whose parents were very involved in their activities had less reason and fewer opportunities to be sexually active.

Other, less direct factors were location of residence when growing up and educational achievement. As stated earlier, women who grew up in rural areas reported an average age of 17, compared with 16 for women raised in urban areas. Women who attended college and went on to earn professional degrees had intercourse after age 17.

While first sexual intercourse does appear to be an experience that occurs during adolescence, delaying sex until late adolescence (18) or early adulthood (19 or 20) helps to ensure that a girl's sexual knowledge is adequate to meet the needs of continued sexual activity. Older adolescents also have a more realistic expectation of how their bodies work and what to expect. They may be mature enough to accept responsibility for the consequences of their own behavior and have more experience in selecting a first partner who shares their common interests and commitment, maturity, and a sense of responsibility in protecting them against unwanted outcomes.

As an adolescent, did your first sexual experience occur under the right circumstances and for the right reasons? It is one experience that people rarely forget. It can be a pleasant memory, or it can be your worst nightmare. And it is almost always better later.

"Everyone Is Doing It"—Did You Feel the Pressure?

Over the past forty years, the age of sexual intercourse for women—African-Americans included—has been declining. In Kinsey's sample, one of the few studies that compared the age of first intercourse for black women, half of the black women interviewed had had sex for the first time by age 18. In my study, by the time they were 18 three out of four women had experienced intercourse.

These findings are consistent with other national studies of sexual practices among black and white adolescents conducted by Melvin Zelnick and John Kantner, beginning in the 1970s. Within each sample, almost half of the women born before World War II had first intercourse between ages 16 and 18. In my sample, more than half of the women born after the 1960s had sex between those ages. If this pattern continues, the shift downward to an average age of 15 might be the anticipated trend for females who will reach adolescence in the next twenty years.

Significant differences in the relationship these women had with their first sexual partner were also noted. The percentage of women whose first experience occurred with their fiancé or husband dropped from 24 percent in the Kinsey study to 8 percent in my sample. More women appear to be having sexual intercourse for the first time at slightly earlier ages and outside of marriage—a trend that is apparent among white women as well and is likely to continue.

According to the 1990 U.S. Census, women are marrying at an average age of 24. Later marriages suggest that because of the gap between puberty and the age of marriage, women will be less likely to wait for marriage in order to experience sex for the first time.

The ratio of African-American men to African-American women is also declining, which may create a different kind of pressure on young women to have intercourse. If they do not comply with their partner's wishes to have sex, the perception is that he can find someone who will.

Did you feel that having sex made you more eligible, especially if "everyone was doing it"? If so, sex then became accepted and expected as a way to maintain a relationship—an experience necessary to make a girl more attractive.

Lessons from the Distant Past

The sexual experiences of black teenage girls, in contrast to their preparation, differ sharply from those of their age-mates in early African societies. Today our first sexual encounters probably occur before marriage and against our parents' wishes. Curiosity or pressure from a partner over-shadows the careful selection of partners and decisions about marriage that were once guided by parents and elders.

I see a slave's inability to control her own sexual decision making mirrored in any black girl's inability to make decisions that are in her own best interest. If she is more curious about gaining sexual information or more determined to please her partner than she is about protecting herself, there are plenty of people who are ready to exploit her needs. I think about a slave's vulnerability when I consider the sexual abuse of any black girl, with its long-lasting effects and subsequent influences on sexual risk taking. That child is captive, too. She has difficulties in exercising her control and self-confidence. Without these skills, she will be unable to advocate for herself when she is challenged by partners who wish to overpower, pressure, coerce, or manipulate her into having sex. An adolescent who does not develop sexual control and the ability to defer sexual activity in favor of goals that are more central to her self-development often becomes an adult who is unable to make her own decisions about sex.

Too many teenagers appear to be searching for a context or a relationship in which they can learn about sex, in the misguided belief that sex can change them and make them mature, more sexy, more acceptable, or more lovable. Very strong cultural messages suggest that having sex outside of a relationship is not acceptable. So girls try to make these relationships last. Even though they are fairly realistic about the pain and discomfort that is sometimes experienced during first-time sexual intercourse, they are willing to endure it. The relationships that they seek, though long-standing, result in marriage only for one in five women. Perhaps because they have little factual information and learn about sex late in childhood, these women are unprepared to manage such long-term quasi-marriages so early in life.

In light of the epidemic of unwanted sexual outcomes, one of the tragic results of sex outside of a committed relationship is that a very young woman, like Sandra, may have to face the consequences of her sexual activity alone.

What These Findings Mean to You

Society has invested less in understanding African-American youths than in stereotyping them. The same forces—poverty and abuse—that shaped the sexual experiences of African slaves in this country four hundred years ago still exist for too many young African-American women. Misinterpreted, their behavior might suggest that the stereotypes are true. But no quick conclusion can outweigh the evidence of the actual circumstances under which these sexual behaviors occur. The facts are more compelling than the myths.

There is no adolescent she-devil, but there are terribly uneducated, misguided kids who are engaging in sex for all the wrong reasons. They should be experimenting with their minds, not their bodies. The question is, who will give them the guidance and encouragement to pursue their personal goals? And where can they turn for more information and education so that they reach adolescence less curious about sex?

For many African-American women, the experience of first intercourse appears to be an extension of delayed early-childhood sexual exploration. Both child sex play and intercourse occurred as a result of curiosity about sex, but the consequences for girls who have reached puberty can be even more devastating to their personal and social development.

Many of the problems posed by adolescent sexual activity are not exclusive to black teens. Poverty, drug use—including marijuana, cocaine, crack, heroin, uppers or downers, and alcohol—poor school performance, and the lack of parental supervision and involvement, as well as the absence of a comprehensive and ongoing sex-education program, are not unique to blacks or any other ethnic group. Perhaps it is time for us to stop categorizing women who become sexually active during adolescence by skin color and begin viewing them as *women,* some of whom are having sex for the wrong reasons.

While black teens are more likely not to use any form of contraceptive, remember that three out of four women who had sex before age 18 and half of those who had sex later—regardless of whether they were black or white—used nothing to protect themselves against pregnancy or sexually transmitted diseases. Sexual irresponsibility is an adolescent problem, not simply a characteristic of black teenagers.

Another problem posed by teenage sex, regardless of ethnicity, concerns our long-term sexual self-awareness. As women mature, they are expected to become more aware of their sexual needs and preferences and more comfortable with the notion that sexual pleasure is one of the joys of life. Ideally, this empowering awareness builds upon early sexual experiences such as first intercourse. But what happens if your first intercourse had little, if anything, to do with your own sexual pleasure? The younger and more naive we are at the time of first intercourse, the less likely we are to know who we are as individuals. The idea of having a trusting, mutually honest friendship would probably not have occurred to us yet. Nor would the idea that bodies need to be ready for sex and its consequences. In addition, few young girls would know how to select a good partner. What, then, happens when these girls enter adulthood? June's story bears the marks of such a childhood and holds a disconcerting answer.

June's Story

June was single, 45, and fed up with believing that there was a man out there who would marry her, or so she said. Instead, she settled for romantic flings that sometimes lasted for years before they ended, usually in the same way—the guy would fall out of love with her and often go on to marry someone else and really settle down.

We talked at length about her first sexual experiences and the pattern of falling in love, having sex, and expecting to get married, even though no one had ever gone through the actual ceremony with her. June loved to be swept off her feet. She admitted that she had sex for the first time because her partner "needed her." She was attracted to guys with a strong line like, "You were born to make love to me and wake up each morning with a smile on your face." Some of the lines were old and phony, but when the lights were low and the music was playing, they sounded good to June.

She loved for guys to do the "heavy press." That included seeing her daily, sending flowers and candy, taking her on champagne cruises and midnight picnics, talking sexy on the phone, and making passionate love in exotic places. This was the treatment that made June move in with them, start cooking scrumptious meals, ironing shirts, and writing home to mother, only to find that her efforts were never rewarded with a marriage proposal.

June laid all of this on me while we were waiting to retrieve our valet-parked cars from a hotel garage below. Knowing that time was of the essence, I asked June what she got out of these relationships. "The satisfaction of pleasing my partner and making him feel like a king," she explained, surprised that I was not impressed with this often repeated rationale.

"With how many of your partners has there been as much concern about meeting your needs as you have for theirs?" I asked.

"Well," she paused, "None. They never got that far."

"You may be too caught up in the romance of the relationship, and misinterpret gestures of affection as an invitation to enter into a sort of

a marriage arrangement, which this is not," I replied. "If you have established a pattern of engaging in sex to please your partner, then it's time to break that cycle. There are many ingredients needed to develop a relationship that might lead to a long-term commitment. Rushing to form a bond while ignoring your own feelings and needs is like tasting a cake that isn't done yet. Just because it's rising does not guarantee that it will be good. It's too soon to tell." I urged her not to give herself away when her partner hadn't really earned her commitment.

My words were wasted. As my car arrived, a tall, good looking, smooth, Barry White-talking brother walked up and asked if she was waiting for something.

"Oh, boy, here we go again," I sighed as I drove away.

I believe that giving yourself away for the wrong reason or to the wrong person is not too different from being taken. Either way, you can end up feeling violated.

Yet, the desire to be sexually experienced and to be in a relationship seem to be part of the fantasies of many African-American girls. Why is it so important to rush to fulfill these dreams in adolescence? To find the answer, we need to understand more about how African-American women define their roles as women, which we will do in the next two chapters.

chapter 7

Becoming Women

The Role of Relationships
in Our Adult Sexuality

Semi's Story, Part I

Semi's life was right on course. Her parents didn't go to college and could
not afford to send their four children, but they instilled in them the determination to work and put themselves through. They all followed suit.

Semi's parents spent their nonworking hours helping their children
with their homework, attending their activities, taking everyone on family
camping trips—each kid could take a friend along—and going to church.
Semi grew up in a close, involved family. What they lacked in money, they
made up for with the love and respect they had for one another. Semi's
parents didn't teach her much about sex, but they kept her so busy that
she had little curiosity as a child and little unsupervised time to get into
much.

The kids teased their parents about holding hands and kissing each
other all the time, but Semi had to admit that she liked seeing the way
her parents looked at each other and still seemed to be in love. One day,
she thought, I'll find someone to look at me that way.

I was really impressed when Semi told me about her family's policy
for watching television—they could watch certain programs on weekends
but never during the week. If they finished their homework, they had
their own collection of books to read, and everyone went to the library on
Saturday to get a new batch.

Adolescence was full of contests, recitals, and group activities, all of
which gave Semi a good sense of the things that she did well. She had
her heart set on being a teacher, and although she was allowed to date
and wear makeup, she said that her parents questioned every guy who

came to the house about his future plans. They did not encourage relationships with guys who did not have the same kinds of goals that their
children had.

Semi finished high school with honors, enrolled in junior college, found
a part-time job, and planned to transfer to a four-year college. She met
a guy who was struggling just as she was to make it on his own. Her
parents liked him, and Semi fell in love. At age 18, they decided to have
sex and planned the time and place and the type of contraceptive they
would use. They dated for three years, until they realized that they weren't
ready for marriage, decided to date other people, and gradually grew
apart.

Defining Our Role as Women

By the time we reach the ripe old age of 18, many of us feel,
like Semi, that we've been waiting all our lives to do exactly
what we choose to do with our bodies. After the curiosity
of childhood, the awkwardness of puberty, and the experimentation of adolescence, we're supposed to have it goin'
on. But what we think that means may be entirely different
from what it should mean.

At this stage, we should be somewhat comfortable with
our adult bodies and have enough knowledge to understand
sex and its consequences. With maturity, we should be increasingly able to refine the ways in which we express our
sexuality and make fewer mistakes that have devastating
and lasting consequences. Our values and religious beliefs
should also be guiding us in making responsible decisions
to protect and control our sexuality, and in developing
positive relationships with people who will help us to achieve
our life goals. In short, we should be firmly on our way to
becoming sexually responsible women.

As adults, we reveal our sexual responsibility through
good decisions and healthy behavior. Semi's decisions, for
example, showed a high degree of responsibility and resulted
in a reasonably safe and healthy pattern of behavior.

In contrast to Semi's responsibility, however, stand the sexual actions of many African-American women. The incidence of sexually transmitted diseases, unintended pregnancies, and abortions in black communities is disturbingly high. According to recent studies, the rate of AIDS in the black population is more than triple that of the white population. Among women, the gap is even wider. Black women face between ten and fifteen times the risk of AIDS reported for white women. We are also particularly at risk for other sexually transmitted diseases—including syphilis, gonorrhea, genital herpes and genital warts, pelvic inflammatory disease, and chlamydia.

By age 20, nearly 40 percent of all American women and about 60 percent of American black women have been pregnant. Minority women in the United States (mainly blacks and Latinas) have an abortion rate of 57 per 1,000 women, 2.7 times higher than that of white women. At first glance, these statistics show that many, many women are not making good sexual decisions.

When I explored black women's sexual behaviors along with their reasons for engaging in sex, it became apparent that that assumption was true—but not for obvious reasons that confirmed negative stereotypes. Instead, I began to see a pattern of decision making emerging from the data. It confirmed that cultural values played a surprising role.

Consider this: When we make decisions that focus on pleasing our partners, we conform to cultural expectations that require us to express our sexuality within the context of a relationship. In the process, however, we may be giving up control of our own bodies. When we make decisions that include our own needs, we have better sexual health, but we diminish our chances of attracting a partner. These dilemmas probably sound familiar to you. In defining their role as women, black women are inevitably torn between cultural values that center on being in a relationship and putting the needs of others before their own needs, and their needs for self-protection.

How African-American women resolve this conflict is a big factor in how we experience sexuality in adulthood, etching the pattern of our decisions about the risks we might take to attract and keep a partner. This chapter encourages you to see if my findings apply to you.

Who Influences Your Sexual Decisions Now?

If you've seen Spike Lee's *Mo' Better Blues* or Terry McMillan's *Waiting to Exhale*, you may have noticed that the conversations the women had about sex, men, and relationships were rich in humor, honesty, pain, anger, and frustration at the problems involved in attracting and keeping the partner of their dreams. But this doesn't necessarily mean that black women discuss the nitty-gritty details, like how much of your sexual history to reveal to a new partner or when you can safely have unprotected intercourse with a partner you've just met, what to do if a condom breaks or leaks, and how to tell whether your partner is bisexual. This would be lifesaving information. Many a woman would be grateful to get such detailed advice and accurate tips, but few do. What do African-American adult women talk about when they talk about sex, and who influences their actions?

I. Friends

Yes, we talk about sex. Most of our sexual discussions center around the mechanics of sex and our feelings about it, but not the risks or ways to protect ourselves. Apart from this, we're very open with each other. Half of us tell our friends the best sexual positions for orgasm, our favorite sexual techniques, where to find a good partner, and our woes if we can't find one. I've heard about a group of friends who drive to work together. On the way in, they discuss how often they have or would like to have sex and their fantasies about sex or their partners. On the way home, they discuss who's lonely, horny, or having problems in her relationships. They can't wait for carpooling each day.

Fewer than one in four of us never discuss sex with friends, or believe that sex is a private matter that shouldn't be discussed with anyone.

One common topic is what I call relationship mechanics—someone describes a current relationship problem and her friends try to solve it by offering advice. This sort of conversation is what takes place on talk shows. There is no guarantee that anyone else is better equipped to solve these problems, but friends nonetheless become experts in advising each other.

Discussions about what to do with an unintended pregnancy, different kinds of contraceptives to use and how and when to use them, or moral issues like whether to have sex with someone are not as common. Of course, when events like the Anita Hill-Clarence Thomas hearing or the O. J. Simpson trial introduce sexual topics such as harassment or interracial marriage into the conversation, they can compete with anything else that might come up.

I've asked women how their friends felt about their current sexual behavior. Most reported that their friends supported the way they handled their sex lives. While more than one in three claimed that their friends weren't in favor of or were opposed to their sex lives, few had friends who thought the way they conducted themselves sexually was wrong.

Many health professionals feel that friends influence each other and increase each other's chances of practicing irresponsible behavior. They assume that black women friends contribute to each other's sexually risky behaviors. Generally, *what* is discussed among friends—is it how to prevent pregnancy or how to attract and keep a partner? In my research, I found that it was the latter. Women seem dependent on their friends for advice about how to keep a romance alive and make a relationship work. Yet if your partner is seen with someone else or is known to sleep around, a typical conversation might gravitate toward how to get him back, how to get even with another woman, or whether you should leave him. But you rarely discuss the fact that his habit of sleeping around could expose you to a sexual disease.

2. Parents

In adulthood, parents are in a supportive role, offering advice and warnings from the sidelines of their daughters' lives. They usually become a marginal source of sexual information. Only one in five of the women I studied reported having discussions that centered around rela-tionships—when to get married or divorced, to stop seeing your boyfriend, or such advice as "You have too many boyfriends, it's time for you to settle down." One in five parents discussed the regulation or control of their sexual behavior with their daughters. Only a few said that they could discuss anything at all with their parents.

3. Religious Institutions

While the church has traditionally focused on restrictions about sex and having babies out of wedlock, the messages that were sent often conflicted with the realities of many relationships. For example, Mona explained that she had church friends and social friends. Her church friends discussed the value of a woman's having sex in marriage and waiting for a husband to satisfy her sexual needs. Her social friends, however, discussed having sex when you feel good about someone and he feels good about you.

While Mona was devout in her church attendance and considered herself to be very religious, she was with her social friends when she met men. She didn't know how to be true to her beliefs and her desire to find a partner at the same time. Consequently, the decisions she made about sex with a partner were influenced more by the opinions of her social friends than by those of her church friends.

4. Partners

Even if friends, families, and religious institutions play a role in socializing women about sex, I doubt that any of these sources have the influence that they could or should have. In adulthood, women concentrate on how they can attract a partner and maintain a relationship. Sex is an expected part of the process. Yet many of the most crucial decisions that might affect their sexual health are made in private, perhaps with their partner, but certainly in isolation from family and other familiar sources of support.

Friends and family are not the primary influence on black adult sexuality. It appears that a partner is. We still view sex as an experience to be shared with someone—in a relationship and in keeping with traditional African principles.

Are You Taking Care of Your Own Sexual Needs?

The majority of the black women I interviewed had a sexual partner. We know little about women who are not sexually active and their reasons for choosing this course. It seems that there just aren't enough men. One in four women said they couldn't find a suitable partner, one in five didn't want a relationship, 15 percent weren't ready for a relationship, and 15 percent had an unavailable partner who was away, ill, or could not have intercourse. Least common were women who had just ended a relationship.

For most white women, regardless of whether they have a partner, taking care of their own sexual needs is an essential part of adult sexuality. Black women ages 18 to 50, however, may never masturbate at any time in their lives. In fact, according to the study I conducted in 1994, 81 percent of black women had never even touched their breasts or genitals to the point of sexual arousal. Why? In the 1984 study, one in three women told me that they had no desire to do so, or even to try. As one said, "It wouldn't be satisfying for me to do it." Others said that they did not feel the need to do so, that they either controlled their sexual urges or had a partner who could satisfy them. A few cited religious beliefs that masturbation was a sin. Finally, a smaller number expressed the opinion that giving a woman satisfaction is a man's job. "That's what men are for—to satisfy women. I don't need to do that for myself," I was told.

Yet some women began to experiment with self-touching in childhood. If they began in adulthood, they were usually between the ages of 18 and 26, and single. Some began using their hand to stimulate their clitoris; others used vibrators or other objects, water from the bathtub spout, breast and genital manipulation, or a combination of these methods. Even then, self-pleasuring was still practiced infrequently—generally less than once a week, though usually to orgasm.

How did women in relationships use masturbation? I wondered. Was it a substitute for sexual gratification if they did not reach orgasm with their partner or did it supplement the need for gratification, regardless of whether the women were satisfied with their sexual partner? If black women are as sexual as the stereotypes make us out to be, you'd assume the latter.

To answer these questions, I asked women how satisfied they were with their current sexual partner and compared their ratings with four masturbatory patterns in childhood, adolescence or adulthood only, or all through life. The results were revealing.

Women who were less sexually satisfied with their current partners were much more likely to masturbate as adults compared with women who were very sexually satisfied. This suggests that for some of us it is a substitute for not receiving satisfaction from our partners, not a primary means of sexual pleasure. Early messages about masturbation had an impact on women's feelings about what they were doing. Almost half of the women I interviewed still felt guilty, even though they reported that it was pleasant, and many were still unsure about whether it's right or wrong. And yet, despite their ambivalence, when they were asked whether their attitudes had changed, most of the women were more positive than they were in the past.

Although masturbation and self-touching for arousal is a matter of personal preference, African-American women face cultural and religious taboos against both behaviors. While women need to examine their bodies by touching themselves all over for lumps or growths that may require medical attention, self-touching is often confused with self-pleasuring or attempts to masturbate. In reality, the two things are not the same. Following cultural and religious beliefs should not result in our neglecting our bodies for fear of practicing a regular routine of self-touching for health maintenance. How can we allow others to touch our bodies if we can't?

Today self-pleasuring is increasingly more acceptable. While relatively few African-American women give themselves sexual pleasure through direct sexual contact, others achieve orgasm through fantasies and dreams. Surprisingly, an even greater number become orgasmic through viewing some form of media—books, magazines, or movies. Once again, it is obvious that the media play a powerful role in socializing and stimulating our sexuality. As children, black girls receive a kind of sex education from the media, and as adults they receive sexual excitement.

Are You Engaging in Risky Behaviors?—
Eight Risky Choices

In the past, women's sex lives weren't open to discussion. For example, the number of sexual partners a woman had wasn't a politically correct topic until sexual diseases became epidemic. Today you need to be prepared to discuss the circumstances of your sex life down to the smallest detail. It's the only way to see how risky your behavior really may or may not be.

1. Number of Partners

One of the stereotypes of African-American women's sexuality is that our alleged sexual impulsivity results in a high number of partners. When African-American women are cited as being at risk for sexually transmitted diseases, including HIV/AIDS, it is difficult not to assume that the reason is that they have had multiple sexual partners who may be drug abusers, bisexual, or gay. That assumption, however, is not necessarily correct. The average number of partners over a lifetime for women ages 18 to 36 is eight. The average over the past twelve years for women ages 18 to 50 is four. In my research, 17 percent reported having only one relationship. About half of these relationships lasted more than a year. A smaller number of these sexual relationships lasted from one night to two weeks.

Women with multiple partners may be the exception and not the rule, as we saw in adolescence. Two out of three black women reported that they did not engage in sex only for sex. Through sex they seemed to be looking for something more, like a committed relationship, rather than solely seeking sexual gratification and pleasure. The sheer number of partners may not be a problem for us in general, but not using condoms or methods that prevent the exchange of body fluids definitely is. Contact with one person who has engaged in risky sexual or drug-related practices can be just as lethal as having many partners. We'll talk more about how African-American women protect themselves against unwanted sexual outcomes.

2. Prostitution or Sex Work

When I asked the women I interviewed if they had ever engaged in prostitution or sex work, 5 percent said yes. These were the same women who reported having partners in the double-digit range. However, none of the women considered prostitution to be their primary job. They had engaged in prostitution for a limited period of their lives, due to financial problems or drug abuse. For example, Gloria said that her job wasn't paying much. She stopped being a sex worker when her husband came home from the armed services. Celina disclosed that she engaged in prostitution throughout college in order to pay her tuition. Most of these incidents were very dangerous and abusive, and increased the women's exposure to infection, as the following story illustrates.

Virginia described how she started hooking because she needed some money.

"I figured that I would go and make me a few dollars. A girlfriend and I went up to Hollywood to get us some johns. My guy said he wanted a date, but I told him no. This turkey took me up into the hills and pulled over and grabbed me around the neck and said, "Okay, bitch, I want you to suck my dick." So I did, but it didn't take me very long. When he was through, he made me get out of the car and I had to walk down that hill with no money. When I got back, my girlfriend fussed at me for goin' with a cheap john."

It was not uncommon for the women who engaged in prostitution to do so at some point because they felt that if they were going to have sex, they ought to get something for it.

Celina remarked, "We had to give it away for too long. Sisters today should profit from what we were once made to do." Some men are literally paying for the abuses that black women have historically experienced.

3. Cunnilingus

Oral sex places women at risk for sexually transmitted diseases, but it is sometimes a preferred method of sexual gratification because pregnancy can be avoided. Almost two out of three black women I interviewed had engaged in cunnilingus. The frequency of this practice ranged from once only to twice daily. When some women were asked why they didn't engage in this behavior at all, most responded that either they or their partner had no desire to do so. Some had moral and ethical reasons, such as "I don't think it is right" or "That is a sin."

4. Fellatio

Almost half of the women had never put their mouth on their partners' genitals. For those who had, the frequency ranged from only once to once a day. For those who hadn't, more than half had no desire to engage in fellatio.

I was struck by the disparate number of women whose partners performed oral sex on them versus the number who themselves performed oral sex. However, while cunnilingus was practiced more frequently than fellatio, if women engaged in one behavior, they were more likely to engage in the other. For the most part, there was reciprocity among women and their partners who practiced these behaviors.

5. Anal Sex

This is one of the riskiest behaviors when it comes to transmitting sexual diseases among men and women. When I asked the women if they engaged in anal sex, the majority said no. Many reported fear of contracting a sexually transmitted disease as the reason for not engaging in anal sex, some simply had no desire to do so, and others cited moral and religious reasons or had never thought about it.

More than one in ten women, however, said that the opportunity to have anal sex never arose, so we do not know what they might have decided if they had a chance. It is important to note that one in five women had engaged in anal sex. The frequency ranged from one attempt to once a month. Only 5 percent of these women, however, did this on a regular basis.

6. Sex with Groups

Sexual practices that involve primary partners along with other people at the same time can be risky for different reasons. They may jeopardize a relationship if a partner becomes attracted to an outside party, or they can threaten sexual health by increasing the possibility of incurring or spreading a sexual disease with yet another partner.

While the majority of the women reported that they had never had sex with more than one person at a time, a little less than 10 percent did so with a frequency ranging from one time to once a month. Most of those who engaged in group sex did so with friends. Few did so with strangers, and a few more had sex with both friends and strangers at the same time.

Predictably, many black women do not participate in group sex or ménage à trois for moral and religious reasons, or lack of desire. Fear of sexually transmitted diseases was barely cited. A few admitted being concerned about what would happen to their relationship if they and their partners engaged in group sex.

7. Partner Swapping

While most black women do not engage in partner swapping—in which two couples have sex with each other's partners—5 percent tried it at least once. The most common reason for not risking it was lack of desire, followed by moral and religious reasons, and lack of opportunity. Once again, few cited fear of sexually transmitted diseases.

8. Extramarital Affairs

When I asked married women if they had ever had an extramarital affair, 40 percent said yes. More than one in five reported one affair, a little over 10 percent reported two affairs, and 5 percent had had three or more. While most of the partners were men, a smaller percentage (7 percent) had had affairs with female partners.

Are you shocked to learn that so many married black women have had affairs? Don't be. We know so little about women's extramarital experiences that in the absence of facts we have assumed that men are the only ones who are unfaithful to their married partners—but my findings don't support that notion.

Is Sex with Your Primary Partner Satisfying?

Do you ever talk about sex with the partner with whom you have spent the most time? What patterns of communication and range of behaviors have you shared over time, as intimacy and emotional commitment grew?

How we indicate our interest in having sex and when we want to have sex can influence what happens when two people get together. Overwhelmingly, black women report that their partners initiate sex most of the time. In fact, nearly 15 percent of the black women in my research never initiated sex with their partner. When they were asked why not, more than half of these women replied that they were not interested in initiating or never had the chance—their partners always beat them to it. Though the majority communicated their sexual needs and desires both verbally and nonverbally (through body language or suggestive clothing), there was a small number who never made any overtures.

One in five verbally discussed sex with their partners. When the psychologist Dr. Sandra Lyons-Rowe and I conducted a study of sexual satisfaction among African-American women, we found that those who were most sexually satisfied with their partners also initiated sex more frequently and verbally communicated their sexual needs to their partners. The fact that they were more direct about their preferences may have contributed to their perceptions of sexual satisfaction. Also, about one in three women reported having intercourse between one and three times a week. Slightly more reported that they had sex with their primary partner four or more times a week, and fewer had sex one time or less per week. Vaginal intercourse was also reported to be their main source of sexual gratification. More than three out of four women were orgasmic at least 50 percent of the time that they had sex.

Do You Have Female Partners?

While most black women have sex only with male partners, a small number in my research had sex with other women, and some were involved with both men and women. Most of their partners were lovers or friends, and the remainder were coworkers or strangers. More than three out of four lesbian relationships were described as intense, with mutual fondling, as well as manual and oral stimulation that resulted in the majority of women reaching orgasm. Almost half of these relationships lasted from six months to over a year. The most frequently cited reason the women gave for engaging in sex with another woman was curiosity or the fact that their female partner had caught them by surprise and hit on them; one in three reported being in love with or turned on by their female partner. One in three had only one partner, but most had between two and six partners in adulthood.

While all of the women who had female sexual partners reported experiencing pleasant feelings as a result of their sexual encounters, more than half also described feeling guilty. Yet, in spite of these feelings, most were not having sex for the sex alone. In fact, two out of three denied that sex was the purpose for these encounters, which suggests that other needs, such as love, emotional support, and nurturance, may have been the motivating factors.

The research that I conducted in 1994 generally confirmed what I found in the '80s: About 5 percent of African-American women reported having had a sexual relationship with another woman once. These adult relationships usually began at age 22, and the average number of partners the women reported was four. Most commonly, they practiced cunnilingus.

Two out of three black women who had sex with a woman also reported having a relationship with a male partner at the same time. Fewer than one in ten reported having sex with another woman outside of the relationship they had with a woman at the time.

Were these women radically different from other black women? Marte wasn't.

Marte's Story

Marte was 40 years old and a very successful businesswoman from the Midwest. She grew up like other girls, playing with dolls, having crushes on boys, and participating in scouting. She had little interest in sex until she got to college, but she did do a little dating in high school. In her words, before she met Jean her life was absolutely "normal."

Marte and Jean were assigned as roommates in college because they had the same major. They became the best of friends—studying together, hanging out with the same crowd, and visiting each other's families for the holidays, something they continue to do. They even got jobs in the same town and decided to get an apartment together. Nobody questioned their "closeness" when they graduated from college, but in truth Marte and Jean had been lovers since their sophomore year. Both were embarrassed and afraid to have other people find out, but they had fallen in love with each other and in love they stayed.

Neither really dated in college, and they both used the excuse that the black guys were into either white girls or each other. Neither was interested in the "marriage and children thing," and they claimed that they wanted to see the world first before they settled down. As the years passed, people began to put pressure on Marte and were always fixing her up with dates, especially at conferences. She would sometimes engage in what she called "conference behavior," and slept with several guys. She wanted to have something to talk to her friends about and admitted that she was a bit curious about men. She wanted to see if she could match what she had, but no relationship or sexual experience she had with a man came close to what she and Jean shared.

Marte decided that she could no longer live with her secret and sought me out to help her tell her family. Jean's family had a "don't ask, don't tell" policy, but Marte's family was relentless in their concerns about her man problem. We discussed the dangers of her conference behavior, which she finally told Jean about. She rehearsed what she would tell her parents and invited them to a session.

Marte explained to her parents how much she loved and respected them and their wishes for her, but she now realized that it was time to live her own life and needed their support and understanding. She said, "If you love me, it won't matter who I love as long as she loves and respects me as you do. I believe that God loves and accepts me as I am. Can you accept the fact that Jean and I are lovers and she is my life partner?"

Her parents struggled, wept, and felt guilty, convinced that they had "caused" Marte to be a lesbian. They grieved about their loss of a chance to have grandchildren, but in time they accepted Marte and Jean as *partners. Fortunately, Marte came out to her parents and did not lose them in her life.*

It took a lot of courage for Marte to make the decisions that she made, and I admired the way she committed to being sexually responsible in her relationship with Jean in order to avoid exposing either of them to undue risks. This is something that everyone should strive for, whether they are in a relationship with a man or a woman.

What White Women's Sexual Practices Tell Us

Generally, black and white women's adult sexual patterns differ markedly, with a few exceptions.

Remember, two out of three white women masturbate in adulthood. Slightly more than 30 percent began in childhood and continued through their teens and beyond. White women are more likely to use masturbation to supplement sex with their partners rather than as a substitute for gratification they aren't getting from their partners. They view it as a primary means of sexual pleasure, whether they are satisfied by their partners or not. They report less guilt and are generally much less conflicted about whether masturbation is right or wrong. In contrast to African-American women, white women are most likely to have an orgasm in their dreams rather than through some type of media stimulation.

There were more white women in my research who were not currently sexually active than there were women with partners—36 percent versus 23 percent for black women—but their reason was the same: Eighty-nine percent reported that there weren't enough men.

Patterns of sexual communication were very similar for black and white women. Most had partners who initiated sex, but white women initiated sex almost twice as often as black women did. Two out of three white women communicated both verbally and nonverbally with their partners about their sexual needs. Few white or black women never communicated to their partners in any way.

The findings on other patterns were markedly different. White women ages 18 to 36 reported an average of nineteen partners in their lifetime. Over the past twelve years, white women ages 18 to 50 reported an average of seven partners. Numbers in the upper ranges were cited by women who engaged in prostitution. One in ten had brief encounters ranging from one-night stands to a few weeks. However, similar to black women, about one in six had only one partner. The primary difference was that white women were more likely to report a combination of long- and short-term sexual relationships in adulthood. Almost half had sex purely for the sake of sexual pleasure, which contrasted with about one in three black women.

While only 8 percent of white women reported that they engaged in prostitution, when the samples of black and white women were compared on prostitution, most were white. In accounting for the difference between the number of white women who engaged in prostitution compared with their black peers, it's important to note that the white women may have viewed themselves as call girls rather than as street walkers. The Mayflower Madam and Heidi Fleiss proved that some women may view it as a business and do not fit the stereotype of the prostitute.

As with black women, none of the white women I interviewed considered prostitution as their job—they had been prostitutes for some of the same reasons that black women gave, but the degree of need differed. For example, Shannon, who lived in Beverly Hills, engaged in prostitution to pay her son's private-school tuition. Even when she no longer needed to, she kept one or two johns on the side to make spending money. Another woman engaged in prostitution with her husband as her pimp. She stopped when he was arrested.

When we compared sexual practices with the primary

partner, vaginal intercourse was still predominant. Similar to their black peers, white women tended to have intercourse between one and three times a week, with most becoming orgasmic at least half of the time. However, of the women who reported that they were orgasmic each time they had intercourse, more than half were black. The latter finding may have something to do with why black women report intercourse as the primary source of sexual gratification.

In contrast, while white women also reported vaginal intercourse as the preferred method of becoming orgasmic, masturbation and being orally stimulated by a partner were reported as the next most preferred methods. Consequently, patterns of becoming orgasmic differed for the two ethnic groups. There were also greater differences in their sexual behavior patterns. Compared with black women, white women were most likely to engage in cunnilingus (87 percent versus 63 percent for black women), fellatio (93 percent versus 55 percent for black women), and anal sex (43 percent versus 20 percent for black women).

Different patterns appeared in sex with primary partners and others. White women were more likely to have sex with more than one person at a time (22 percent versus 9 percent for black women), only slightly more likely to engage in partner swapping (7 percent versus 5 percent for black women), and slightly less likely to have an extramarital affair (37 percent versus 40 percent for black women). Those who had affairs, however, were more likely to have three or more (76 percent versus 23 percent for black women). Five percent had extramarital affairs with women (versus 7 percent for black women).

Both groups were at risk for sexually transmitted diseases if they had unprotected sex, but many of the potential sources of infection differed. For black women the primary source seemed to be vaginal sex, whether with the primary partner or not. For white women, the primary source ranged from vaginal to oral and anal sex with their primary partner and others.

What Recent Findings Confirm

When we asked African-American women about their sexual practices with their primary partners in the study conducted in 1994, the same pattern emerged. Fewer than half of the women had ever masturbated or engaged in oral sex—specifically cunnilingus, where they were the receiver, or fellatio, where they were the giver. Those who had oral sex did so only about once a month, on average. Few women engaged in anal sex or group sex.

When we compared black women with white women of similar ages, sexual patterns again differed:

- They were less likely to engage in all of these behaviors than were white women.
- They were more likely to be married if they engaged in oral sex. White women were more likely to be single if they engaged in fellatio.
- They had fewer sexual partners over their lifetime than did white women.

We noted the same pattern among African-American survivors of breast cancer, and the same differences when black and white breast-cancer survivors were compared. It appears that across the age span, African-American women reported a preference for vaginal intercourse, just as they were observed to engage in hundreds of years ago in Africa by some of the missionaries who first wrote about African sexuality. Those who were more likely to practice another form of sexual activity, including oral, anal, or group sex, were likely to be better educated, less religious, or more affluent. Single women had more multiple sexual partners than married women, as you might expect.

Over time the changes in the patterns of black women's sexual behavior dramatize a disturbing trend. When I compared college-educated black women with studies done by Kinsey and his associates, it became clear that an increasing proportion of black women were engaging in unprotected intercourse. A fairly consistent proportion had female partners, including some who had no current male partner but continued to have sex exclusively with women. Women who had had female sexual partners since adolescence often had sex with males as well. They married and had children but continued to have sexual contact with women. In short, risk taking seems to be deeply embedded in the way we live.

Are You Taking Risks or Taking Responsibility?

Sexual risk taking obviously occurs regardless of ethnicity. If black women's and white women's sexual practices are different but both are risky, then the question remains: Why are black women increasingly at greater risk of having unintended pregnancies and sexually transmitted diseases, including HIV? At the beginning of this chapter, I suggested that the answer lies in our decision making about our relationships and whether we choose to protect and control our reproduction. As we have seen too often, by adhering to cultural values that stress maintaining a relationship and ignoring the consequences, African-American women choose not to protect their reproduction.

The longer and harder I look at this pattern, the more I realize how much black women need this insight. The next chapter looks at contraceptive use, pregnancy and abortion histories, and other indicators of our readiness for or our resistance to making sexual choices in our own best interest. Those of us who are prepared for our relationships need confirmation and confidence that we are going to be fine even if the relationships don't last, and those of us who aren't prepared need knowledge and healing.

chapter 8

Giving Our Love
Surviving Our Choices

Semi's Story, Part II

I first met Semi over the telephone. She had heard me speak and called all over UCLA until she found me. She explained that she wanted therapy but had no money and wanted to save up to see me in about six months— and six months to that day, she and I met face-to-face. She sat down and unrolled a list of topics for us to discuss. I got the sense that this perky lady was serious about reaching certain goals in her life and needed someone to get her on the right track. The rest she would do for herself.

Semi was 27 years old and single when we met. She was trying to end a relationship that showed no promise of leading to marriage, but because so many of the men whom she met seemed uninterested in making a commitment she also feared that she might not find a husband, which was one of her life goals. She wanted to deal with the possibility that she would remain single or would have to modify some of the expectations she had of a partner. This was a major decision that she was seeking help to make, because it could change the course of her life. Semi was about to finish working on her teaching credential and had received a job offer.

"What brought you in to see me?" I said, not yet having heard anything that would explain why this young woman had worked so hard to save the money for therapy.

"I want a baby and I haven't found anyone to marry," she said. "I want to get on with my life, but I don't believe in having children out of marriage, so I want to adopt a little boy."

She realized that this adoption would decrease her chances of finding someone to marry, and needed to discuss whether she should lower the standards she had set for herself and the partner she wanted or go on with her plans and accept being single. We discussed the pros and cons of single motherhood, and she finally worked out a plan to manage every one. She tearfully decided to go on with her life and adopt a baby.

So, at age 28, and with her family's support, Semi adopted a baby, John Henry, "because he looked like he was going to be big and strong," she explained.

Several years passed with cards and pictures exchanged so that I knew that Semi and John Henry were doing fine. She was teaching and loving it, and loving her baby.

On a plane trip to attend her grandmother's funeral, Semi's life changed in an unexpected way. John Henry lost one of his toys, and while Semi was searching the floor she heard a voice say, "Are you looking for this?"

Semi looked up into the eyes of a black man with a knock-out smile. They exchanged numbers and began to have lunch dates when they talked endlessly about everything. They became friends and decided to get tested for HIV and other sexually transmitted diseases in the event their relationship developed into something deeper. They waited for the results, showed each other the reports, and planned their first sexual encounter.

Semi and I laughed over the phone at how nervous she was. She felt that she had gotten "rusty," it had been so long since she'd had sex. We discussed the pros and cons of sex before marriage, even though Semi was not a virgin. She wanted to be sure about her decision so that she would have no regrets later.

A few months later John proposed to Semi and John Henry, and they accepted. John told her that he loved her not in spite of John Henry but because she had enough love to give to a little child who otherwise might not have had a family to raise him. They already had the ring bearer, so the rest of the wedding plans were pretty uncomplicated but beautiful.

I was proud of Semi because she made some really difficult decisions about her life goals and stuck to them. She had to make many sacrifices in the process, but in the end she did not compromise on the things that she wanted in life. She was prepared to remain single and filled her life with lots of activities, good friends, and her family. She was actually more attractive to John because she had taken control of her life and was confident that the choices she had made were best for her.

Semi and I worked on her sexual knowledge, which is something that few black women do, but I respected her because what she did not re-

ceive from her parents she got for herself. Semi is a good example of a woman who is committed to being sexually healthy.

Making the Right Decisions

Semi's choices clearly showed that she valued sexual responsibility, just like millions of other African-American women. By respecting themselves, women like Semi show respect for the parts of our culture that help us survive. They are:

- family life
- committed relationships where children represent the bond between partners
- knowing that there is a right time for sex and for children

On the other hand, they are not bound by certain other beliefs that are also sanctioned by our culture and expected of our gender, namely, transferring control of our lives to a partner. This part of our culture may have served us better when women were raised only to marry, but it hinders our ability to cope today. In our society at this time, our well-being depends on our willingness to accept responsibility for ourselves, whether we are in a permanent relationship or not. So when sexually responsible women make choices, they also think about:

- protection from unwanted outcomes
- exerting sexual control
- improving their sexual knowledge

Stolen women's lives tell a different story, as you will also hear in this chapter. We'll look closely at how African-American women tend to respond to a set of basic adult sexual decisions and dilemmas. Think about how your own choices fit into the picture. You may discover that, like Semi, you have already developed the inner resources to work your way through life's sexual challenges when the need arises. Or you may discover that you need help and more life-affirming ways of thinking about your options.

Deciding to Use a Contraceptive

Sexually responsible women try to protect themselves against sexual diseases and the possibility of an unwanted pregnancy. I asked the women in my research about condom use along with many other methods of birth control. I asked them not only to tell us which contraceptive method they currently used but to give us their contraceptive history—which methods they had used since they first had sex. I was stunned by the answers.

We found that not even half of the black women in our 1980s study were using a method that was prescribed by a health professional, and only one in four used something that had been bought over the counter. One in three used nothing at all. Five percent of them had never used any contraceptive in their lives. Those who used contraceptives selected methods that they could control without breaking the flow of the sexual act, such as IUDs, birth-control pills, and tubal ligation. They were least likely to use the rhythm method and withdrawal, diaphragms, and condoms, the method that is recommended today.

You might wonder, have women's choices changed since we became aware of HIV/AIDS? Some have; some have not. In our 1994 study, we asked women about their partners' condom use. About one in three African-American women reported using condoms less now than they did a year ago. One in four used them more now than a year ago. In spite of the risks of contracting sexually transmitted diseases—including HIV—African-American women seem to have difficulty demanding that their partners use condoms.

The most common reasons I heard were:

- "They were not available"—meaning that she would have had to interrupt the sexual act or purchase something beforehand in order to use a contraceptive at that moment.
- "I don't like contraceptives (or a specific type)," and
- "I wanted sex to be natural."

Few if any women could boast that with every heated sexual encounter they used a contraceptive. In fact, 96 percent said that they had sex at least once without using contraceptives (94 percent of white women said the same). Perhaps a single incident can be attributed to chance. However, total nonuse raises serious concerns.

Taken together, more than half of the women in my research made a deliberate decision not to use anything. Less than 20 percent did not use birth control but didn't mind becoming pregnant, and a small percentage wanted a baby or used a contraceptive but it failed to protect them against pregnancy. It's also possible that some of the women did not use their contraceptives properly. If they forgot to take their birth-control pills, for example, they may have taken two the next day in an effort to catch up.

Significantly, however, about two out of three black women did not use contraceptives but did not wish to become pregnant. This pattern of not using contraceptives even though they did not wish to become pregnant tended to persist with each pregnancy the women reported. In other words, their behavior did not change from one pregnancy to the next. Not surprisingly, young women born after the 1960s and single women were most likely not to use contraceptives or plan to become pregnant.

It's hard not to wonder exactly what women are thinking about when they choose not to protect themselves even though they do not want to become pregnant. It became apparent from the interviews that these women viewed the consequences of sex as separate from the sexual act itself. Some women, especially those who were young and single, seemed to have been concentrating more on what was going on between themselves and their partners at the time than on birth-control methods. In the context of a relationship, it is likely that sexual control and protection against unwanted outcomes can be overshadowed by a partner's wishes and feelings.

With this in mind, we asked a slightly different question: If you weren't thinking about becoming pregnant, did your partner influence your decision not to use contraceptives? We also asked how many times a woman's partner influenced her pregnancy.

More than one in three black women said that their partners encouraged them to have at least one pregnancy; more than one in four said that their partners influenced them to have two pregnancies, and another quarter said that their partners encouraged them to have between three and nine pregnancies (these women were usually married). Less than 10 percent of the women said that their partners never encouraged their decision to become pregnant.

Further research confirms these findings. On average, African-American women, regardless of marital status, had two unplanned pregnancies compared with one for white women. These findings are supported in part by the fact that more than half of single black women had at least one child outside of marriage. Are some African-American women deferring the decision to control their reproductive ability to their partners, because a child is perceived as a link to that partner regardless of marital status? Children have long been a cherished symbol of the bond between married partners.

Today, however, more women can afford to raise children without guaranteed involvement on the father's part. Children are still valued, but their presence does not necessarily ensure marriage. Some black women accept this reality; others refuse to accept it and constantly try to cement a relationship by having children.

Deciding to Have an Abortion

It was once assumed that black women opposed abortion because they wanted to keep their children, no matter how many they had or whether they could afford them. But when we asked the women if they had ever had an induced abortion, half of them said yes. A little more than half of the white women also reported having at least one abortion. On average, there were two legal procedures per woman. Of the women who were born after 1954 but who became pregnant before *Roe vs. Wade*, ten percent had both legal and illegal abortions, and the remaining few were self-induced. More than half of these womrn were white.

When we asked the women why they decided to obtain their first abortion, almost half cited "not being ready" to have a baby; close to 12 percent cited pressure from parents or their sexual partner to abort, as well as their own reluctance to have a baby (23 percent); and a little more than 11 percent did not want the child of that particular partner. The latter were most likely to be women who became pregnant as a result of being raped. The reasons for second abortions were similar to those for the first abortion.

If we consider the number of unintended pregnancies among black women, and the fact that first intercourse often occurs because of curiosity about sex and partner pressure, these findings once again suggest that African-American women are not controlling their own bodies, especially their reproduction, and are instead deferring to their partners.

However, the women did not appear to feel good about the limited choices they had once they became pregnant. The idea of making a baby may initially sound romantic, but many of these women simply weren't ready for the reality of what was to come in nine months. When they were asked to comment on their feelings about abortion, they described a variety of negative reactions such as guilt, insecurity about whether what they were doing was right or wrong, and fear of the consequences—especially their ability to conceive children in the future.

Middle-class women reported fewer negative feelings and more relief at terminating an unwanted pregnancy. They seemed more aware that an unintended pregnancy could interrupt long-term goals.

My research, in contrast to other literature on abortion, does not support the notion that black women have sought abortions more or less than white women. In fact, both groups are very similar in this regard. Both use abortions and contraceptives to control their reproduction and to protect themselves against unwanted sexual outcomes.

For African-American women, the overall pattern appears to be pro-children, pro-families, and pro-choice. We have always valued the right to choose to bear children, whether legally or illegally. Within that pattern, abortion appears as a last decision in a series of events that may have been avoided if we had had more information about our bodies and exercised more caution in giving control of our bodies and our reproductive ability to partners who may desire some of the results, like children, but not the total context, such as a committed relationship in which to properly care for them.

Deciding How to Deal with Sexual Problems with a Primary Partner

Asked which sexual problems they or their partners *ever* had in their primary relationships, more than one in ten women reported that at one time sex had been painful; more than half claimed that on occasion they did not want to have sex and were not sexually aroused. One in three of the women claimed that their lovers did not have adequate control of ejaculation, and about one in five said that their partners did not want to have sex on at least one occasion. About 15 percent reported that their partners ejaculated prematurely before entering the vagina, could not lose their erection, or could not get an erection at least once. One in ten said their partners had at one time had difficulty becoming aroused.

Clearly, black women are not always ready for sex—nor are their partners. In fact, these are common sexual problems shared by many. Adequate practice of the right techniques minimizes them. Relaxation, good health, and communication with one's partner can make a positive difference. However, we found that instead of seeking help or advice, black women who reported these problems, particularly those whose partners could not control their erection or ejaculation, were most likely to have extramarital affairs.

Nancy's Story

Nancy, a 27-year-old nurse, had been married for almost two years. However, she and her husband were having sexual problems and she was very unhappy. She described her difficulty in becoming sexually aroused and being lubricated before sex, primarily because her husband usually did not want to have sex and had trouble controlling his ejaculation. Sometimes if he was really excited he would ejaculate as he penetrated her vagina, which really frustrated Nancy. Consequently, they were currently not having sex at all. However, Nancy reported having three relationships with men outside of her marriage, and she also masturbated to satisfy her sexual needs.

This is an example of a relationship in crisis—neither partner was enjoying sex with the other. Their problems increased the likelihood that Nancy would continue to seek a sex life outside of her marriage. In spite of his ejaculatory difficulties (which a physical exam and medication or sex therapy would probably remedy) and the need to prove himself as an adequate partner, Nancy's husband could have sought other sexual relationships as well. By not obtaining help for these problems, they gave up on maintaining a monogamous relationship and both were risking their sexual health.

It is possible that some black women, believing the stereotypes about the black stud, are intolerant of their partner's sexual dysfunction. It's also possible that these men are unwilling to seek help, or they find that sex therapy is too expensive. For whatever reason, problems may exist needlessly for long periods, eroding the woman's sexual satisfaction and increasing the number of partners she becomes involved with, sometimes without contraceptives or barrier methods that prevent sexually transmitted diseases. Women who do not masturbate may be left with few options for sexual gratification if they are not satisfied in their primary relationship—they can either have an affair or forgo having sex. The latter option is far safer but is usually not desired.

Sometimes one partner detects symptoms of a disease but fails to notify the other, since disclosure might lead to an admission that he or she has had an affair. For women, nondisclosure can markedly increase the chances of contracting sexual diseases that eventually prevent pregnancy and create other health problems. Unfortunately, the symptoms of many sexually transmitted diseases, including HIV and AIDS, are sometimes undetected or misunderstood until they have severely impaired a woman's reproductive system or resulted in a loss of life.

Coping with a History of Sexual Abuse

In studies of the effects of sexual abuse, we found that women who had a history of abuse in childhood were at risk of being victimized again and again, particularly if, like Heather, no one helped them develop effective coping strategies to deal with a dangerous world.

Heather's Story

Heather, a 27-year-old woman, was told the usual things about sex when she was young but was treated in a manner that was at odds with this information. Her parents were alcoholics, and at age 5, when no one else was at home, her stepfather often masturbated in her presence. He would also drag her into the bedroom, take out his penis, and make her shake it and give him oral sex. Then he would perform oral sex on her. This went on for seven years.

Sometimes when her uncle was over and her stepfather had passed out, the uncle would fondle Heather's breasts and genitals, try to kiss her, take his penis out, and offer her money if she would give him oral sex. Her uncle reasoned with her that he could not get an erection and needed her help. Luckily, someone always came home just when he had decided to try something else. This also occurred for more than seven years—"whenever he could catch me," according to Heather.

When Heather was 9, she and her girlfriend spent the night at a church mother's house. Other kids fondled her body while she slept, and she woke up shocked and frightened, but she never told anyone about this incident. When she was 14, her brother's friends once asked her to play touch football. They tackled her and pretended they were wrestling, but they were actually rubbing their genitals against her in a sexual way.

With each of these incidents, Heather withdrew more and more. She spoke to few people because she was afraid that she would tell all of the things that were happening to her. Her uncle and stepfather warned her that if she told they would hurt her as she'd never been hurt before.

She did make friends with a neighbor, and after school one day she went over to watch TV with his family. When the other members of the family went to bed, her friend shut the doors and threatened to beat her. He would not allow her to leave the house, and he raped her.

Heather began to take drugs and drink to cope with her problems. She trusted no one. She could not watch sex or violence on television and remained so thin that no man would notice her—or so she thought. She figured that all men wanted her body, so she did nothing to make herself look attractive. She had graduated to PCP ("sherm") when her 25-year-old cousin raped her. She began using drugs more and more to relax, to go to sleep, and to get up. After she was hospitalized, her drug habit decreased, but the problems she had in coping with her abuse did not subside.

Finally, at age 25, Heather began to contemplate suicide. She was at home alone and had not eaten for days. She wanted to call a friend for food, but she blacked out because of a cocaine overdose. Heather recalled that if she'd had a gun she would have blown her brains out, but somehow a friend came to her rescue.

Today Heather is a single mother of two. She has no church affiliation and few friends. She counted at least twenty-five sexual partners in her life, ranging from one-night stands to four-year relationships. Currently, she has no partner, is afraid to initiate sex, and is absolutely revolted by oral sex because of what happened to her when she was young. She uses no birth control because she hopes to find the right man one day and believes that sex should be natural. So far she's had four unintended pregnancies and two abortions for which she felt guilty, but she could not afford to care for another child.

Heather is still waiting for someone to care for her.

Heather's story represents the long-term effects of an estranged and dysfunctional family that increased her risks of repeated incidents of sexual abuse and exploitation. The incidents diminished her self-esteem and resulted in drug and alcohol abuse for most of her adulthood. In spite of Heather's past experiences, the decisions she made about protecting her reproductive ability and reducing her chances of becoming infected with HIV or other STDs were poor and unlikely to improve unless she sought professional help.

She needed sexual knowledge, parental guidance regarding sexual responsibility, and protection from abuse. Because she did not have this support, Heather has had difficulty making sound, healthy sexual decisions throughout her life. She remains at risk of compromising both her health and her reproductive ability. This inability to make positive decisions can only increase her vulnerability to sexual and mental-health problems, and undermine her ability to parent her children in a more effective way than she herself was parented.

In my work with UCLA psychologists Michael Newcomb and Monika Riederle, we found that sexual abuse by family members was the strongest predictor of sexual risk taking, including nonuse of contraceptives, unintended and aborted pregnancies, multiple partners, and high-risk patterns of sexual behavior much like Heather's. A team of researchers and I examined whether African-American women in our 1994 study who were sexually abused in either childhood or adulthood were also more likely to engage in high-risk sexual practices and found that indeed they also reported higher numbers of unintended pregnancies than women without any history of abuse.

Coping with a History of Physical Abuse

African-American women who reported that as children their mothers disciplined them by scolding, spanking, beating, or otherwise physically punishing them were also likely to report being in relationships where their partners threw, smashed, hit or kicked things or physically attacked them. Sometimes their partner used a knife or a gun to threaten them with harm. Women with a lifetime history of physical battering were also more likely to have difficulty discussing sex with their partners. They also reported a high number of sexual partners and unintended pregnancies.

It appears that being harshly punished and battered early in life can influence a woman's perception of her ability to be an assertive partner in a relationship later in life. In fact, fear of being harmed diminishes not only a woman's willingness to engage in sexual discussions with her partner about preferred sexual practices but also the likelihood that she will use contraceptives. These are the women who choose to have sex, whether it is risky or not, to please their partners, avoid arguments, or to make up with their partners after a fight.

For example, Angela, a survivor of abuse, once told me

that the best sex she ever had with her husband was after he had beaten her. She never dared to use any birth control or suggest that he use a condom. A pregnancy, however, did not stop him from beating her. In fact, the beatings increased if she couldn't have sex whenever he wanted to. Relationships like these are extremely dangerous for women in many ways and very similar to those that our ancestors experienced hundreds of years ago. In many ways, battered women feel captive in abusive relationships, though most are not.

Deciding to Keep Sexual Harassment in Check

As long as men believe that African-American women are sexually available wherever and whenever, we'll be randomly exposed to their sexual statements or overtures. If we believe the same thing, we'll behave in ways that make us vulnerable. Even if we don't, little changes. At work, where conversations regarding sexual matters or sexual behavior are not expected, we'll still be magnets for sexual comments. And in social settings, where our sexual availability might be expected, we'll still attract comments or actions of a sexual nature that are exaggerated, unwanted, and unwelcome. That's the definition of sexual harassment.

Of the black women we interviewed, about one in three claimed to have been sexually harassed at work. These incidents, reported primarily by single women, usually involved promises of promotions in exchange for sexual favors. Sometimes the remarks were almost casual. For instance, Sally, who works for the California Youth Authority, was harassed by another agent, who suggested that she fly to San Francisco with him.

"Oh, my goodness," she said.

The agent replied, "It is not your goodness that I am after." Sally laughed and tried to play it off.

The most common incidents also involved being touched, rubbed, kissed, and being subjected to the attempt. In a fairly typical scenario, Marva told me that her boss repeatedly tried to kiss her. She warned him that if he didn't stop she would report him. He didn't, so she did. She was later called into the main office and fired. Eventually the man's record of sexual harassment came to light and he too was fired. But for Marva, justice arrived too late.

Given that women clearly find these incidents at work emotionally upsetting, how do most black women respond? More than a third take no action to report it compared to one in four white women. More than one in four are either fired or quit their jobs; about the same number either reprimand or threaten the harasser, or attempt to get him fired. Some manage to ignore the harassment and register no emotional response. Most experience a variety of negative consequences, including becoming depressed. Most rely less on the system and more on themselves by confronting the harasser.

Sexual harassment in social settings is even more prevalent than it is in the workplace. More than half of the African-American women in our study reported at least one incident of sexual harassment in public settings such as bars, gyms, or parties, or on the street. These incidents usually include catcalls, sexual propositions, vulgar comments, or even being grabbed on the street by strangers. Only rarely do such comments come from friends.

The women usually ignore the incidents, largely because there is no one to turn to in a public place. For instance, Esther went to a club one night wearing a dress with an elastic top. A stranger walked over and grabbed the dress, pulling the top down to her waist. He proceeded to comment on what he would love to do to her breasts. She managed to pull herself together and left the club.

One of my most striking findings sheds some light on this pattern. Some researchers have found that black women report more sexual harassment than white women. I haven't.

In a study published with Dr. Monika Riederle, I found

that black women do not report more incidents of harassment at work than their white peers. More than half of white women claimed to have been harassed, versus one in three black women.

How can I explain such a striking contradiction? One possible interpretation is that harassment simply occurs more among whites than among blacks. But I think there's more to it than that. Different perceptions of what constitutes harassment could influence who reports it; or black women could have less information about how harassment is defined.

Another interpretation, however, seems more plausible to me. Black women may be devaluing their own feelings about the effects that harassment has on them. Just as they were less likely to report incidents of sexual abuse to their parents, the police, or other authorities, they may feel that because stereotypes about their sexual availability are so commonplace, there would be little support even if they came forth. The fact that black women tend not to report sexual abuse is just one more indication that they have internalized society's devaluation of them as sexual objects.

Francine reported that because she was single and well endowed, she *expected* men at work to "hit on her." When they did, she simply discounted these overtures. She did not view them as incidents of harassment.

If black women perceive sexual advances simply as an expected nuisance, they may acknowledge only incidents of harassment in which there are tangible outcomes, like losing a job or being physically assaulted. These differences in perception might also account for the difference between the number of black and white women who reported the incidents. Harassment that is simply upsetting emotionally or makes a woman less willing to work in certain settings may seem like "her problem." It may not seem worthy of being mentioned to anyone else.

This may explain why some black women, particularly in the working class, did not support Anita Hill's allegations of sexual harassment against then–Supreme Court nominee Clarence Thomas. They felt that sexual harassment simply comes with having a job. If you're paid well, according to their view, "Just shine somebody like Clarence on, and don't complain."

My concern is that there may be an unhealthy tolerance of harassment in the black community. In the workplace, sexual harassment has always occurred, and in some ways we have come to expect it. Fear of losing a job is as real today as it was hundreds of years ago—especially if you're modestly educated, unskilled, or know what it means to be the last hired and the first fired.

Only certain prior experiences appear to heighten black women's reactions to verbal sexual advances. For example, Dr. Riederle and I found that African-American women with a history of sexual abuse before age 18 were much more likely than women with no history of abuse to describe incidents of sexual harassment in the workplace by their superiors, coworkers, clients, and male employees in positions subordinate to theirs. They felt that they were perceived as fair game by others, regardless of their job status.

In social settings, men continually relate to us in inappropriate ways. For example, black men may be surprised to learn that making open remarks about a woman's physical assets or lack of them while she is being introduced or as she walks by is not an authentic part of our culture. That behavior is both disrespectful and rude. It's reminiscent of the days when African women were examined on the auction block before being sold. It should not be excused as a "black thing" simply because it has gone on for so long.

An African-American woman does not need to be evaluated solely or publicly for her sexual prowess by her own man—or any man, for that matter. This is not the way our ancestors treated one another, and it's not the way we should be treated now. Every black woman in her lifetime will need to make certain decisions about sexual harassment:

- How will she handle these statements and gestures on the spot?
- How will she try to minimize them in the first place?
- Will she choose job security or more harassment?

We need specific preparation to cope with harassment today. But we resist because many of us have witnessed or personally experienced negative consequences of acknowledging and reporting it. We would rather overlook it than take action, fearing that it will eventually backfire. We seem to expect to be punished for speaking out against something that has been tolerated for too long. There is still sufficient reason to dissociate our feelings from the incidents, as our ancestors may have done years ago, in order to maintain social companions or job security.

Yet the truth is, the only way to change being viewed as sexual objects is to report or confront harassment whenever possible.

Coping with Negative Expectations about Our Relationships

I talked with a representative sample of black women in two separate focus groups to find out what personal views affected their choice of sexual partners. Forty-three women who ranged in age from 25 to 58, with a median age of 32 (almost half were single, 25 percent were married, and the remainder were divorced) shared their basic beliefs with me.

We Tend to Assume That White Men Haven't Changed

While several women described close friendships and relationships with white men, they voiced suspicions that white guys still considered black women as sexual objects, much the way they did hundreds of years ago. In fact, the women seemed to be acutely aware of the historic mistreatment of black women by white men. Their responses referred more to past than current incidents or relationships.

"No matter how friendly they are to me, I basically think of white men as trying to get us. They may be chummy, but they are always trying to find a method to do us in," said one woman. Another commented that she feared white men because of what happened to our ancestors during slavery. Another echoed that sentiment. "White men," she said, "have been a source of many of the stereotypes, and because of their economic control of the media, they continue to perpetuate these myths. Our problem," she went on, "is the white men tell us about ourselves and some of us go on and believe it."

Comparing black with white men as lovers, the women concluded that brothers were more sensitive and warm, while white men were cold and less in touch with both their feelings and their sexuality. One woman, however, felt that these comparisons were not meaningful because the socialization experienced by black and white men is so different. The general consensus was that each could offer something unique, and women should not "close any doors" if they want a relationship with a man.

One woman reported that as teenagers neither she nor her brother could date white people. She could not recall anything that their parents, especially their mother, had said about interracial dating, but she and her brother felt guilty, as if something about it wasn't right.

"I just can't get rid of those ghosts," one woman admitted.

"When I see a sister with a white guy, I say 'right on,' but I don't say that when I see a brother with a white girl," said another. The women rationalized that if a sister was with a white guy, it was probably because she had been unsuccessful in her search for a brother and had decided to settle for someone she hoped would love her, regardless of color. If a sister dated *only* white guys, the women surmised that it was due to an identity problem—"self-hatred," as one woman put it.

Some of the women remarked that "dating out" can also be learned if sisters grew up in an all-white setting where they never had a chance to meet or learn to appreciate black men.

"Brothers are in your face with their agenda," one woman said. "White guys are more indirect, but they want the same thing."

We Tend to Believe That Black Men Have Negative Feelings about Us

"I think they have a problem with us. Brothers stereotype us as mean and with an attitude," one woman exclaimed. "They don't really want us for sexual partners."

I immediately had visions of Sapphire, rocking back on her heels with her hands on her hips, giving someone a tongue-lashing.

"Black men see us as hostile and negative because we put down a black man's dreams," one woman said.

"Why?" I asked.

"A lot of painful things have happened between black men and women, beginning with slavery, and sisters are angry," she said. "Both can see each other's pain from trying to adjust to living in a racist world, but neither has enough strength to help the other. We don't know what the other one really needs."

Another woman explained further: "My husband tells me that while I prefer black to white men, I castrate them, and I imagine that I do. My expectations of what I want are very rigid, and there is still that indoctrination that a black man is supposed to be my salvation—that I should stay with him even when he is less than perfect and never have any thought about going somewhere else."

We Feel or Fear Rejection by Black Men

Among the women we interviewed, the effects of being rejected by black men were apparent. This emotion centers on our need to have our beauty and importance validated by black men when the world's standards favor whites. "Who is going to confirm the African-American woman's beauty if the African-American man doesn't appreciate her as she is?" one woman asked. "If her man says that she is not beautiful, who will say that she is?" Her thoughts echoed throughout the conversation.

I got the impression that we were resentful because some black men prefer white women and rationalize their preference as "getting back at white men." This preference, however, was unacceptable and devastating to the sisters in this focus group. Many had attended large universities and described themselves as "nice little black girls, getting all dressed up with nowhere to go" because the black guys were all dating white girls, "saying how they hated white people and sleeping white at the same time."

Someone added, "I wonder what it's going to be like for my daughter?" A momentary but loaded silence was broken by someone else, who described her anger at sitting in a restaurant eating alone when a brother walks in with a white woman.

"Why do they need to do that?" another commented. "We come in all colors and sizes."

"Black men say that they turn to white women because they can't find a black woman they can talk to. My response to that is when they were 16 or 17 they went with every black girl they could. Now that they're ready to settle down, they say there are no black women around. I say they haven't taken time to find out who we are . . . who we grew up to be."

Another woman added, "They want someone who isn't going to challenge them. They want someone who's going to stay home and have babies."

"I would stay home," someone answered. "I'm tired of working. I wish someone would take care of me."

"But if what we want is that warmth and sensitivity," another sister said, "maybe we need to listen more and stop expecting black men to have everything . . . it's really not that important to me. If a person is intelligent, that's enough. If he is warm and sensitive and cares about me, then he's going to see me as his queen and be my king. That's what it's all about. I don't give a damn if he never went to school, you know. I think a lot of people get off into socioeconomic class and education, and I wonder where they are in terms of love and what they really want in a partner."

"Are we looking for an ideal that is not there?" one woman asked.

"At this point, maybe I need to reevaluate my priorities," a single woman added. "But we haven't been socialized to prioritize, and that needs to change. We have been socialized within our culture to be strong, but not to buy into the white middle-class dream. I bought it, though, and was lucky enough to find a man who could afford to buy me things my mother wanted me to have.

"But a lot of sisters aren't that lucky. I'm playing a dream most of the time, and complaining when I should be thanking God that I found someone who is good to me and good to my children. But I think in our culture we have to evaluate relationships in a different way, and when we don't we create distance between men and women.

"We cannot forget that brothers may not have had a lot of opportunities, but I don't buy that women have had it any easier. I don't think we have ever had control of our bodies, and we are the only group that can say that. White women are asking to get off their pedestal . . . we have never been asked to step up to one.

"So we have to tell our daughters, our peers, our teachers, or any black woman that to get closer to black men, you have to appreciate our culture, our experience, and remember our history. You can't forget that he is suffering because he's being denied the middle-class dream—he may not be educated, he may speak dialect, and may not know how to dress. Those are things that others have said are important. But they are not necessarily important for us, in order to keep our culture alive. Everything that the dominant culture says and does is not necessarily good for us. If we think that black men are beautiful, then we have to take them as they are and work with them."

"But they need to return the love and support," another woman added.

"I guess you're saying that if we want to create less distance between black men and women, someone needs to change and perhaps we should begin that process." I said.

"Besides," said a woman who was married to a physician, "I think that you give up something to get something. I am at the mercy of the beeper and squeezed in between practice hours. He'll say, 'Honey, I'm sorry, but I have to take care of this. . . .' So, having an educated man isn't as rosy as it looks."

These women agreed that their relationships with black men were intense because of the warmth, the sharing of feelings and common experiences, and even the pain of racism.

"Nobody else can relate to me in that way," one woman said. A lot of heads nodded in agreement.

Because the pool of educated and employed black men is small, the women talked about the alternatives. Some middle-class sisters who were dating white men urged, "It's okay, why don't you try it?" Other women, however, grew up in homes where their mothers were middle-class and from the South. "Southern middle-class people were not into dating white," one woman explained. "So it isn't okay for me." One remembered her mother telling her, "I wanted something better for you, so we left the South. What we left behind was having to date white." It appeared that her mother was referring not only to black women and white men dating, but to having sexual liaisons.

While some of the women were willing to consider interracial dating and marriage, they were not willing to accept the notion that there are too many black women for too few men. Instead, their solution was to reconsider men who were initially thought to be unacceptable—regardless of ethnicity—and not to feel as if they were failures if they could not find a life partner.

As one women summarized, "These are some of the issues that have rarely been discussed. We need a lot more time to discuss what black women and men are doing to each other and what we can do to get closer. It's difficult, but if we don't do it, it won't get done."

When I asked the women which ethnicity they preferred their partners to be, most African-American women selected African-American men. Five percent didn't care about their partner's ethnicity, and even fewer preferred white men. Despite the problems, this finding is a strong testament to both our resilience and our desire for black men.

The stereotypes that we endorse about each other only get in our way. How we deal with them will either widen the gap or help forge the bond between us.

Deciding to Expand Our Sexual Knowledge

Many of us take responsibility for our own sexuality even if we have little knowledge, because as children our curiosity about sex was adequately monitored and we were protected from sexual exploitation and abuse. But achieving genuine satisfaction in our relationships can easily require more knowledge than we have. Fortunately, as Maya's story proves, that door is open to any woman who is determined to seek it.

Maya's Story

I met Maya in a doctor's waiting room, of all places. We were the last two patients to be seen and spent the time chatting about what it was like to be married for over a quarter of a century. She was the better story-teller, and I was the better listener.

Maya met Jude, a Nigerian national, in college when she was 18 and he was 21. He met the criteria for being "tall, dark, and handsome." He had a regal stride, a deep voice, a gentle nature, and an eye for Maya since the day they met. Schooled by her parents that self-development was more important than finding a husband, Maya found that the busier and more committed she became, the more Jude pursued her. Maya had a passion for her music. Her dream was to play in Carnegie Hall. Jude, on the other hand, was just in the United States to get his education and until he met Maya he had planned to return home.

He was a perfect gentleman on their dates, but his request to have sex with Maya was met with a resounding "no." That was not in her plans, she explained. Nothing to complicate her life right now. She was not interested in casual sex. She had also heard that African guys liked submissive women who would tolerate other women on the side. "I'm an African-American woman, and don't you forget it," she'd exclaim. "I don't believe in sharing." Their relationship deepened, nevertheless.

The more in love they fell, the more determined Jude became to win her over. He entered graduate school and continued to date Maya while she finished college. They finally had sex and Maya found that together they could make music of their own. As she halfheartedly planned to move away to pursue her career, Jude realized that the only way that he could convince her to stay was to propose marriage. He did, and she accepted, but their struggle with sexual responsibility was not over.

Maya caught him having an affair; she was devastated, depressed, and determined to let Jude and the other woman know that she didn't play that game. He apologized, but they never really resolved their differing views about monogamy. The second time she caught him, she packed up the children and left.

She realized that her marriage was over. She had not dated another man for over two decades and had absolutely no interest in starting now. Jude, however, wanted to try again, promising that he would change his ways, but Maya knew better. They needed counseling. Jude ranted and raved, but eventually went. In time, they began to date and to discover each other all over again. She realized that she was as committed to her beliefs as he was to his. Neither love nor having children was enough to *bridge the gap. Somebody was going to have to blink, but it wasn't going to be Jude, or so he said.*

Of all the times for the doctor's receptionist to call Maya, it was now. We said goodbye, exchanging cards and hugs. I wanted to ask, "How did your story end?" but I didn't.

I was leaving the building when someone called me from a parked car. It was Maya. She introduced me to her husband, Jude. "I bet you want to know which one of us blinked," she said in a teasing voice.

"We both did," Jude said. "Maya told me that you two discussed how we almost lost each other. I promised to dedicate myself to Maya alone if she promised to make our marriage exciting, different and new."

"Actually," Maya said, "after counseling, we kept dating. We'd meet for secret lunches, phone each other and leave mysterious messages, and really made our marriage an affair. Jude taught me what he liked about having other women on the side, and I took what I was comfortable with. I became his wife, his lover, his best friend and the mother of his children. With counseling, I regained my focus on my career and have found that my independence excited him, as it had when we first met. Some people just love to pursue what they can never totally possess."

As they drove off, promising to keep in touch, I just stood there, grateful for the lesson that I learned. You can be your own person, but you must continue to grow and change. Being responsible and true to your principles does not mean that you can't be exciting, too. In fact, that's what renews a lasting relationship.

part three

Taking Back
Our Lives

chapter 9

How Are You Doing?

Taking Sexual Responsibility

Now that you've nearly completed *Stolen Women*, I hope that you feel you've gotten a great deal of significant information. For instance, before you started reading it, did you know that:

- African-American parents tend to voice strong opposition to pre marital intercourse?
- African-American women are less likely to be actually taught about sex by their parents than by someone outside of their homes?
- African-American women who do not experience sexual abuse before the age of 18 are less likely to engage in behaviors that heighten their risks for sexually transmitted diseases, including HIV, than those who do?
- African-American teens are more likely to have intercourse for the first time out of curiosity about sex than for passion or love?
- The age of first intercourse for African-American and white women is nearly the same?
- Fewer African-American than white women are likely to report an incident of sexual harassment in the workplace, even though they probably experience it just as often?
- African-American women tend to have fewer sexual partners over their lifespans than white women do?

To put the facts into perspective, along the way, I asked

you to consider dozens of personal questions that involved your past, present, and future behaviors, decisions, and influences. Let's take some time now to put your thoughts together and locate your position on the path to sexual responsibility. Here's a questionnaire to guide you. It's made up of questions I designed especially for readers of *Stolen Women* and should not be confused with the questionnaire that I used to conduct my research. Answer each question as honestly as you can, then total your scores.

Test Your Sexual Responsibility

Sexual Knowledge

1. How much do you know about your body?
   a. I don't need to know   5
   b. I have as much knowledge as I need   3
   c. I know everything about how the female body
       works   0

2. How often do you examine your sexual organs—your vagina, labia, and clitoris—to make sure they are clean and healthy?
   a. Never   5
   b. Sometimes   3
   c. Daily   0

3. Do you know how your genitals look or smell when you have an infection?
   a. I know how they look and smell if infected   0
   b. I know how they look, but not how they smell   1
   c. I know how they smell, but not how they look   2
   d. I don't know how they look or smell   3

4. How often do you touch and examine your breasts?
   a. Never   5
   b. Sometimes   3
   c. Regularly   0

5. Do you know how to touch yourself to feel sexual pleasure?
   a. Yes   0
   b. No   1

6. What do you know about how the male sexual organs (penis and testes) work? Answer the following questions true or false.
   a. If he says he's had a vasectomy, there is no way you can tell from looking at his body.
   True   0
   False   1

   b. Men need to ejaculate on a regular basis in order to avoid pain or discomfort from a buildup of semen, called "blue balls."
   True   1
   False   0

   c. Men need to be on top of you in order to impregnate you.
   True   1
   False   0

   d. You can get a sexually transmitted disease only if a man penetrates you.
   True   0
   False   1

   e. If you are beginning menopause or have not had a menstrual period for a year, you do not need to use a condom to protect yourself against a sexually transmitted disease.
   True   0
   False   1

   f. If a woman says she is a lesbian, the chances are that she does not have a sexually transmitted disease, including HIV.
   True   1
   False   0

g. If you are married, you don't have to worry about becoming infected with a sexually transmitted disease, including HIV/AIDS.

True	1
False	0

7. How much information are you supposed to have about:

a. How to please a woman sexually

1. None	2
2. A little	1
3. Everything	0

b. How to please a man sexually

1. None	2
2. A little	1
3. Everything	0

c. How to have an orgasm

1. None	2
2. A little	1
3. Everything	0

d. How to help a man have an orgasm

1. None	2
2. A little	1
3. Everything	0

e. How to have sex where you put your mouth on a woman's vagina

1. None	2
2. A little	1
3. Everything	0

f. How to have sex where someone puts his or her mouth on your vagina

1. None	2
2. A little	1
3. Everything	0

g. How to have sex where someone puts his penis or an object into your bottom or anus

      1. None   2

      2. A little   1

      3. Everything   0

h. How to avoid becoming pregnant
1. None   2
2. A little   1
3. Everything   0

i. How to avoid becoming infected with a sexually transmitted disease, including HIV/AIDS
1. None   2
2. A little   1
3. Everything   0

8. Have you ever put a condom on a partner?
a. Yes   2
b. No   0

9. Can a woman be a sexpert (an expert on sex) and still be a lady?
a. Yes   0
b. No   1

10. From whom were you told what not to do sexually while growing up? Total all that apply:
a. My parents or parent figure(s)   0
b. My religion   1
c. Friends   2
d. School   3

11. If you are age 35 or older, do you get yearly mammograms?
a. Yes   0
b. No   2

12. How much do you know about the history of your ancestors—how they were stolen and came to America—and what has become of your family?
a. I really don't know anything except that somebody came from Africa   5

| b. I know parts, but not all | 3 |
| c. I know the entire story | 0 |

Total _____

Sexual Experiences

1. How long should you be a virgin? (Circle one)

a. Until you marry	0
b. Until you find someone who turns you on	1
c. Until you find someone to love you	1
d. Until you are ready	1
e. Until you are able to take responsibility for being sexually active	0
f. Until you and your partner take responsibility for being sexually active	0
g. Until you are sure that your partner does not have a sexually transmitted disease	0

2. At what age did you first have intercourse?

a. Never	0
b. Before age 16	5
c. After age 16	0

3. How often do you have intercourse with someone to see what sex would be like with that person?

a. Never	0
b. Sometimes	3
c. All the time	5

4. How often do you have trouble saying no to requests for sex if someone asks you to—especially if that person is attractive and likes you?

a. Never	0
b. Sometimes	3
c. All the time	5

5. How often do you have a sexual relationship with a partner without getting to know him or her?

| a. Never | 0 |

b. Sometimes 3
c. All the time 5

6. How often do you forget or simply fail to use a contraceptive even when you have sex and don't want to become pregnant?
   a. Never 0
   b. Sometimes 3
   c. All the time 5

7. Before you were age 18, how often did you and a family member engage in a sexual act against your will or without full understanding of what you were agreeing to?
   a. Never 0
   b. Sometimes 3
   c. Often 5

8. Before you were age 18, how often did you and a nonfamily member engage in a sexual act against your will or without full understanding of what you were agreeing to?
   a. Never 0
   b. Sometimes 3
   c. Often 5

9. How firmly do you believe that it is your partner's role to decide when and how you will have sex?
   a. Not convinced at all 0
   b. Very firmly convinced 5

10. How often have you faked an orgasm with someone?
    a. Never had one 4
    b. Each time I have sex 5
    c. Sometimes 3
    d. Never 0

11. How often do you have unprotected sex for money?
    a. Never 0
    b. Sometimes 3
    c. Each time I have sex 5

12. How do you express your sexual needs? (Circle one)
    a. I wait for my partner to ask me   1
    b. I don't express my sexual needs   1
    c. I say something sexy   0
    d. I do something sexy   0
    e. I just come out and say I want sex   0

13. How often do you use a contraceptive that prevents both pregnancy and a sexually transmitted disease when you're with a partner you don't know well?
    a. All the time   0
    b. A lot   2
    c. Sometimes   4
    d. Never   5

14. Whether you're married or not, how often do you and your partner honestly and openly discuss any potential sexual or drug-related experiences or relationships that either of you had before you got together or since?
    a. Never, are you kidding?   5
    b. Never, I would be hurt (beaten or harmed) if I did   5
    c. I don't want to know—we have a don't ask, don't tell policy   5
    d. I can trust my partner, I don't need to know   5
    e. We did once   4
    f. Only when I'm suspicious of his/her behavior   5
    g. Regularly, every six months or so   0

                                        Total _____

Sexual Risk Taking

1. How often do you have sex in the dark with someone you don't know?
    a. Never   0
    b. Sometimes   3
    c. All the time   5

2. Has anyone ever forced or threatened you with force or a weapon to have sex against your will since age 18? (Circle one)
   a. Yes   5
   b. No   0

3. Have you ever had sex with a group of people who engage in unprotected sexual contact?
   a. Yes   5
   b. No   0

4. Have you ever had sex while being tied up, strangled, or smothered?
   a. Yes   5
   b. No   0

5. How often do you have sex when you think you can't get pregnant?
   a. Never   0
   b. Sometimes   3
   c. All the time   5

6. Have you ever had sex while riding in a car, elevator, plane, or any other place where you could be easily discovered?
   a. Never   0
   b. Sometimes   3
   c. All the time   5

7. How often are you hit, kicked, slapped, punched, or thrown around so that bruises appear on your body or limbs are broken?
   a. Very often   5
   b. Sometimes   3
   c. Never   0

8. How often do you get high on drugs and have sex?
   a. Never   0
   b. Sometimes   3
   c. Very often   5

9. How often do you drink alcohol and have sex?
   a. Never   0
   b. Sometimes   3
   c. Very often   5

10. Does it matter whether you have (answer all of these)
   a. Unprotected sex with men?
      1. Yes   0
      2. No   1

   b. Unprotected sex with women?
      1. Yes   0
      2. No   1

   c. Unprotected sex with both men and women?
      1. Yes   0
      2. No   1

11. How often have you engaged in sex but couldn't remember with whom or what you did sexually?
   a. All the time   5
   b. Once   3
   c. Never   0

12. How often do you have unprotected anal sex?
   a. Never   0
   b. Once   1
   c. Sometimes   3
   d. Whenever I can   5

                                          Total _____

Attitudes about Sex, Children, and Love

1. How important is it for you to have a love interest in your life all the time?
   a. Very important   5
   b. Somewhat important   3
   c. Not important at all   0

2. Are you a real woman if you don't have a baby?
   a. Yes   0
   b. No   1

3. How important is it to have a baby to love you and fill your life?
   a. Very important   5
   b. Somewhat important   3
   c. Not important at all   0

4. Is having a sexual relationship more important than
   a. Your health?
      1. Yes   1
      2. No   0

   b. Getting your hair done?
      1. Yes   1
      2. No   0

   c. Getting an education?
      1. Yes   1
      2. No   0

   d. Getting and keeping a job?
      1. Yes   1
      2. No   0

   e. Having money?
      1. Yes   1
      2. No   0

   f. Having children?
      1. Yes   1
      2. No   0

   g. Being happy with yourself?
      1. Yes   1
      2. No   0

5. Would you have sex with your boss in order to get a promotion or raise?

a. No   0

b. Yes, in a heartbeat   1

6. Is it acceptable to plan ahead to have sex?
    a. Yes   1
    b. No   0

7. How well do you express what you want in a sexual relationship with a partner you care about?
    a. I express myself well   0
    b. I'm okay at it, but I could do better   3
    c. Not well at all   5

Total _____

Doing the Right Thing

1. How often do you do what you're told even when it's not what you want to do?
    a. Never   0
    b. Sometimes   3
    c. Always   5

2. How often do you quote religious passages about not engaging in sexual practices that are not approved of by your religion and yet engage in them anyway (especially if your partner is fine)?
    a. None of the time   0
    b. Never, but I've been tempted   1
    c. Some of the time   3
    d. Each time I have sex   5

3. How important is it for you to be liked and accepted?
    a. Not that important   0
    b. Somewhat important   3
    c. Very important   5

Total _____

Relationships

1. Which one sounds most appealing to you:
   a. To be interdependent   0
      Independent but still dependent in some ways
      with some people who are dependent on you.
   b. To be independent   1
      Able to care for yourself whether you're in a
      relationship or not
   c. To be totally dependent on someone to take care
      of you   2

2. How often do you find yourself in relationships where
   you feel that your partner makes all the decisions, tries
   to control you, and is possessive of how you spend your
   time?
   a. All of my relationships   5
   b. Some of my relationships   3
   c. None of my relationships   0

                                            Total _____

Sexual Attractiveness

1. Circle all the things you need to do to feel like a woman:
   a. Wear tight clothes   3
   b. Show your cleavage or push up your breasts to
      show as much as possible   3
   c. Sit in sexy positions that suggest that you might
      be a good sexual partner   3
   d. Say sexy or suggestive things   3
   e. Get very close to your partner's face while you're
      talking   2
   f. Be complimented on your beauty   1
   g. Pierce your tongue, nipples, or genitalia and wear
      a ring on these parts of your body   3

    h. Press your body against someone when you are greeting him or her with a hug   3

2. Have you ever had unprotected sex with someone who you know has an STD, including HIV/AIDS?
    a. Yes   5
    b. No   0

3. Have you ever injected nonprescription drugs with a needle?
    a. Yes   5
    b. No   0

4. Have you ever had unprotected vaginal, oral, or anal intercourse with someone who injects nonprescription drugs with a needle?
    a. Yes   5
    b. No   0
    c. Who knows?   5

5. Have you ever had unprotected vaginal, oral, or anal intercourse with someone who has unprotected sex with a man or men?
    a. Yes   5
    b. No   0
    c. Who knows?   5

6. Do you have an STD (including HIV/AIDS) and have sex without your partner's using a condom?
    a. Yes   5
    b. No   0

7. How sexy might someone find you if you have had a mastectomy (removal of one or both breasts)?
    a. Very sexy   5
    b. Somewhat sexy   3
    c. Not sexy at all   0

8. How sexy might someone find you if you have had cosmetic surgery to enhance your body?

a. Not any sexier than if I didn't have surgery   0
b. Not sexy at all   0
c. Somewhat sexy   3
d. Very sexy   5

Total _____

You and Your Appearance

1. How important is it for you to get your hair washed so that it is clean?
   a. It's not important   5
   b. It's somewhat important   3
   c. It's very important   0

2. How often do you wear whatever you can find or whatever is handy when you go out?
   a. All the time   5
   b. Some of the time   3
   c. Never   0

3. Is it acceptable to smoke, even though the tobacco industry was built on slave labor?
   a. It's acceptable; give me a break   5
   b. It's somewhat acceptable   3
   c. It's not acceptable   0

4. Is it acceptable to drink even though the liquor industry was built on slave labor?
   a. It's acceptable; give me a break   5
   b. It's somewhat acceptable   3
   c. It's not acceptable   0

5. How often are you drunk to the point of slurring your words, stumbling a bit, and talking a little too loudly?
   a. All the time   5
   b. Sometimes, on occasion   3
   c. Never   0

6. How often do you wear clothes that show the curves of
   your behind, the nipples of your breasts, or the area
   between your legs?
   a. Anytime I can   5
   b. Sometimes   3
   c. Never   0
   d. Only if I'm trying to attract someone   5

7. How important is it for you to have clean clothes, especially items that don't have rings around the collars and
   sleeves?
   a. Very important   5
   b. Somewhat important   3
   c. Not important   0

8. How overweight are you?
   a. I'm not overweight   0
   b. I'm a bit overweight, but it's okay   1
   c. I'm overweight and working on it   2
   d. I'm overweight and I don't care   3
   e. My weight is totally out of control   4

9. How often do you exercise to the point of sweating?
   a. Never   5
   b. At least once a week   3
   c. At least three times a week for twenty minutes   0

10. How often do you wear rollers, head rags, or a plastic
    bag on your head, a baseball cap when your hair needs
    to be done, or house shoes when you leave the house?
    a. Never   0
    b. Sometimes   3
    c. Whenever I need to   5

                                          Total _____

Understanding Your Score

What might each score mean?

• *Sexual Knowledge.* The total score is 58 points. If your score is between 38 and 58, you are at great risk both of not knowing and not thinking that you need to know enough about sex and your family history to survive. You need to study or discuss with your doctor how the human body functions, how pregnancy occurs, and how men and women derive sexual pleasure. Regardless of whether you are in a relationship, you can't know too much about sex. You also need to know where your ancestors came from and their health histories, as well as how they've survived. It will give you a perspective on your purpose in life. Make it a priority.

If your score is less than 38 you probably have enough sexual knowledge to get by. But concentrate on the specific items that you scored higher on and get the information you need to improve your knowledge. Also, remember that we are constantly learning about sexual health and just because you scored well does not mean you don't need to continue to read accurate articles and books on the subject.

If you are in a committed relationship, there may be sexual strategies that you think your partner does not expect from you or that you are uncomfortable practicing. Ongoing conversations about what each partner wants and needs should take place. Sometimes no communication results in miscommunication.

If you are not in a relationship or are dating casually, you can practice having conversations with friends to hear yourself ask frank questions about sex. These are skills that women often have to learn. Sometimes *how* a question is asked or how a statement is made is just as important as *what* is asked. Try to develop a style that suits you and is both honest and sincere.

Remember that much of what you might have been told about sex by people who are important to you may contradict what you need to know in order to survive. You have to give yourself permission to learn about sex and develop relationships with people who are as concerned about staying as healthy as you are. People who are ashamed of their sexual behavior are more likely to hide the truth from others and themselves. Keep taking this part of the test until you get every answer correct.

• *Sexual Experience.*   The total number of points is 57. If your score is between 38 and 57, you are engaging in risky sexual practices that might increase the chances of an unwanted outcome like pregnancy or a sexually transmitted disease. Regardless of whether you are in a long-term, committed relationship where both you and your partner are monogamous (and you *know* this), you need to spend time making sure that your decisions about sex are not pressured. Take time to evaluate your sexual wants and to determine whether you are ready for an unintended pregnancy. If you responded "sometimes" to items about sexual abuse and have not had any therapy to help you to deal with a history of sexual trauma, you may be particularly at risk for being in relationships where your partner may assume control over your sexual decision making. It's important that you gain experience in identifying your own sexual needs and how to communicate them.

If your score is less than 38 you may be taking risks, but not as many as women who have higher scores. The margin for risk taking has to diminish in a world with sexual diseases that can kill or seriously complicate your chances of having your own children when you're ready to take this step. Look at the items to which you answered "sometimes." Think about the circumstances under which you participate in these activities. You may still need help in reducing these behaviors.

• *Sexual Risk Taking.*   The total number of points for these very risky practices is 58, and if your score is between 37 and 58 you are engaging in very risky sexual behaviors that might increase your chances of being raped or battered physically. You might not be alert enough to determine whether you are at risk, especially with a partner whom you may not know very well and whose judgment might be influenced by drugs or alcohol.

You may also have had some sexual experiences that you were forced to engage in or didn't understand fully at the time. These experiences can reinforce the notion that you cannot or should not be in control of your body.

Most likely, you are not making decisions in your best interest because you may be at risk of becoming infected with a sexually transmitted disease or becoming pregnant. These sexual practices depersonalize you and isolate sex as an event that is often void of feelings, intimacy, and commitment. These experiences increase the risks to your sexual health. Most risky of all is that you may not be truthful with yourself. Considering how you are risking your sexual health, try to avoid letting other people control you. Keep taking this part of the test to see whether you are changing your behavior and becoming more responsible for yourself.

If your score is less than 37, you still need to look at the items you answered "sometimes." If you like thrills and excitement, try to take up a sport or hobby that satisfies your need for risk taking. Items in this section are really dangerous, even if you are in a committed relationship. Chances are, you aren't experienced in making decisions based on your own well-being. If you can't do this, how can you expect someone else to?

• *Attitudes about Sex, Children, and Love.* Of the 25 possible points, if your score is between 17 and 25, it's possible that sex itself is more important to you than finding out who you are as a total person—that is, apart from a sexual being. Your womanhood and identity may be centered around the ability to produce children and to please others. It might be difficult for you to help your children become sexually responsible unless you spend more time developing yourself and being less dependent on others for acceptance.

Women with scores of less than 17 may not place sex above all else in their lives, and that's good. Look at the items on which you had higher scores and ask yourself how important it is for you to be in control of your life. If it's important, sex is worth planning ahead for.

• *Doing the Right Thing and Relationships.* These two sections total 22 points, and if your score is between 11 and 22, you may need to assess how comfortable you are about depending only on yourself and making your own decisions. You should be very comfortable. It's also important to accept that we are sexual from birth and that our sexual beliefs and practices are influenced by socializing forces, particularly by those who are close to us. It's equally important to know your values and stick by them. If your score is less than 11, you are more likely to consider yourself in your decisions. Before you say yes to someone, make sure that you fully understand the consequences.

• *Sexual Attractiveness.* If your score is between 15 and 56, you may be using your body to feel more attractive and buying into the notion that you should be barely clothed or look a certain way in order to be acceptable to others. You may wear "auction-block attire"—skimpy outfits that allow others to gawk at your body. Our ancestors were forced to reveal their bodies against their will. Why are you revealing yours? Look in the mirror before leaving the house and ask yourself how much of you people need to see before they can accept and like you. If you answer "all of me," you're not surviving sexual slavery.

Women with scores of less than 15 are most likely to use their bodies less to make a statement about themselves. Check the items on which you scored highest to make sure that your appearance makes the statement that you want to make about yourself.

• *You and Your Appearance.*   If your score is between 39 and 49, your body image may be out of your control and your appearance and behavior may not be important enough for you to adopt a personal style that becomes you and makes you feel good about yourself. You don't have to wear designer clothes to be clean and neat. Self-respect comes with caring for yourself and your health on a daily basis. Pamper yourself and take more time to groom your ancestral hair, discover and maintain your body's natural weight, and look your best each day. Regardless of your score, with age, stress, poor nutritional habits, and an inadequate exercise regimen, anyone can lose control of her body image and face major health problems. Surround yourself with friends and family members who want to break the legacy of weight and health problems that we have had since we came to these shores. We need to take responsibility for our sexuality, and that includes our bodies and the image they create.

If you want to demonstrate daily that you remember and will no longer tolerate the pain, suffering, and oppression of our ancestors, avoid purchasing and using cigarettes and liquor—products from two industries that have profited from our slavery and poverty. Their use, along with the misuse of legal and illegal drugs, has contributed to the health problems, spread of diseases, destruction of families, unemployment, and level of violence in our communities that equals or surpasses what our ancestors experienced during slavery. In many ways, these substances are themselves instruments of oppression and a reminder that we can renew our captivity by engaging in behaviors that addict us. An addiction is another form of slavery.

If your score is less than 39, go back and review those questions to which you responded "somewhat important," "some of the time," "on occasion," "somewhat acceptable," or "sometimes." Think about the occasions when you have engaged in these behaviors and ask yourself if you can afford to be somewhat inconsistent about these practices. If not, try to be more consistent in your behaviors by remembering each time to engage in behaviors that honor one of your ancestors.

- *Overall you should strive for these answers:*

  Sexual Knowledge—1=c; 2=c; 3=a; 4=c; 5=a; 6a=t; 6b=f; 6c=f; 6d=f; 6e=f; 6f=f; 6g=f; 7a=c; 7b=c; 7c=c; 7d=c; 7e=c; 7f=c; 7g=c; 7h=c; 7i=c; 8=a; 9=a; 10=a, a,b, or a,b,d; 11=a; 12=c

  Sexual Experiences—1=a, e, f, or g; 2=a or c; 3=a; 4=a; 5=a; 6=a; 7=a; 8=a; 9=a; 10=d; 11=a; 12=c,d,e; 13=a; 14=g

  Sexual Risk Taking—1=a; 2=b; 3=b; 4=b; 5=a; 6=a; 7=c; 8=a; 9=a; 10a=a; 10b=a; 10c=a; 11=c; 12=a

  Attitudes about Sex, Children, and Love—1=b or c; 2=a; 3=c; 4a=b; 4b=b; 4c=b; 4d=b; 4e=b; 4f=b; 4g=b; 5=a; 6=a; 7=a

  Doing the Right Thing—1=a; 2=a; 3=a and b

  Relationships—1=a; 2=c

  Sexual Attractiveness—1=f or none; 2=b; 3=b; 4=b; 5=b; 6=b; 7=a; 8=a or b

  You and Your Appearance—1=c; 2=c; 3=c; 4=c; 5=c; 6=c; 7=a; 8=a,c; 9=c; 10=a

Do You Need Help to Change?

If you examine your scores and find that you need extra help to change, there are many resources in your community with information, support, counseling services, and referrals to give you the help that you need. Check your local listings for:

- Planned Parenthood
- Hotlines for child abuse, domestic violence, rape, suicide, depression, sexually transmitted diseases, and HIV
- Churches and missions that offer counseling
- Web sites that offer health information on the internet

Some of the national organizations that may give you local referrals are:

Association of Black Psychologists
P.O. Box 55999
Washington, DC 20040-5999
(202) 722-0808

Black Psychiatrists of America
2730 Adeline Street
Oakland, CA 94607
(415) 465-1800

National Association for the Advancement of Colored People
Director
The Prison Program
4805 Mt. Hope Drive
Baltimore, MD 21215
(410) 358-8900

National Association of Black Social Workers
15231 West McNichols Avenue
Detroit, MI 48235
(313) 836-0210

National Association of Black Women Attorneys, Inc.
3711 Macomb Street, N.W., 2nd fl.
Washington, DC 20016
(202) 966-9691

National Black Women's Health Project
1237 Ralph David Abernathy Boulevard, S.W.
Atlanta, GA 30310
(404) 758-9590

National Council of Negro Women, Inc.
1001 G Street, N.W.
Suite 800
Washington, DC 20036
(202) 628-0015

National Medical Association
1012 10th Street, N.W.
Washington, DC 20001
(202) 347-1895

National Political Congress of Black Women, Inc.
600 New Hampshire Avenue
Suite 1125
Washington, DC 20037
(202) 338-0800

National Urban League, Inc.
500 East 62nd Street
New York, NY 10021
(212) 310-9000

Schomburg Center for Research in Black Culture
515 Malcolm X Boulevard
New York, NY 10037-1801
(212) 491-2200

chapter 10

Putting It All Together
Affirming Our Sexuality

"I like our style. I like the black woman's strut. I like the fact that nothing gets us down for very long. I like the way we look; the way we talk; our ambition and our dreams. The young women today are using the best of the rest of us to wrestle through with their identities and responsibilities. . . . I like the way we aren't afraid to seek answers. And aren't afraid of the answers we find. I like our courage. In a world that continually assaults all that we are and that we stand for, I like the fact that we have stood and we are standing for ourselves."

—*Nikki Giovanni*

Society refuses to acknowledge that time alone does not heal the effects of being stolen women. So we must. It's the first step in regaining control of our bodies and our lives. It may not be easy, but as the poet Nikki Giovanni observed, we have a long tradition of standing for ourselves.

Sexual marketing, sexual exploitation, and abuse continue to be a national pastime. Some people are still unconvinced that society—including her own family and intimate partners—can sometimes undermine a woman's confidence in her ability to control her sexuality. They don't see that sexual experiences at an inappropriate age can contribute to poor timing of sexual events later in life. But we must.

This book has identified numerous sexual patterns and

stereotypes that are falsely associated with African-American culture. According to my findings, and contrary to many people's perceptions, the following practices are *not* encouraged or condoned by our culture:

- Having sexual knowledge at a young age
- Having an unusual interest in sex
- Having first intercourse outside of marriage
- Having a high number of sexual partners
- Engaging frequently in oral and anal sex or other unconventional sexual practices

Contrary to the portrait of our womanhood that is reflected in negative stereotypes, we want to be sexually responsible and see role models of women who are sexually healthy.

The Five Principles of Sexual Responsibility

What determines whether we survive sexual slavery? What will help us heal ourselves and be the role models the next generation needs?

1. Having the Courage to Get Adequate Sexual Knowledge

In the past, according to our culture, having little or no sexual knowledge indicated that women were sexually inexperienced. Today inadequate sexual knowledge is one of the major reasons our children, adolescents, and adults engage in sexual practices without fully understanding the consequences of their behavior and the impact of poor decision making where sexual matters are concerned. Knowledge alone does not necessarily change risky behaviors, but it can provide the basis for decisions that promote sexual health.

Most African-American women and children do not have enough sexual knowledge to break the cycle of unintended pregnancies and sexual diseases, some of which can kill them; nor do they understand how sexual stereotypes promote and encourage irresponsible sexual practices.

2. Connecting Our Family Values to Sexual Socialization and Sexual Behavior

Parents who assume that teaching their daughters when and how to behave sexually can be reduced to admonitions not to have children before marriage are missing the point of our history and the reality of our times. Marriage has not been—nor is it likely to be—a realistic gauge of when girls will need sexual knowledge, when they will be sexually active, or when all of our problems will be solved.

Parents need to take a much more active role not only in offering guidance to their children on a continuous basis but in discussing any and all sexual topics that arise. If they do not, they may miss opportunities to reeducate their children and protect them from exploitation or abuse.

This, of course, assumes that the parents themselves are reliable models of sexual responsibility. Most important, parents need to be involved in all aspects of their children's lives, gradually allowing the children to be responsible for themselves. We cannot depend solely on schools and churches to educate our children about human sexuality—what they learn may not sustain them. We need to encourage and develop human-sexuality courses that address our history and what is needed to protect and control our sexuality. We also need to be a part of the educational process so that we can learn about sex and ensure that what our children learn while they're away from home is also discussed at home. From these efforts, a new generation of knowledgeable and responsible youths can emerge.

3. Protecting One Another from Abuse or Exploitation

One in three of us are likely to be sexually abused at some point in our lives. In fact, black women are more likely to be sexually abused than they are to get married or go to college.

In the face of statistics like these, we need a completely different kind of education to prepare us for living in America. While parents, especially mothers, may remember what happened to us in the past, all youngsters are not receiving the specific information they need to understand who and what they must avoid in our communities and homes. They need to learn that there are appropriate ways for other children and adults to express their love or affection. Regardless of whether the perpetrator of abuse is related, children should have a very specific idea of inappropriate ways of expressing affection. We also have to stress the importance of disclosing negative incidents to a responsible person, and teach our children to do so. In that way, their chances of becoming victims again can be lessened.

We can no longer tolerate sexually suggestive media—television, music, videos, movies, books, magazines, or the Internet—that overexpose us and our children to inaccurate, negative images and stereotypes. Unfortunately, these are only misinterpreted or used as an excuse for misguided behavior. We have to aggressively control our children's exposure to any messages that would have them believe that they cannot be sexually responsible individuals. Sexual irresponsibility is not a part of our culture.

4. Valuing Our Ability to Control Our Own Sexual Decision Making

Sexual decision making is a skill that is developed slowly throughout childhood, adolescence, and adulthood. It helps us control our sexuality. It gives us the ability to select a partner who will also respect us and help us avoid unwanted sexual outcomes.

Adolescents are too often motivated by curiosity and the pressure to perform sexually, as expressed by friends, love interests, and the media. They think they are ready for sex because someone else tells them they are ready. They are not learning to control their sexuality and protect their reproductive systems in a responsible way; nor are they reinforced by our society when they do. Rarely do adolescents who defer early sexual activity and avoid early pregnancies receive attention from the media and their communities for setting a good example for others by their sexual responsibility and efforts to develop themselves as future leaders. As adults, adolescents who do not control their sexuality often continue these patterns and abuse their sexuality or allow it to be used by others, and thus fail to exercise decision-making skills that benefit themselves rather than others.

Learning to control your sexuality may sound restrictive and rigid, but any powerful source becomes more powerful when it's channeled in the right direction. Sex is no exception.

5. Creating Respectful and Mutually Satisfying Relationships That Also Include Sex

Only when we respect ourselves can we have healthy relationships. Do you recognize your needs and not just your wants? Do you believe in your skills and your worth as an individual? Learn to say yes to these questions.

Healthy relationships also involve learning how to compromise with partners while not ceding all our control to them. Our cultural and religious values emphasize relationships in our lives, which suggests that our self-esteem and self-worth hinge on these contacts. But while these relationships are crucial to the survival of the African-American family, *our* survival as women is contingent upon something else—self-protection and decision making in our best interest. Give yourself permission to form the kind of relationships that you need, whether you find a life partner whom you want or not.

The Power of Healing

We've come a long way since we arrived on these shores. Like the women in my research, some of us are coping, and some of us aren't. We have a long way to go before the wounds that were inflicted on us during the passage away from our culture can fully heal. But we are free.

In many ways, we have very traditional views of the importance of relationships and families. In adapting to the twenty-first century, we need to be prepared to reassess our traditional expectations. We can make whatever changes are necessary, and we can help others who need encouragement.

Each time I doubt that I can overcome my own negative experiences with the way others perceive me as a sexual being, I try to remember my ancestors. I visualize them watching and showing me how to be free, to celebrate my womanhood, and to reach out to others. Most important, I bow my head only to God, find peace within myself each day, and count my blessings.

God didn't bring us across the oceans that divide Africa and America to leave us alone. We embody a spirit, a strength, and a resilience that have allowed us not only to survive but to move forward. If you think we've got a long way to go, look how far we've come. As an African-American woman, I experience a sense of healing and renewal each day, as I recite this creed:

> I believe that
> What I think and feel about myself
> And how I care for and protect my body

Frees me to love myself as God loves me,
To gain the respect that I deserve,
And to help others do the same.

It may be as valuable for you as it has been for me. Now, I wonder what I did with that emerald-green dress and those matching green shoes . . .

About the Studies

The first study. In 1980, the National Institute of Mental Health approved my first federally funded project on women's sexuality, and I've been continuously funded through three presidencies. This is significant, because apart from the projects that are related to pregnancy, sexually transmitted diseases, or AIDS, very little research on sexuality has been funded by the government. Most of the large studies, such as the one that Kinsey and his colleagues conducted, as well as the 1995 national survey spearheaded by Robert Michael, John Gagnon, and Ed Laumann, were funded by private foundations. They were not held to the same scrutiny as projects funded by the U.S. government. I was prepared for this. I knew that to be a credible expert I would need to be trained specifically to do this type of research. I was selected for the research-scientist program, also funded by the National Institute of Mental Health, to learn how to survey large populations, develop interviews, train interviewers, collect data, use sophisticated statistical procedures, and interpret the findings within the context of the population that I had studied. I met with some of the world's most respected researchers in sexuality, and I took additional courses beyond my doctorate at U.C.L.A.

When I began my research I wanted to do something that few had done before me: conduct studies of black women using a face-to-face interview designed to highlight their personal experiences. I therefore ran several focus groups, talking to women of different ages and walks of life about their sexual experiences during childhood, adolescence, and adulthood to get a sense of how the black experience could be incorporated into research on sexuality.

In addition, I wanted to use a research format that approximated everyday conversation as closely as possible. As an African-American myself, I knew that few African-Americans are accustomed to discussing their sex lives at all, especially with strangers. I wanted the women my colleagues and I talked with to be as comfortable as possible without blurring the lines of communication. I also wanted the data-collection phase of my study to allow for clarification of sexual terms and other information.

This is more than an ethnic issue. You see, America is still in a quandary about how sex should be discussed in our society. Because there is no expected level of sexual knowledge in this country, everyone develops his or her own language of sexual practices and patterns of behavior. My research team and I therefore had to develop definitions of sexual terms that most women would understand so that we would be speaking the same language.

Face-to-face interviews were the most natural way to have an ongoing conversation about sex. The interviews were tape-recorded so that we could use a woman's own words in describing her experiences. I ensured consistency of responses by asking the same questions in different ways. In other words, if I asked a woman how many pregnancies she'd had, then asked how many of them were intended and how many were unintended, the figure she gave had to match the total number of pregnancies or the interviewer had to clarify the discrepancy. In general, I found, people do not willfully give inaccurate answers; they may just need to review what they have said and have the discrepancy pointed out to them.

In the past, researchers assumed that most women would feel comfortable with a middle-aged white male asking them about their sexual experiences. I felt, however, that a woman would be more likely to discuss certain topics and give more accurate answers if the interviewer were someone like herself. I decided that my interviews would be conducted by women.

In my first study, I chose four women, each of whom had a master's or doctoral degree in psychology as well as training in human sexuality. Then, over a three-month period, I personally trained them to conduct the interviews. Two of the interviewers were black and two were white. I had been troubled by studies that lump all black women in one category and claim that they are studying African-Americans, as if there were no cultural differences between women who were born in Haiti and those who were born in Texas. Slavery existed all over the world, but I wanted to obtain a sample of African-American women who grew up in the United States. The women in our study were either born in the United States or spent at least six of their first twelve years of life here. Women who spent their childhood in the West Indies, South America, or Africa, for example, were not included.

While I had been extremely critical of the numerous studies that simply compare white and black women, I realized that I needed to return to some of these comparisons for clarification, so I included white women to show where differences due to ethnicity or culture might possibly contribute to women's sexual patterns.

Both groups also had diverse backgrounds, which allowed us to study a range of experiences. The women were matched for age, educational level, marital status, and whether they had children. We attempted to match income levels as well, but there is at least a $10,000 difference in the income of the average white and black family of four, so we matched incomes as best we could, ranging from under $10,000 to above $50,000 per year. Educational level ranged from women who had less than a tenth-grade education to those who had graduate and professional degrees. At last, middle-class and affluent women could be included in a study with poor women without merely being compared with them. Some were married and some were not remotely interested in marriage. Some had sex with other women and some did not. I did not want to overlook anyone.

In the first study we included two generations. The women ranged in age from 18 (when they could legally consent to participate in a study without their parents' knowledge) to 36. We wanted to examine sexual differences between women born after World War II and women born after the 1960s, who had time to become sexually active if they chose, to be independent enough to make their own decisions about their sex lives, and to develop long-term, committed relationships if they were not married.

I also thought that it was important to obtain a sample of women who, given their demographics, could be taken as representative of an even larger number of women. The 248 women in this study were compared with women who lived in Los Angeles County and were found to represent the demographic characteristics. This allowed us to generalize some of the patterns we found to larger groups of African-American women in the same age bracket.

Ethnic matching of the interviewer and the interviewee became especially important when we asked about the stereotypes that women had heard, and about incidents of sexual harassment or abuse. There was one basic reason for this approach. Sometimes women are reluctant to discuss how they feel about another ethnic group or to use terminology that they feel is known only to their own ethnic group, especially when the topic is sex, because their answers might sound racist or, at the very least, strange to an outsider. My research team and I wanted to minimize the chances that the women we talked to would be reticent about expressing their true attitudes.

Finally, with ethnic matching I hoped to show the women being interviewed that black women can discuss sexuality in an open and professional way. Sex is a topic like any other, and we should discuss it without fear that we will be considered loose if we do. It's a healthy conversation to have with the right person.

The women who lived all over Los Angeles County were recruited using U.S. Census information about the county, which indicates areas where ethnic minorities and nonethnic minorities reside. The Institute of Social Science Research (ISSR) at U.C.L.A. was contracted to call telephone numbers with L.A. County prefixes and five random numbers to locate African-American and white women who were matched for age, education, marital status and, as closely as possible, income. The ISSR called 11,834 phone numbers to find women with these characteristics who would agree to participate in a study about women's sexuality. Not everyone was game—27 percent of the women who were eligible declined the interview. This, however, is a modest refusal rate, considering the process. Once the women were recruited over the phone, an interviewer met them at their homes, at an agreed-upon location, or at U.C.L.A. for the interview. The study does not include women who identified themselves as being a member of any ethnic group other than African-American or white. The women interviewed were also ineligible if they were moving out of Los Angeles when contacted, if their husband or partner would not allow them to speak on the telephone to learn about the study and decide whether they wished to participate, and if they repeatedly asked us to call back (more than nine times).

This is one of the few studies to focus on the sexual practices that women willingly engage in along with those they were forced to engage in. We also asked about specific incidents so that we could describe and define sexual behaviors. We did not ask a single question like "Have you ever been abused?" Studies that used very broad and vague questions about abuse tended to get few women to answer affirmatively because there are varying definitions of abuse. We also asked the women to recall each and every incident of sexual abuse, whether it took place during childhood, adolescence, or adulthood.

While I acknowledge that some women had difficulty in recalling all the information needed, many more called back to offer additional details after the interview was over. By discussing the incidents openly in a nonjudgmental environment, they were able to remember more specifics. During the interview, we used techniques to stimulate their memory of past events. For example, we asked all our questions about childhood at one time so that the women could focus on events that occurred before age 13. We also used significant events in their lives, such as the birth or death of a family member, to help them recall their sexual experiences during that period. Each question was read to the women so that those who had trouble reading or could not read at all would not feel embarrassed.

All were given cards with responses, so that if their answer to a question was something they were not proud of, they could give the number of a response from the card without having to repeat their answer aloud. The interviews lasted between three and eight hours, during which time the women and the interviewers got to know one another and feel comfortable discussing personal topics. The women were paid $20.00 in cash, reimbursed for baby-sitting and transportation, and given referrals for counseling if they expressed an interest in talking more about their experiences (fewer than 5 percent asked for referrals). Some of the women had never discussed sex with anyone, and many had never disclosed their experience of sexual abuse. Few had received counseling or therapy before.

The second study. For the second study, conducted in 1994, Drs. M. Belinda Tucker, Gloria Romero, Claudia Mitchell-Kernan, and I received funding by NIMH to study patterns of women's sexual decision making that would increase their chances of having an unintended pregnancy or contracting a sexually transmitted disease, including HIV. We used stratified probability sampling to recruit comparable samples of African-American, Latina, and white American women 18 to 50 years of age who lived in Los Angeles County. The sample was obtained through random telephone-dialing procedures conducted by the Institute of Social Research at the University of California, Los Angeles. Stratification of the sample was initially based on the proportion of households in the tract that were either African-American or Latino, with either tract subsequently used for the county. More than 10,000 telephone calls were made to locate the desired sample. Of those, 3,334 were households in which a woman resided. Women were screened over the telephone for their eligibility, and 1,172 who matched the target age range were recruited for the interview. A total of 905 were actually interviewed; there were 305 African-American, 300 Latina, and 300 white American women. The refusal rate was 29 percent. To be considered eligible to participate in the face-to-face interview, respondents had to be female between the ages of 18 to 50 years, and identify themselves ethnically as either non-Latina white American, African-American/black, or of Mexican origin. The sample was compared with U.S. Census data for L.A. County women who matched these characteristics and was found to be comparable.

Each participant was interviewed face-to-face using portions of the Wyatt Sexual History Questionnaire included in the Los Angeles Structured Interview by a trained female interviewer of the same ethnicity; interviews took place at the woman's home, at U.C.L.A., or at another designated location. The interviews ranged from three to eight hours in length and were tape-recorded to ensure the accuracy of the interviewer's transcription of responses during data collection. Respondents were paid $32.00 for their time and given referral information for mental-health services upon request. (Fewer than 5 percent made such a request.)

The third study.   After responding to a mail survey about their sexuality and health, a sample of seventy-one African-American and seventy-six white women who participated in a larger study of breast-cancer survivors who had surgery one to five years ago (conducted by Drs. Patricia Ganz, Julia Rowland, Beth Meyerowitz, and me) were recruited for face-to-face interviews about their sexuality before and after surgery. The women were recruited from offices of private physicians and hospital registries. They were first contacted by telephone and invited to participate in the interview. The details of the study were described during this conversation, with special attention given to confidentiality and the voluntary nature of participation. If a woman expressed a willingness to participate, she was then assigned an interviewer who matched her ethnicity and an interview was scheduled. The interview itself included items about coping with breast cancer and women's sexuality. The sexual history items were adapted for this population from the Wyatt Sexual History Questionnaire.

Background and Statistics

Chapter 3: Doctor–Nurse

Self-Touching and Masturbation

There were women in our study (21 percent) who did not recall touching their own bodies, while 80 percent did recall touching their bodies at some point in childhood. Close to three out of four (73 percent) did not recall masturbating before age 13. Of those who recalled masturbating, about one in five (21 percent) began between the ages of 9 and 12. A few women (3 percent) recall masturbating between the ages 6 and 8. Another 3 percent recalled masturbating at or before age 5.

Of the women who masturbated, the most common method of masturbation was also the most direct—the hand (65 percent). The remainder of the women recalled using other methods, such as inserting their finger or an object into their vagina (9 percent); squeezing their thighs together (6 percent); rubbing against an object like a bed or a toy (2 percent); or manipulating their breast or genital area (9 percent); and 6 percent used a combination of these methods. Three percent used other methods to masturbate. In addition, of those women who masturbated, many did so once a week to once a month (79 percent). Almost half of these women (49 percent) did not recall having an orgasm. Although in about one out of four instances they did reach orgasm (24 percent), others reached orgasm 50 to 75 percent of the time (9 percent), and the remainder reached orgasm each time they masturbated (18 percent).

Sexual Arousal

Almost two out of three women (62 percent) did not recall experiencing any kind of sexual arousal during childhood. Of those who did, almost half (44 percent) were between the ages of 9 and 12 and were with a friend when they had this experience. Some (24 percent) recalled becoming aroused with a family member. The remaining 32 percent experienced arousal through other means, such as watching a movie.

Contrary to stereotypes of sexually active black girls, most of the women we interviewed (75 percent) did not engage in mutually exploratory sexual experiences during childhood, though 25 percent did. Of those who did take part in mutual exploration, the most common age was between 9 and 12 (75 percent); only a few (4 percent) reported mutual exploration between the ages of 3 and 5, and about one in five (21 percent) reported mutual touching between the ages of 6 and 8. Of those who participated in mutual exploration over one-third (37 percent) recalled participating with someone who was of the opposite sex; less than one-third (30 percent) experimented with the same sex; and the remaining third (31 percent) were with a group. Two percent gave other responses.

Coping with Trauma

Although there may be many reasons teenagers do not like their bodies, research on the long-term effects of sexual abuse suggests that sexual trauma can sometimes result in low self-esteem and depression, as well as eating disorders and body-image problems. In our study, women who reported at least one incident of sexual abuse before age 18 were most likely to report that they did not like their bodies as adolescents. This finding certainly suggests that body image may be affected by physical trauma.

Chapter 4: Childhood Messages

Although white women received little information regarding sex during their childhood, the information they did receive was more than likely to come from their parents. Slightly fewer than half of the white women we interviewed (47 percent) did not recall their parents saying anything about premarital intercourse, as compared with 53 percent of the African-American women. Similarly, most white women did not recall anything being said about homosexuality (79 percent), masturbation (89 percent), or nudity (25 percent).

The Power of Five Strong Messages You Might Have Heard about Sex

1. Messages about Nudity

About one out of four African-American women (26 percent) did not recall her parents saying anything about nudity. Over half (59 percent) recalled their parents issuing a warning or saying something negative, such as "It is not right," or that they should put a robe on to cover up their bodies. A very small percentage of women (1 percent) recalled hearing their parents say it was okay to be naked, and 6 percent remembered that their parents said it was okay to be nude sometimes. The remaining 8 percent gave other responses.

2. Messages about Masturbation

A majority of the African-American women (90 percent) did not recall their parents saying anything about masturbation during their childhood. Those who grew up in a home with two parents rather than one were more likely to remember being told not to masturbate. Of those who recalled being told not to masturbate, 8 percent received a negative message, such as "It is a sin" or "This is something that you just don't do." No one recalled their parents saying that masturbation was allowed in their home. The remaining 2 percent were told something other than the above.

3. Messages about Homosexuality

For 71 percent of the women, homosexuality was not an issue that they recalled hearing their parents discuss. About one in five women (21 percent) recalled their parents saying something negative, such as that homosexuals should be "locked up." A small percentage (8 percent) recalled their parents being neutral about the matter.

4. Messages about Premarital Intercourse

Most of the women (88 percent) recalled discovering the real meaning of intercourse after age 9. Of that percentage, almost half (45 percent) learned what the word means after age 13. Some women (32 percent) did not recall their parents saying anything about premarital intercourse during childhood. Other African-American parents or parental figures were more outspoken about their opposition to sex before marriage than they were about other sexual practices. In fact, many African-American women (38 percent) recalled their parents saying something, such as "Don't do it." Others (20 percent) recalled being told to "wait until marriage." The remaining 10 percent recalled their parents giving indirect messages and/or saying that it was okay and up to the individual.

5. Messages about Sexual Abuse

"Don't talk to strangers" and "Don't take candy or money from strangers" were warnings that almost everyone recalled as a child. Almost every respondent in the study (87 percent) heard such proscriptions during their childhood, while only one in ten girls (10 percent) were given specific explanations of what being molested meant. The remaining 3 percent did not recall hearing anything. Although three out of four (76 percent) understood that molestation meant that they could die or be raped or harmed in some way, 24 percent had no idea what this meant.

Did You Experience the Joy of Seeing Affectionate Parents?

Some of the women in the study (37 percent) did not recall seeing their parents behave in a way that suggested that they had a sexual or affectionate relationship. One in five parents (20 percent) gave the impression either that sex was negative or they just lacked affection for each other. Some parents (17 percent) tried to hide their sexual attraction to each other by projecting the message that sex was okay under certain conditions—i.e., there was a time and a place for sex . . . behind closed doors. Over one in five women recalled their parents having a positive relationship (23 percent). Some of the parents discussed sex even though they were not demonstrative. The remaining 3 percent reported something other than the above.

What Did Your Church Say?

Almost half of the women interviewed (44 percent) did not recall anything being said in church about sex when they were children, while 50 percent heard some type of religious social proscription, such as it was a "sacred act, reserved only for marriage." The remaining 6 percent were given factual information or biblical teachings—the story of Adam and Eve, for example.

School—Mostly Dancing Tampons?

Some women (34 percent) did not recall having any sex education in school, although one in five (21 percent) did recall such a class. Some (19 percent) recalled learning about sex from a film, and the remainder (18 percent) remembered some religious social proscription, such as sexual behaviors like masturbation are considered a sin. The remaining women's questions were either referred to their parents or they were told something other than the above (8 percent).

Friends—Peer Pressure and Sexual Hype?

Many of the respondents (40 percent) did not recall their friends discussing sex. Of the 60 percent whose friends did discuss sex, some (25 percent) had conversations that dealt with things they were curious about, while others (26 percent) were given accounts of other people's sexual activities that actually occurred. Six percent were told something negative about sex, such as that it was painful. The remaining 3 percent were told something other than the above.

Many women (40 percent) felt that their friends were in favor of engaging in sexual activities, while some (34 percent) felt that their friends did not express one opinion or another. Twenty-four percent felt that their friends were opposed to engaging in such activities. The remaining 2 percent did not recall exactly how their friends felt. Women who identified parents rather than peers as having the greatest influence on them from childhood until age 18 also tended to delay first intercourse until late adolescence (53 percent).

Chapter 5: Our Adolescent Development

Unfortunately, there have been few studies on the socialization of black adolescents, so we have little with which to compare our findings. However, it is important to examine national studies of adolescent growth and development in order to understand the changes that have taken place in the onset of puberty during the past forty years. In 1973, the National Center for Health Statistics noted only a three-month difference between the average age at which menstruation began for women born between 1893 and

1918, and those born between 1939 and 1955. In my study there is a four-month difference between the average age of menstruation for older women (those born between 1939 and 1955) and my sample (who were born between 1947 and 1965). This difference suggests that the average age of first menstruation may decrease about every twenty years for black women, but the changes are gradual. The declining age of first menstruation may be influenced by the women's diet, height, and weight, but there are secondary implications. Twelve-year-old girls may appear to be more mature than they actually are, and their appearance may motivate others to initiate sexual activities with these preadolescents. Physical appearance can increase the risk of early pregnancy among these girls if others assume that they are sexually precocious and are therefore ready for sex. For this reason, it is important for African-American girls to receive early and ongoing sex education in childhood, so that as they mature sexually they will also be more prepared to resist being influenced by those who wish to rush them into sexual activity.

Coping with Your Biological Development

More than one in five women (22 percent) reported that they first noticed their breasts developing between the ages 7 and 10, and some were 11 years old (25 percent). The majority of women recalled noticing their breast developing between the ages of 12 and 14 (48 percent) and 15 to 20 (5 percent).

Choosing Your Confidants

In this study, more than half of the African-American women (56 percent) discussed the changes in their breasts with either their mother or a mother figure. This finding differed from what the white women in the sample reported. They were twice as likely to discuss breast development with a friend rather than a parent.

The onset of menstruation ranged from ages 9 to 18, with the average age being 12. Six percent began their period between the ages of 9 and 10, 77 percent began between ages 11 and 13, 10 percent at age 14, and the remaining 7 percent began between the ages of 15 and 18. Interestingly, 14 percent of the women who grew up in rural areas versus 5 percent of the urban women began to menstruate between the ages of 15 and 18.

Did You Like Your Body?

Most African-American teens (80 percent) were more likely than their white peers (52 percent) to feel good about themselves, especially if they grew up in small towns and were born before the 1960s. It is likely that thirty years ago, in a close-knit environment, teenagers received less conflicting information and sexual stimulation and stood a greater chance of self-acceptance.

Most of the African-American women (42 percent) reported that they liked their teenage bodies, although a little more than one in five (27 percent) did not feel one way or another about their bodies, and the remaining 31 percent did not like them. Thirty percent of their white peers reported liking their bodies; 22 percent were neutral, and almost half of them (48 percent) did not like their bodies.

What Were Your Expectations about Sex?

When the women were asked if they had ever thought about having sex and decided against it, almost half (44 percent) said they had never thought about having intercourse prior to their first experience. However, about one in three (30 percent) gave "fear" as the reason they thought about but did not have intercourse at that time. Another reason was that though they had thought about having sex, they did not feel they were ready or they lacked the necessary knowledge (10 percent). In addition, some women reported being deterred by some type of social or religious prohibition, such as the belief that it was a sin (15 percent). The remaining 1 percent reported either getting caught or a combination of the reasons above.

Sixteen percent of the African-American women did not recall knowing what to expect during their first sexual encounter, as compared with 21 percent of their white peers. Forty percent of African-Americans recalled thinking that it would be a pleasant and enjoyable experience, as compared with 53 percent of the white women in the study. Of those who expected the first intercourse to be unpleasant, three out of four were black (35 percent). The remaining 8 percent of African-American women thought that it would be painful but pleasurable. Only 15 percent of white women expected their first time to be unpleasant.

To further understand what young women expected sex to be like, I separated the women who had intercourse before age 18 from those who had intercourse when they were 18 or older. We found that the women in the older group were more likely to have expectations that were consistent with what actually happened than were those who were younger than age 18.

Did You Have Personal Goals?

The most common goal among women in this study was to have a career that required at least a college education (40 percent), followed equally by those who wanted to obtain an education or have a career in the creative arts (26 percent), have a family (9 percent), or just get a job (6 percent). As teenagers, some of the women could only react to the chaotic circumstances of their family life by simply wanting to escape what they had endured so far (18 percent). One woman reported having no goals and longed for acceptance by others.

What Were Your Messages from Home?

Sexual standards are the strategies that women have used for years to motivate men's interest or to gain their respect. If followed properly, these standards are also expected to ensure a good reputation and attract a suitable husband. Here are some of the specific rules and expectations that African-American parents have passed on to their adolescent daughters: Sexual instructions and prohibitions such as "a boy won't respect you if you go too far" (62 percent) and instructions about how to be "ladylike" in their behavior and physical appearance and by being married in a white dress (28 percent). The remaining women (10 percent) did not recall being inculcated with any standards of sexual behavior.

In my study, the average age at which African-American women were allowed to wear makeup was between 14 and 15 (39 percent). Twice as many of their white peers (29 percent) were allowed to wear makeup before age 15 compared with black girls (12 percent). Of those who recalled the age at which they began to wear makeup 33 percent did so between the ages of 16 and 19; some (6 percent) have never worn makeup. One in ten (9 percent) reported that they had no desire to wear makeup, either because of religious beliefs that prohibited its use or because it was their personal choice not to paint themselves up.

Parents' Rules and Warnings

Most women (60 percent) were told that boys would assume that they "would go all the way" if they engaged in petting. Few women (1 percent) reported that their parents were open to discussing any sexual topic with them during adolescence. The remaining 39 percent of African-American women received mixed parental messages or verbal or nonverbal warnings against such activity.

There were three fears that parents had for their teens: "Kissing would lead to other things"; their daughters would not be able to control their sexuality if they started petting with boys; and their daughters might be sexually molested or raped. African-American women were, however, much more likely to be given specific information about how to protect themselves from sexual assault (64 percent) than their white peers (36 percent).

Learning From Siblings

Adolescents learn a lot about sex from their siblings. Some of the women in this study had brothers who were either caught having sex at home with someone or word got back to the parents that their brothers were sexually active (14 percent). In most of these cases (81 percent), parents discussed their son's behavior and admonished him. In only one in five cases (19 percent), however, were brothers punished corporally for their behavior or denied privileges.

Many of our respondents (60 percent) did not recall the consequences of their sister's behavior; although pregnancy was the most common result of a sister's sexual activity in 17 percent of the women's families. The second most common offense was to be caught kissing a boy (14 percent). The remaining 9 percent reported that their sisters were warned about their sexual activity or caught having someone sleeping over. In contrast to how their brothers were disciplined, however, many of the girls received corporal punishment for their sexual behavior (39 percent), or a verbal reprimand by the parents (45 percent). The remaining 16 percent of the women reported that their sisters either received a warning or were not caught.

Learning from School

Almost half of the women (45 percent) reported that they had at least one sex-education class. The second most common form of sex education was viewing a single film (17 percent). The third was religious instruction in parochial schools, which included more warnings than anything else (14 percent). Still, about one in five (17 percent) received no formal sex education between the ages 13 and 17. The remaining 6 percent reported a combination of the above or were referred to their parents.

Learning from Religious Sources
More than half of the women (55 percent) recalled receiving religious proscriptions about kissing, touching, and sexual intercourse; 45 percent heard nothing at all.

Learning from Friends
More than half of the black women (57 percent) claimed that their friends discussed their own sexual experiences or sex in general, compared with 43 percent of the white women.

What These Findings Mean to You

Fifty percent of African-American girls decreased their church attendance or stopped going to church during their teenage years. Thirty-two percent of the women recalled their church attendance remaining the same, and 18 percent recalled their attendance increasing.

Chapter 6: Ready or Not

1. What Was Your Age?
The average age of first intercourse for women in my study was 16½ years. The earliest age at which a woman reported having had voluntary intercourse was 10 and the oldest was 25. One woman was a virgin at the time of the interview. Of those who had sex almost one in three women (30 percent) had intercourse by the age of 15, and two out of three (65 percent) had had this experience by age 18.

Only one in five of the women (20 percent) married their first partner, and thus first intercourse for most of them (80 percent) occurred outside of marriage.

2. What Were Your Reasons?
There were four common reasons for first intercourse. The most popular were curiosity and the desire to find out what sex was all about (39 percent); pressure from a partner (25 percent); love— 16 percent of the women claimed to be in love with their partner and were motivated by those strong feelings; lust, or being

sexually excited, was the fourth most common reason for women. Among these women (14 percent), a typical explanation was, "I was ready, turned on, and wanted him." The remaining 6 percent reported something other than the above, such as being tired of being a virgin.

3. Where Were You?

Nearly three out of four women (72 percent) reported that they had sex for the first time either in their own home or at that of their partners. A few (11 percent) lost their virginity at the park or the beach. Less common locations were a car, a motel, and school (7 percent). The remaining 10 percent either reported "other" or did not state a location.

4. Who Was Your Partner?

Most women had sex for the first time with steady boyfriends (84 percent) or with partners whom they knew well (14 percent). Included in these numbers are participants having had their first sexual encounter with the following people: a fiancé or husband (4 percent); or a stranger or relative (7 percent). And 4 percent recalled having their first intercourse with a casual acquaintance. The remaining 2 percent reported someone other than the above or did not identify this person.

As adolescents, almost half of the women (49 percent) maintained a relationship with their first partner one to five years after first intercourse. Others (17 percent) had relationships with their first partner that lasted five or more years. Women whose relationships lasted from six to twelve months made up 18 percent of the report. And relationships that lasted at least one to six months were reported at 7 percent. Thus, most women had long-term relationships with their first partners. Only a few women (9 percent) had sex for the first time with a one-night stand.

5. Did You Use Birth Control?

Most of the women (80 percent) reported that neither they nor their partner used any method of birth control when they had sex for the first time.

First Intercourse for Black and White Teens

Among the white women in the study, the earliest age for first intercourse was 12 and the oldest was 27. In contrast to black adolescents, white teens' most common reason for first intercourse was pressure from a partner (32 percent), followed by being in love and/or lust (22 percent). "One thing leading to another" (13 percent) and curiosity about sex tied for the least common reasons for first intercourse (13 percent). The remaining 20 percent felt they were ready for intimacy and wanted to participate in the sexual act.

Having sex with steady dates (62 percent) was most common for white women, and for almost one out of three of these women (30 percent), this person was someone they had known well. The remainder of the women (8 percent) lost their virginity with a stranger, a relative, or a casual acquaintance.

African-American women were more likely to have relationships that lasted years (68 percent versus 32 percent for white women). Of those women who had only a single occasion in which they had sex with their first partner, more than half (55 percent) were white. However, while they tended to have more sexual relationships in adolescence, almost two out of three white adolescents (64 percent) used some form of birth control the first time they had sex.

First Sex with a Female Partner

Although almost all of the African-American women interviewed for this study had their first sexual experience with a male, about 9 percent also had a sexual experience with another female during adolescence. Almost all same-sex encounters (91 percent) occurred with a friend, and only a few of the incidents involved someone the women had just met (9 percent). The majority of African-American women (63 percent) who had a sexual experience with a female during adolescence had only one such encounter.

Masturbation

As in childhood, most African-American adolescents (83 percent) did not masturbate. Of those who did masturbate, hand manipulation of the genitals was the most common method (49 percent). Other methods involved techniques and/or the use of equipment not reported in childhood, such as vibrators and water flowing from the bathtub faucet (3 percent). Stimulation of the breasts and genitals (21 percent) was another method described, as well as thigh squeezing (8 percent). The remaining 19 percent used other methods, like rubbing against an object, breast stimulation

only, a combination of methods, or insertion of objects, to masturbate.

Contraceptive Use

For those who had sex before age 16, more than half (56 percent)
used birth control after the first encounter. Most black teens (88
percent) who had sex after age 16 were likely to use contraceptives
closer to but still after their first intercourse.

Abortions

The age range of the women who had had abortions ranged from 15
to 32, with an average of two abortions per woman. Women who
had sexual intercourse before age 16 were most likely to have had
an abortion before age 17, and women who ended their education
before graduating from high school were likely to have had an abortion between the ages of 15 and 17. More than one in four women
in this study (27 percent) had a pregnancy before their eighteenth
birthday that ended in an abortion; 73 percent of them did not.
Most of the women, however, had first intercourse before age 16 (93
percent).

Multiple Partners

More than half of African-American adolescents (56 percent) had
only one partner between the age at which they had their first intercourse and age 17. Sixteen percent of African-American women
reported having two partners, and 19 percent reported three or four
partners. Only eight percent reported five or more sexual partners.
As for their white peers, one in three (38 percent) reported one
partner; 12 percent reported two partners; 11 percent reported three;
12 percent reported four; and 27 percent reported five or more sexual
partners during adolescence.

Length of Adolescent Sexual Relationships

More than half of African-American women (54 percent) reported
having a long-term relationship with a single partner during their
teens, while only 2 percent reported that all of their sexual relationships during adolescence were brief—meaning they were
one-night stands or lasted only a few weeks. Fifteen percent of
the women reported having multiple long-term relationships. The
remaining 24 percent reported having short- and multiple-term
relationships.

In contrast, more than one in five white women (22 percent)
reported having brief relationships during their teens, and only one

in three (36 percent) described having had a long-term relationship during adolescence. Six percent reported having multiple long-term relationships, and the remaining 35 percent reported having multiple short- and long-term relationships.

Sex for Sex Alone

We asked the women whether they had ever had sex for sex alone—meaning sex solely for sexual gratification—during adolescence. Most of them (91 percent) responded no; only 9 percent said yes. More than one in four white women (26 percent) reported that they had sex for sex alone during adolescence, which may help to explain the higher number of partners these women reported.

What These Findings Mean to You

Our study confirms that black teens are more likely not to use any form of contraception (62 percent compared with 38 percent for white women). But it is important not to lose sight of the fact that—regardless of whether they were black or white—three out of four adolescents who had sex before age 18 and half who had sex at age 18 or later used nothing to protect themselves against pregnancy or sexually transmitted diseases.

Chapter 7: Becoming Women

I. Friends

Almost half of the women in our sample (45 percent) generally shared with their friends such information as the sexual positions most conducive to orgasm, their favorite sexual techniques, where to find a good partner, and their woes if they could not find one. Fewer than one in four women (23 percent) never discussed sex with friends. They believed that sex was a private matter that should not be discussed with anyone. For 18 percent of the women, another common topic was what I called relationship mechanics—the type of conversation that takes place on talk shows today. Another 6 percent had general issues that touched on sex, and the remaining 8 percent discussed a combination of things like getting pregnant, which contraceptives to use, or when to have sex with someone.

Almost half of the women (47 percent) reported that their

friends supported the way they conducted their sex lives, while 13 percent claimed that their friends weren't in favor of or were opposed to their sex lives. Thirty-six percent felt that their friends were neutral, and the remaining 4 percent did not know how their friends felt.

2. Parents

Parents are usually a marginal source of sexual information, and that was true for most (60 percent) of these women. Only one in five women (20 percent) reported that discussions centered around relationships—when to get married, divorced, or when to stop seeing a boyfriend, for example. And 20 percent discussed the regulation or control of their sexual behavior.

Are You Taking Care of Your Own Sexual Needs?

At least 83 percent of the black women we interviewed currently had a sexual partner. Of those who did not have a partner, one in four (25 percent) reported not being able to find a suitable partner. One in five (20 percent) didn't want a relationship, 15 percent weren't ready for a relationship, and 15 percent had an unavailable partner who was away, ill, or could not have intercourse. Least common were women who had ended a relationship (5 percent); 20 percent reported other reasons.

We know that more than half of these women (59 percent) never masturbated. For those who never masturbated, the most common response among about one in three women (32 percent) was that they had no desire to touch their bodies in that way. The second most common reason the women (29 percent) gave for not masturbating was that they could control their sexual urges and did not need to manturate or they had a partner who could satisfy them if they wanted sex. One in four (24 percent) were governed by the religious belief that masturbation is a sin, and 15 percent described giving a woman satisfaction as a man's job.

For fewer than one in five women (16 percent), masturbation began in childhood and continued in adulthood. Those who began masturbating in adulthood did so between the ages of 18 and 26 (21 percent), and were single. Four percent of the women began to masturbate in adulthood between the ages of 27 and 36. The methods used in adulthood were similar to those used during adolescence—close to half of the women (47 percent) used their hand to stimulate their clitoris. Other common methods were vibrators or dildos (7 percent); water from the bathtub spout (5 percent); breast and genital manipulation (18 percent); and inserting objects into the vagina (12 percent). The remaining 11 percent of the women used methods such as thigh squeezing, or they wouldn't specify a method.

Each woman was asked four questions to describe the emotions she might have felt about masturbating. When asked about each of these emotions, almost half of the women (43 percent) felt guilty about masturbating, even though they reported that it was a pleasant experience; the rest of the women did not feel guilty. Twenty-four percent were still unsure whether masturbating was right or wrong, while everyone else was sure, one way or the other. However, eighty-one percent of African-American women viewed this practice more positively than they did in the past. The range of these feelings reflects the ambivalence that black women had about masturbating even though some of them engaged in it.

Almost one in ten women (9 percent) reported achieving orgasm through fantasies and dreams, but, surprisingly, almost one in four (23 percent) could become orgasmic by viewing some form of media—books, magazines, or movies. The remaining 67 percent did not report becoming orgasmic through any means other than direct sexual stimulation.

Are You Engaging in Risky Behaviors?

1. Number of Partners
Women reported that the average number of partners was eight; 15 percent reported only one relationship; 8 percent reported having two partners; 16 percent reported three; 47 percent reported more than three but less than thirteen partners; and 14 percent reported more than thirteen partners. About half of these relationships lasted for years; about one in three women (32 percent) had a combination of long-term and shorter relationships, which lasted a year or less, and 13 percent had dalliances that lasted an average of about from one night to two weeks. Among the remaining 6 percent, relationships lasted anywhere from one to twelve months. In addition, two out of three women (69 percent) reported that they did not engage in sex for sex alone with their sexual partners.

2. Prostitution or Sex Work
Five percent of the women engaged in prostitution or sex work at some point in their lives (these are the women who reported

having partners in the double-digit range), while 95 percent did not.

3. Cunnilingus

Sixty-three percent of the women we interviewed engaged in cunnilingus. The frequency of this practice ranged from once only to twice daily. Among the women who did not engage in this activity, half of them, or their partner (57 percent) had no desire to do so. Thirteen percent had moral and ethical reasons for not engaging in cunnilingus, such as, "I don't think it's right." Nine percent reported that the opportunity never arose, and an equal number thought about it but never participated. The remaining 12 percent either reported something other than the above or did not make a statement on the subject.

4. Fellatio

Almost half of the women (45 percent) never put their mouth on their partner's genitals. For those who did (55 percent), the frequency ranged from only once to once a day. Among those who didn't engage in this practice, more than half (55 percent) had no desire to do so; some (19 percent) reported moral and ethical reasons; others (11 percent) never thought about it; fear deterred 7 percent; and for 5 percent of the women the opportunity simply never arose. The remaining 3 percent reported reasons other than the above.

5. Anal Sex

Eighty percent of the women did not engage in anal sex. Thirty-seven percent reported fear of contracting a sexually transmitted disease as the reason for not practicing this form of sex; 32 percent had no desire; 17 percent cited moral reservations; and 11 percent had never thought about it. Three percent, however, said that the opportunity to have anal sex never arose, so we do not know what they might have decided. One in five women (20 percent) engaged in anal sex. For those who did, the frequency ranged from one attempt to once a month. Only 5 percent of these women, however, engaged in this practice on a regular basis.

6. Sex with Groups

While 92 percent of the women in our study reported that they did not have sex with more than one person at a time, 8 percent did so with a frequency ranging from one time to once a month. Sixty percent of those who engaged in group sex did so with friends, 10 percent with strangers, and 30 percent had sex with both friends and strangers at the same time. Predictably, 40 percent of the women did not participate in group sex or ménage à trois for moral and religious reasons; 38 percent had no desire to do so. Fear of sexually transmitted diseases was the reason given for only 2 percent of the women who did not participate. Five percent of the women never thought about group sex or never had the opportunity (15 percent).

7. Partner Swapping

While 95 percent of the women said that they did not engage in partner swapping, 5 percent engaged in this practice at least once. Almost half of the women (43 percent) who didn't claimed that they had no desire to do so; 36 percent cited moral and religious reasons; 8 percent said that they never had an opportunity; 7 percent said they thought about partner swapping; and only 3 percent cited fear of sexually transmitted diseases. The remaining 3 percent did not state whether they participated in partner swapping.

8. Extramarital Affairs

While 60 percent of women did not have extramarital affairs, 40 percent did. Fewer than one in five (23 percent) reported having one affair; 11 percent reported two affairs; and 5 percent had three or more affairs. While most of the partners were men, 7 percent of the women had affairs with female partners.

Do You Have Female Partners?

Of the 7 percent of women who reported having female partners in adulthood, 89 percent of their partners were lovers or friends and the remainder were strangers. More than three out of four (77 percent) of the relationships were described as intense—that is, the women engaged in mutual fondling, as well as manual and oral stimulation, that resulted in orgasm (78 percent). Along with cunnilingus, other behaviors practiced were using dildos on each other (7 percent); fondling one's partner (14 percent); being fondled by a partner (14 percent); and rubbing bodies together (21 percent). In the 1994 study of African-American women, 85 percent reported that their partners were either friends or lovers, and that 15 percent were coworkers or acquaintances.

While some of the women (44 percent) engaged in sex with another woman out of curiosity or because their female partner caught them by surprise and "hit on them" (11 percent), 33 percent reported being in love with or turned on by their partner. The remaining 12 percent also reported some other positive feeling. One in three (33 percent) had a same-sex relationship with only one partner, but most (67 percent) had between two and six partners in adulthood. More than half (55 percent) described their feelings as guilty. And two out of three (67 percent) denied that sex was the purpose of these encounters.

What White Women's Sexual Practices Tell Us

Twenty-six percent of the white women did not masturbate in adulthood. Of the 74 percent who did, 37 percent began between the ages 18 and 26, and 6 percent began between the ages of 27 and 36. Thirty-one percent of these women began masturbating in childhood and continued throughout their teens and into adulthood. Of those who did not masturbate, the reported reasons consisted of not needing to (42 percent); religious and ethical beliefs (31 percent); and 27 percent just didn't participate.

White women (43 percent) reported less guilt than African-American women (57 percent) and were much less conflicted about whether masturbation is right or wrong (64 versus 36 percent for African-American women). When asked if they had experienced orgasm without sexual contact, 70 percent said no. For those women who reported being orgasmic without sexual contact, 24 percent said in their dreams rather than through some type of media stimulation (6 percent).

Among white women, patterns of sexual communication were very similar to those reported by black women. Although two women were virgins, all had partners who initiated sex; fewer white women never initiated (8 versus 13 percent for black women). Forty-five percent of the white women initiated sex 25 percent of the time (versus 33 percent of African-American women). Forty-seven percent of white women initiated sex 50 to 75 percent of the time (versus 54 percent of African-American women). Two out of three white women (64 percent) communicated both verbally and nonverbally with their partners about their sexual needs, while only 36 percent of African-American women communicated either verbally or nonverbally.

White women reported an average of nineteen partners in their lifetime. Numbers in the upper ranges were cited by women who engaged in prostitution or sex work. There were more white women who were not currently sexually active with a partner—36 versus 23 percent for black women. Of those who had ever been sexually active since they first had sex, 15 percent were with one partner; 8

percent had two partners; 6 percent had three partners; 33 percent had more than three but less than thirteen partners; and 38 percent had more than thirteen partners. Almost half of the women (47 percent) had sex purely for the sake of sexual pleasure (sex for sex alone).

Similar to their black peers, white women (51 percent) tended to have intercourse between one and three times a week, with most (81 percent) achieving orgasm half of the time. However, of those who reported being orgasmic each time they had intercourse, 55 percent were black. When asked what was the easiest way for women to be orgasmic, women also reported that vaginal intercourse was the easiest method of reaching orgasm (33 versus 52 percent of African-American women), followed by masturbation (19 versus 7 percent of African-American women); oral stimulation by a partner (19 versus 15 percent of African-American women); fantasy (2 versus 1 percent of African-American women); a combination of all methods (9 versus 6 percent of African-American women); and oral stimulation of a male or a female (15 versus 14 percent of African-American women). No method was reported for 3 percent of white women (versus 2 percent of African-American women).

Compared with black women, white women were most likely to engage in cunnilingus (87 versus 63 percent for black women); fellatio (93 versus 55 percent for black women); and anal sex (43 versus 20 percent for black women).

White women were more likely to engage in sex with more than one person at a time (22 versus 9 percent for black women), only slightly more likely to engage in partner swapping (7 versus 5 percent for black women), and slightly less likely to have extramarital affairs (37 versus 40 percent for black women). Those who had affairs were more likely to have three or more (76 versus 23 percent for black women). Five percent of the women had extramarital affairs with women (versus 7 percent for black women).

What Recent Findings Confirm

The following information is based on the 1994 study. Forty percent of African-American women participated in masturbation (compared with 83 percent of white women).

Thirty-three percent of African-American women have never participated in cunnilingus (compared with 10 percent of white women), while 35 percent have engaged in this activity at least occasionally (compared with 42 percent of white women); 15 percent engage two times per month (compared with 18 percent of white women); and 16 percent of African-American women engage in this activity four or more times per month (compared with 31 percent of white women).

Forty-two percent of African-American women have never engaged in fellatio (compared with 11 percent of white women), while 37 percent of African-American women engage in this activity at least once per month (compared with 32 percent of white women); 10 percent engage two times per month (compared with 18 percent of white women); and 11 percent of African-American women engage four or more times (compared with 39 percent of white women).

When they were asked if they used a condom the last time they engaged in sexual intercourse, 77 percent of African-American women and 84 percent of white women said no.

Ninety-four percent of African-American women have not engaged in a ménage à trois (compared with 84 percent of white women); 93 percent of African-American women have not had an extramarital affair (compared with 93 percent of white women).

Chapter 8: Giving Our Love

Deciding to Use A Contraceptive

We found that while almost half of the women (45 percent) were using a method that had to be prescribed or inserted by a health professional, and about one in four (24 percent) used something that had to be bought over the counter, about one in three (31 percent) were currently using nothing at all. The different types of contraceptives they reported using were natural methods, 4 percent; withdrawal, 2 percent; diaphragm, 10 percent; foam/jelly, 5 percent; condom, 3 percent; IUD, 12 percent; the pill, 19 percent; and tubal ligation or other, 14 percent. One out of three used no protection (31 percent), although no one was abstaining from intercourse.

There are few women who can boast that with every heated sexual encounter they used a contraceptive. Indeed, most African-American women (96 percent) said that they had sex at least once without using contraceptives (94 percent of the white women said the same).

The reasons black women gave for not using contraceptives

are the following: "They were not available"—meaning that a woman would have had to interrupt the sexual act or purchase something in order to use a contraceptive at the moment (35 percent); "I don't like contraceptives (or a specific type)" (14 percent); and "I wanted sex to be natural" (9 percent). There were also women who made a deliberate decision not to use a contraceptive (14 percent) and chose not to act either because they wanted a baby (13 percent) or had inaccurate information on which to act (15 percent).

Two out of three black women (67 percent), and 60 percent of the white women, regardless of marital status, had been pregnant at one time in their lives, and one-third of them never had a pregnancy. More than half of the women (54 percent) had no planned pregnancies; about one in three had one pregnancy (32 percent); 14 percent had two or more pregnancies that were planned.

The number of unplanned pregnancies for these women ranged from none to nine, with only 9 percent of the women reporting no unplanned pregnancies and more than one in three (36 percent) reporting one unplanned pregnancy. Twenty percent of the black women reported two unplanned pregnancies, and 28 percent reported three to nine pregnancies. The remaining 7 percent indicated "other" or did not report an answer.

About two out of three black women (63 percent) did not use contraceptives but did not wish to become pregnant; 17 percent did not use birth control but didn't mind becoming pregnant; 6 percent wanted a baby; and 8 percent used a contraceptive but it failed to protect them against pregnancy. The remaining 6 percent answered something other than the above.

More than half of single black women (52 percent) had at least one child outside of marriage, fifteen percent of the women reported having two children outside of marriage, and 6 percent reported having three or more.

Deciding to Have an Abortion

Half of the black women (50 percent) reported having had an induced abortion. A little more than half of the white women (51 percent) also reported having had an abortion. When we asked the women why they decided to obtain their first abortion, almost half (46 percent) cited "not being ready" to have a baby; 12 percent cited pressure from parents or a sexual partner to abort; 23 percent did not want the baby; and 11 percent did not want the child of that particular partner. The remaining 8 percent reported another reason.

Deciding How to Deal with Sexual Problems with a Primary Partner

More than one in three of the women (39 percent) reported having difficulty with lubrication before sex. More than half (55 percent) claimed that on occasion they did not want to have sex. Other problems included not being sexually aroused (48 percent) and painful intercourse (19 percent).

For the primary partner, adequate control of ejaculation was a substantial problem (31 percent). Almost one in five (19 percent) said that their partners did not want to have sex; 15 percent reported that their partner ejaculated prematurely before entering the vagina; 14 percent could not lose the erection; 12 percent could not get an erection; and one in ten (10 percent) said their partner had difficulty becoming aroused.

Deciding to Keep Sexual Harassment in Check

About one in three women (35 percent) claimed to have been sexually harassed at work. Of those women, most (86 percent) reported that a boss or coworker made direct or indirect remarks to them— "I want to eat you up," for example—or promised them a job or a promotion in return for sex and/or slapping their behind and/or attempting to embarrass them. The remaining 14 percent who experienced sexual harassment at work reported that their boss or coworker breathed down their neck or rubbed his body up and down their back.

Although women were emotionally upset by these incidents, they took no action in reporting them (14 percent). More than one in four (29 percent) were either fired or quit their jobs. Seven percent either reprimanded or threatened the harasser, or attempted to get him fired (only one harasser was a woman). Thirty-four percent of the women had an emotional response, 7 percent had a physical reaction, and the remaining 7 percent changed their behavior. Only 2 percent reported the haassment to officals.

More than half of the African-American women (51 percent) reported at least one encounter of sexual harassment in public settings such as bars, gyms, or the street. Of the women who were harassed, three out of four of these incidents (75 percent) included catcalls, sexual propositions, vulgar comments, or even being grabbed on the street; 25 percent consisted of other behaviors. Most of the women (72 percent) were harassed in social settings by strangers, and least often by friends (3 percent). Acquaintances constituted 8 percent of the harassers; neighbors 5 percent; business associates 5 percent; other people made up 7 percent.

References

Chapter 1: Stolen Woman

Africa—The World She Remembered

there were strict rules for sex. Mbiti, John S., *African Religions and Philosophy.*

there were rules governing the person with whom you could experiment. Mbiti, John S., *African Religions and Philosophy;* Forde, Daryll, *African Worlds.*

punishment for breaking the rules was severe. Mbiti, John S., *African Religions and Philosophy.*

forbade sexual contact before marriage. Amadiume, Ifi, *Male Daughters, Female Husbands in an African Society.*

stolen something precious from her. Forde, Daryll, *African Worlds.*

father financially responsible when the child was born. Amadiume, Ifi, *Male Daughters, Female Husbands in an African Society;* Forde, Daryll, *African Worlds;* Richards, Audrey, *Chisungu.*

not regarded as sexual objects but as symbols of life. Mbiti, John S., *African Religions and Philosophy.*

joke about your parents' genitals. Ibid.

"I Am Because We Are"

therefore I am. Mbiti, John S., *African Religions and Philosophy,* p. 127.

but by other women as well. Ibid.

responsibilities as wives and mothers. Parkin, David, and David Nyamwaya, *Transformation of African Marriages.*

learned to plan and space their children. Mbiti, John S., *African Religions and Philosophy.*

retaining their virginity. Amadiume, Ifi., *Male Daughters, Female Husbands in an African Society.*
land her in trouble." Ibid.

The Rites of Passage

was the principal ritual. Knudsen, Christiana O., *The Falling Dawadawa Tree: Female Circumcision in Developing Ghana.*
ready for marriage. Jacobs, Harriet, *Incidents in the Life of a Slave Girl;* Mbiti, John S., *African Religions and Philosophy.*
between the ages of 4 and 8. Toubia, Nahid, *Female Genital Mutilation: A Call for Global Action.*
draining urine and menstrual blood. Hay, Margaret J., and Sharon Stichter, *African Women South of the Sahara;* Toubia, Nahid, "Female Circumcision As a Public Health Issue."
external genitalia made a woman "unclean." Toubia, Nahid. *Female Genital Mutilation: A Call for Global Action;* Giorgis, Belkis Wolde, Female Circumcision in Africa; Post, May Thein Hto, "Female Genital Mutilation and the Risk of HIV."
and therefore, less desirable. Giorgis, Belkis Wolde. *Female Circumcision in Africa.*

Treasured, Protected, and Prepared

or teenage brothers and sisters. Mbiti, John S., *African Religions and Philosophy.*
sexual functions with his wife. Ibid.
sexual boundaries were clearly drawn. Ibid.
sex with domestic animals was also taboo. Ibid.
usually by the mutual agreement of both families. Ibid.
a prized young person's adulthood and productivity. Ibid.
social consequences of these rules as well. Fortes, Meyer, *Social Structure;* Mickelwait, Donald, Mary Ann Riegelman, and Charles F. Sweet, *Women in Rural Development;* Parkin, David, and David Nyamwaya, *Transformation of African Marriages.*
assumed that they were sinful. Thomas, A., and S. Sillen, *Racism and Psychiatry.*
could not control their sexual urges. Ibid.
"hot, unconstitutioned ladies." Thomas, W. H. *The American Negro.*

The New World—The New Sexual Order

I. Sex Became a Negative Experience

no rights over your body. Engerman, Stanley, and Eugene Genovese, *Race and Slavery in the Western Hemisphere;* Wriggins, J., "Rape, Racism and the Law."

wanted to have sex with white men. Staples, Robert, *The Black Woman in America.*

to the worst plantation. White, Deborah. *Arn't I a Woman?*

The girl was put to death. Federal Writer's Project, *Slave Narratives,* Kentucky Narratives, VIII, Reel 7, pg. 53.

Celia was charged with first-degree murder. Hine, Darlene Clark, *Black Women in America: Historical Encyclopedia.*

sentenced to death and hanged. Ibid.

sexual relationships with them. Jacobs, Harriet, *Incidents in the Life of a Slave Girl;* Feldstein, Stanley. *Once a Slave;* Blake, Jane. *Memoirs of Margaret Jane Blake.*

would themselves be slaves. Weld, T. D., *American Slavery as It Is.*

exercised excessively to terminate unwanted pregnancies. Jacobs, Harriet, *Incidents in the Life of a Slave Girl.*

to have the marsa'. Gutman, Herbert, *The Black Family in Slavery and Freedom, 1750–1925.*

one every other year. French, Austa, "Slavery in South Carolina and the Ex-Slaves," pp. 46, 93–94, 180–187, 190–191 in Gutman, Herbert, *The Black Family in Slavery and Freedom 1750–1925,* pp. 84–85.

control of their sexuality and reproductive rights. Morrison, Toni, *Beloved.*

slaves created increased demand. Curtin, Philip, *The Atlantic Slave Trade.*

ready for market. Roberts, James, *Narrative of James Roberts,* p. 111.

mix the genes of Africans and whites. Thomas, A., and S. Sillen, *Racism and Psychiatry;* Haller, J, "The physician versus the negro: medical anthropological concepts of race in the late nineteenth century."

valued like prize animals. White, Deborah, *Arn't I a woman?*

on his plantation as well. Sutch, Richard, "The Breeding of Slaves for State and Westward Expansion of Slavery, 1850–1860." In Engerman, Stanley, and Eugene Genovese, *Race and Slavery in the Western Hemisphere.*

2. Privacy and Modesty Were Not Respected

neither comfortable or decent." Weld, T. D., *The American Negro.*

big enough to work. Botkin, B. A., *Lay My Burden Down.*

made a wretched appearance." Weld, T. D., *The American Negro.*

broken over her body." Anderson, William, *Life and Narrative of William Anderson,* p. 14.

women were handled at auction. White, Deborah, *Arn't I a woman?* Feldstein, Stanley, *Once a Slave;* Fisk University, *Unwritten History of Slavery.*

indication of their willingness to exhibit themselves. Jones, Jacqueline, *Labor of Love, Labor of Sorrow.*

unheated, and poorly constructed. Wade, Richard, *Slavery in the Cities.*

3. Group Solidarity Was Difficult to Maintain

"safe havens" in the North. Blassingame, John W., *The Slave Community;* Franklin, John Hope, *From Freedom to Slavery.*

again, through ignorance." Still, Peter, *The Kidnapped and the Abandoned,* pp. 171–173.

had less strenuous housework. Fox-Genovese, Elizabeth, *Black and White Women of the Old South.*

"privileged abusive or coerced relationships." French, Austa, "Slavery in South Carolina and the Ex-slaves," pp. 46, 93–94, 180–187, 190–191 in Gutman, Herbert, *The Black Family in Slavery and Freedom, 1750–1925.*

sexual relationship with their husbands. Jones, Jacqueline, *Labor of Love, Labor of Sorrow.*

4. Women Were Often Unprepared for Their Roles

which some of them did. Walker, Alice, *Possessing the Secret of Joy.*

what it was." Gutman, Herbert, *The Black Family in Slavery and Freedom, 1750–1925.*

it was felt to be necessary. Ibid.

5. Sexual Contact Between Family Members Became Inevitable

I was my master's son." Blassingame, John, *Slave Testimony,* p. 152.

you are my own son." Feldstein, Stanley, *Once a Slave,* p. 12.

6. Marriage Was No Longer Protected by the Family

terms husband *and* wife. Franklin, John Hope, *From Freedom to Slavery;* Blassingame, John, *The Slave Community.*

if one of them was free. Ibid.

for each other and for their children. Ibid.

protect his wife and children from sexual abuse." Jacobs, Harriet, *Incidents in the Life of a Slave Girl*, p. 59.

whenever he saw fit." The story of John Lindsay (1863) in Blassingame, John, *Slave Testimony*, p. 400.

bloody act of cruelty." Bayliss, John F., *Black Slave Narratives*, p. 100.

helplessly witness the daily mistreatment of their mates. Jacobs, Harriet, *Incidents in the Life of a Slave Girl.*

slave mother were her property. Weld, T. D., *The American Negro.*

the joint responsibility of the parents. Hine, Darlene Clark. *Black Women in America.*

The Psychological Burden

or the death of a loved one. Bayliss, John F., *Black Slave Narratives;* Blassingame, John, *Slave Testimony;* Botkin, B. A., *Lay my Burden Down;* pp. 53, 174–187; Feldstein, Stanley, *Once a Slave;* Jacobs, Harriet, *Incidents in the Life of a Slave Girl;* Miller, Randell M., ed., *"Dear Master" Letters of a Slave Family;* Still, Peter, *The Kidnapped and the Abandoned,* pp. 171–173; Weld, T. D., *The American Negro.*

above such things, if she could. Botkin, B. A., ed., *Lay my Burden Down,* p. 91.

Freedom—A Different Captivity

plundered towns and plantations. Hine, Darlene Clark, *Black Women in America,* pp. 243–248.

does not invite sensuous embraces. Thomas, A., and S. Sillen, *Racism and Psychiatry.*

feed their families. Billingsley, Andrew, *Black Families in America.*

in the homes of white families. Jones, Jacquelyn, *Labor of Love, Labor of Sorrow;* Billingsley, Andrew, *Black Families in America.*

if they did not "put out." Hine, Darlene Clark, *Black Women in America,* pp. 243–248.

90 percent of slaves were illiterate. Fox-Genovese, Elizabeth, *Black and White Women of the Old South.*

dealing with the ex-slaves." Billingsley, Andrew, *Black Families in America,* p. 70.

a married partnership. Gutman, Herbert, *The Black Family in Slavery and Freedom, 1750–1925;* Blackwell, James E., *The Black Community.*

Chapter 2: The Price We Pay

The Permissive Stereotype

black heroine who was sleeping. Independence Day. Centropolis Film Productions, 20th Century Fox film, 1996.

The Mammy

the ideal slave and the ideal woman." Wallace, Michele, *Black Macho and the Myth of the Superwomen.*
a dark complexioned woman with African features. West, Carolyn, "Mammy, Sapphire and Jezebel," *Psychotherapy.*
to other cities and plantations. Fox-Genovese, Elizabeth, *Black and White Women of the Old South.*
was not interested in freedom. Ibid.
the movie epic Gone with the Wind. Selznick International Pictures, 1939.

The She-Devil

research on sexual stereotypes. Campbell, Bebe Moore, *Essence,* pp. 71–72, 108, 113.
run around a great deal." Blassingame, John, *Slave Testimony,* p. 376.
that I could be proud of." Rita Cochran in Diana Russell, *Against Pornography,* pp. 47–48.

The Workhorse

tolerate rape or physical abuse. West, Carolyn, "Mammy, Sapphire and Jezebel," *Psychotherapy.*

Invisible Chains

their disadvantaged sanctuary in the ghetto." Poussaint, Alvin, "Blaxploitation Movies," *Psychology Today.*
supposedly crafty and manipulative tendencies. Ali, Shahrazad, *The Blackman's Guide to Understanding the Black Woman.*

expectations about their own performance. Steele, Claude M., and Joshua Aronson, "Stereotype Threat and the Intellectual Test Performance of African Americans," *Journal of Personality and Social Psychology.*

Chapter 3: Doctor–Nurse

Self Touch and Masturbation

reported masturbating before age 13. Kinsey, A., et al., *Sexual Behavior in the Human Female.*
low self-esteem, anxiety, and sexual abuse. Friedreich, W., et al., "Normative Sexual Behavior in Children," *Pediatrics.*

Sexual Arousal

sexual activity in childhood and adolescence. Leitenberg, H., E. Greenwald, and M. Tarran, "The Relation between Sexual Activity among Children during Pre-adolescence and/or Early Adolescence and Sexual Behavior and Sexual Adjustment in Young Adulthood," *Archives of Sexual Behavior.*
does not indicate sexual preference. Masters, W. H., V. Johnson and R. Kolodny, *Child Sexuality.*

Coping with Trauma

a teacher or a minister. Wyatt, G. E., "The Sexual Abuse of Afro-American and White American Women in Childhood." *Child Abuse and Neglect: The International Journal.*
counseling for their early sexual trauma. Wyatt, G. E., "The Aftermath of Child Sexual Abuse of African American and White American Women," *Journal of Family Violence.*

Did You Grow Up in a Risky Environment?

linked with abusive early-childhood experiences. Wyatt, G. E., M. Newcomb, and M. Reiderle, *Sexual Abuse and Consensual Sex.*

Chapter 4: Childhood Messages

Our Reluctant Guides on Childhood's Path to Knowledge

did not teach their children about sex. Kinsey, A., et al., *Sexual Behavior in the Human Female.*

What Did Your Church Say?

fornication, uncleanliness, lasciviousness. Gal. 5:19, KJV.
woman that is a harlot or profane. Lev. 21:7, KJV.

School—Mostly Dancing Tampons?

or excessively touching one's body. Gen. 38:9, KJV.

Chapter 5: Our Adolescent Development

Coping with Your Biological Development

the appearance of breast development. Morrison, J., et al., "Mother-Daughter Correlation of Obesity and Cardiovascular Disorders in Black and White Households," *National Heart Lung and Blood Institute.*
that black women's sexuality attracts. Grier, William, and Price Cobbs, *Black Rage.*

What Were Your Expectations about Sex?

size of African men's penises. Thomas, W. H., *The American Negro.*

Chapter 6: Ready or Not

Masturbation
most African-American adolescents did not masturbate. Wyatt, G. E., "Changes in HIV Related Sexual Practices and Condom Use of African American and White Women over a Decade," under review.

1. Wealth and Education

until they were 17 or older. Wyatt, G. E. "Re-examining Factors Predicting Afro-American and White Women's Age of First Coitus." *Archives of Sexual Behavior.*

helps girls defer sexual activity. Ibid.

2. Number of Caring Adults

sharing the responsibilities of raising their children. Kanter, John F., and Marvin Zelnick, "The National Survey of Adolescent Female Sexual Behavior," *Inter-Consortium for Political and Social Science.*

3. Protection from Abuse in Childhood or Adolescence

relationship between sexual abuse and adolescent pregnancy. Boyer, Debra, "Adolescent Pregnancy," *National Resource Center on Child Sexual Abuse of the National Center on Child Abuse and Neglect.*

sexually impulsive, and sexually irresponsible activity. Wyatt, G. E., et al., "Sexual Risk Taking and Health Protection for Single and Married African American Women," under review.

"Everyone Is Doing It"

had sex for the first time by age 18. Kinsey, A., et al., *Sexual Behavior in the Human Female.*

before World War II (48%) had first intercourse between ages 16 and 18, whereas over half of women born after the 1960s in my sample (56%) had sex between those ages. Kanter, John F., and Marvin Zelnick, "The National Survey of Adolescent Female Sexual Behavior," *Inter-Consortium for Political and Social Science;* Wyatt, G. E., S. D. Peters and D. Gutherie, "Kinsey Revisited, Part I," *Archives of Sexual Behavior;* Wyatt, G. E., S. D. Peters, and D. Gutherie, "Kinsey Revisited, Part II," *Archives of Sexual Behavior.*

dropped from 24% in the Kinsey women to 8% in my sample. Kinsey, A., et al., *Sexual Behavior in the Human Female;* Wyatt, G. E., S. D. Peters, and D. Gutherie, "Kinsey Revisited, Part I," *Archives of Sexual Behavior;* Wyatt, G. E., S. D. Peters, and D. Gutherie, "Kinsey Revisited, Part II," *Archives of Sexual Behavior.*

marrying at an average age of 24. U. S. Department of Commerce, Bureau of the Census.

he can find someone who will. Wyatt, G. E., "The Socio-Cultural Relevance of Sex Research," *American Psychologist;* Wyatt, G. E., et al., "Sexual Risk Taking and Health Protection Among Single and Married African American Women," under review.

Chapter 7: Becoming Women

Semi's Story, Part I

pelvic inflammatory disease, and chlamydia. Wyatt, G. E., "The Socio-Cultural Relevance of Sex Research," *American Psychologist.*
than that of white women. Ibid.

Are You Taking Care of Your Own Sexual Needs?

who were very sexually satisfied. Wyatt, G. E., and Lyons-Rowe, S. L. "African American's Sexual Satisfaction as a Dimension in their Sexual Roles," *Sex Roles.*

4. Fellatio
more likely to practice oral sex with their partners. Wyatt, G. E., et al., "Sexual Risk Taking and Sexual Health Protection among African American Women," under review.

Is Sex with Your Primary Partner Satisfying?

sexual needs to their partners. Wyatt, G. E., and Rowe, S. L., "African American Sexual Satisfaction as a Dimension in their Sexual Roles," *Sex Roles.*

Do You Have Female Partners?

Most commonly, they practiced cunnilingus. Wyatt, G. E., "Changes in HIV Related Sexual Practices and Condom Use of African American and White Women over a Decade," under review.

What White Women's Sexual Practices Tell Us

about one in three black women. Ibid.

Chapter 8: Giving Our Love

Deciding to Use a Contraceptive

compared with one for white women. Wyatt, G. E., et al., "Re-examining Predictors of African American Women's HIV Risk Taking," under review.

2. Coping with a History of Sexual Abuse

deal with a dangerous world. Wyatt, G. E., "The Aftermath of Child Sexual Abuse of African American and White American Women," *Journal of Family Violence;* Wyatt, G. E., C. M. Notgrass, and G. Gordon, "The Effects of African American Women's Sexual Revictimization," *Prevention in Human Services.*

Heather's Story

sexual behavior much like Heather's. Wyatt, G. E., "Child Sexual Abuse and its Effects on Sexual Functioning," *Annual Review of Sex Research;* Wyatt, G. E., and M. Newcomb, "Internal and External Mediators of Women's Sexual Abuse in Childhood," *Journal of Consulting and Clinical Psychology;* Wyatt, G. E., and M. H. Reiderle, "Reconceptualizing Issues That Affect Women's Sexual Decision Making and Sexual Functioning," *Psychology of Women Quarterly.*

women without any abuse histories. Wyatt, G. E., et al., "Re-examining Predictors of African American Women's HIV Risk Taking," under review.

3. Coping with a History of Physical Abuse

discussing sex with their partners. Wyatt, G. E., et al., "Re-examining Predictors of African American Women's HIV Risk Taking," under review.

Deciding to Keep Sexual Harassment in Check

versus one in three black women. Wyatt, G. E., and M. Reiderle, "The Prevalence and Context of Sexual Harassment among African American and White American Women," *Journal of Interpersonal Violence.*

in positions subordinate to theirs. Ibid.

Resources

Books

Akbar, Na'im. *Chains and Images of Psychological Slavery.* New Jersey: New Line Productions, 1984.

Ali, Shahrazad. *The Blackman's Guide to Understanding the Black Woman.* Philadelphia: Civilized Publications, 1989.

Amadiume, Ifi. *Male Daughters, Female Husbands in an African Society.* New Jersey: Zed Books, 1987.

Anderson, Robert. *From Slavery to Affluence: Memoirs of Robert Anderson, Ex-Slave.* Hemingsford, Nebraska: Hemingsford Ledger, 1927.

Anderson, William. *Life and Narrative of William Anderson; or Dark Deeds of American Slavery Revealed, Written by Himself.* Chicago: *Daily Tribune* Book and Job Printing Office, 1857.

Bass, B. A., G. E. Wyatt, and G. J. Powell. *The Afro-American Family: Assessment, Treatment and Research Issues.* New York: Grune & Stratton, 1982.

Bayliss, John F. *Black Slave Narratives.* New York: Macmillan, 1970.

Bennett, Lerone, Jr. *The Shaping of Black America.* New York: Verso, 1975.

Bernard, Jessie. *Marriage and Families among Negroes.* New Jersey: Prentice Hall, 1966.

Billingsley, Andrew. *Climbing Jacob's Ladder.* New York: Simon & Schuster, 1993.

———. *Black Families in White America.* New Jersey: Prentice Hall, 1968.

Blackwell, James E. *The Black Community: Diversity and Unity.* New York: HarperCollins Publishers, 1991.

Blake, Jane. *Memoirs of Margaret Jane Blake.* Philadelphia: Innes & Son, 1897.

Blassingame, John. *The Slave Community: Plantation Life in the Antebellum South.* New York: Oxford University Press, 1979.

Blassingame, John, ed. *Slave Testimony: Two Centuries of Letters, Speeches, Interviews and Autobiographies.* Baton Rouge: Louisiana University Press, 1977.

Botkin, B. A., ed. *Lay My Burden Down: A Folk History of Slavery.* Chicago: University of Chicago, 1968.

Catterall, Helen Tunncliff. Vols. 3, 5, *Judicial Cases Concerning American Slavery and the Negro.* Washington, D.C.: Carnegie Institution of Washington, D.C., 1932.

Colley. "Homes of the Freed." In Jones, Jacqueline. *Labor of Love, Labor of Sorrow: Black Women, Work and Family from Slavery to the Present.* New York: Vintage Books/Random House, 1985.

Comer, James P., and Alvin Poussaint. *Raising Black Children: Two Leading Psychiatrists Confront the Educational, Social and Emotional Problems Facing Black Children.* New York: Plume, 1992.

Cope, John. *King of the Hottentots.* Capetown: Howard Timmins, 1967.

Curtin, Philip. *Africa Remembered.* Madison: University of Wisconsin Press, 1968.

———. *The Atlantic Slave Trade: A Census.* Wisconsin: University of Wisconsin Press, 1969.

Engerman, Stanley, and Eugene Genovese. *Race and Slavery in the Western Hemisphere: Quantitative Studies.* New Jersey: Princeton University Press, 1975.

Federal Writer's Project. *Slave Narratives: A Folk History of Slavery in the United States from Interviews with Former Slaves.* Typewritten records prepared by the Federal Writer's Project; 17 vols., microfilm edition. Washington, D.C.: Library of Congress, 1936–1938.

Federal Writer's Project, Kentucky Slave Narratives, vol. 8, reel 7, p. 53.

Federal Writer's Project, North Carolina, vol. 11, part 2, p. 78.

Feldstein, Stanley. *Once a Slave: The Slaves' View of Slavery.* New York: William Morrow & Co., 1971.

Fisk University. *Unwritten History of Slavery: Autobiographical Account of Negro Ex-Slaves.* Nashville, Tennessee: Social Science Institute, Fisk University, 1945.

Forde, Daryll. *African Worlds: Studies in the Cosmological Ideas and Social Values of African Peoples.* New York: Oxford Press, 1968.

Fortes, Meyer. *Social Structure: Studies Presented to A. R. Radcliffe-Brown.* New York: Russell & Russell, 1963.

Fox-Genovese, Elizabeth. *Black and White Women of the Old South: Within the Plantation Household.* Chapel Hill: University of North Carolina, 1988.

Franklin, John Hope. *From Freedom to Slavery.* 6th ed. New York: McGraw Publishing Co., 1988.

Giorgis, Belkis Wolde. *Female Circumcision in Africa.* United Nations Research Studies, Economic Commission for Africa, 1981.

Grier, William, and Price Cobbs. *Black Rage.* New York: Bantam Books, 1969.

Gutman, Herbert. *The Black Family in Slavery and Freedom, 1750–1925.* New York: Vintage Books, 1976.

Haftin, Nancy J., and Edna Bay, eds. *Women in Africa: Studies in Social and Economic Change.* California: Stanford University Press, 1976.

Harrison, Alferdteen. *Black Exodus: The Great Migration from the American South.* Jackson: University of Mississippi Press, 1991.

Hay, Margaret J., and Sharon Stichter. *African Women South of the Sahara.* New York: Longran, 1981.

Hernton, Calvin. *Sex and Racism in America.* New York: Doubleday & Co., 1965.

Hine, Darlene Clark. Vols. 1, 2, *Black Women in America: Historical Encyclopedia.* New York: Carlson Publishing, 1993.

Huggins, N., M. Kilson, and D. Fox. *Key Issues in the Afro-American Experience.* New York: Harcourt Brace Jovanovich, 1971.

Hurston, Zora Neale. *Their Eyes Were Watching God.* Connecticut: Fawcett Publications, 1965.

Jacobs, Harriet. *Incidents in the Life of a Slave Girl.* New York: Schomburg Library/Oxford University Press, 1988.

Jones, Jacqueline. *Labor of Love, Labor of Sorrow: Black Women, Work and Family from Slavery to the Present.* New York: Vintage Books, 1985.

Keckley, Elizabeth. *Behind the Scenes, or Thirty Years a Slave and Four Years in the White House.* New York: Oxford Press, 1988.

Kinsey, A., C. Martin, W. Pomeroy, and P. Gebhard. *Sexual Behavior in the Human Female.* Philadelphia: W. B. Saunders Co., 1953.

Knudsen, Christiana O. *The Falling Dawadawa Tree: Female Circumcision in Developing Ghana.* Denmark: Intervention Press, 1994.

Masters, W. H., V. Johnson, and R. Kolodny. *Child Sexuality.* New York: HarperCollins Publishers, 1992.

Mbiti, John S. *African Religions and Philosophy.* London: Heinemann Press, 1985.

Mickelwait, Donald, Mary Ann Riegelman, and Charles F. Sweet. *Women in Rural Development: A Survey of the Roles of Women in*

Ghana, Lesotho, Kenya, Nigeria, Bolivia, Paraguay and Peru [Case Study]. Colorado: Westview Press, 1976.

Michael, R., J. H. Gagnon, E. O. Laumann, and G. Kolata. *Sex in America: A Definitive Survey*. New York: Little, Brown & Company, 1994.

Miller, Randell M., ed. *"Dear Master" Letters of a Slave Family*. Ithaca: Cornell University Press, 1978.

Morrison, Toni. *Beloved*. New York: Alfred A. Knopf, 1987.

Nwapa, Flora. *Efuru*. London: Heinemann, 1966.

Parkin, David, and David Nyamwaya, eds. *Transformation of African Marriages*. Manchester University Press for the International African Institute, 1987.

Radcliffe-Brown, A. R., and Daryll Forde. *African Systems of Kinship and Marriage*. New York: KPI distributed by Routledge & Kegan Paul, 1987.

Richards, Audrey. *Chisungu: A Girl's Initiation Ceremony among the Bemba of Northern Rhodesia*. London: Faber & Faber, 1956.

Roberts, James. *Narrative of James Roberts: Soldier in the Revolutionary War and Battle of New Orleans*. Chicago: The Book Farm, 1858.

Russell, Diana. *Against Pornography: The Evidence of Harm*. New York: Russell Publications, 1993.

Saadawi, Nawal. *The Hidden Faces of Eve: Women in the Arab World*. Translated by Sherif Helata. London: Zed Press, 1980.

Staples, Robert. *The Black Woman in America: Sex, Marriage and the Family*. Chicago: Nelson-Hall Publishers, 1973.

Staples, Robert, and Leanor B. Johnson. *Black Families at the Crossroads: Challenges and Prospects*. San Francisco: Jossey-Bass Publishers, 1993.

Still, Peter. *The Kidnapped and the Abandoned: The Personal Recollection of Peter Still and His Wife "Vina," after Forty Years of Slavery*. Syracuse: Harvard Press, 1856.

Stow, George, ed. *Native Races in Africa: A History of the Hottentots & Bantu into the Hunting Grounds of the Bushmen, the Aborigines of the Country*. New York: Macmillan, 1905.

Sutch, Richard. "The Breeding of Slaves for Sale and Westward Expansion of Slavery, 1850–1860." Chapter 8 in Engerman, Stanley, and Eugene Genovese. *Race and Slavery in the Western Hemisphere: Quantitative Studies*. New Jersey: Princeton University Press, 1975.

Teyegaga, B. D. *Dipo Custom and the Christian Faith: The Nature of a People Is in Their Traditions, Religion, and Customs*. Accura: J'Pitter Printing Press, 1985.

Thomas, A., and S. Sillen. *Racism and Psychiatry.* New York: Bruner/Mazel, 1972.

Thomas, W. H. *The American Negro: What He Has, What He Is and What He May Become.* New York: Macmillan, 1910.

Toubia, Nahid, ed. *Women of the Arab World: The Coming Challenge: Papers of Arab Women's Solidarity Association Conference.* New Jersey: Zed Books, 1988.

Toubia, Nahid. *Female Genital Mutilation: A Call for Global Action.* New York: Women, Inc., 1993.

Wade, Richard. *Slavery in the Cities: The South 1820–1860.* New York: Oxford Press, 1964.

Walker, Alice. *Possessing the Secret of Joy.* New York: Pocket Books, 1992.

Walker, A., and P. Parmar. *Warrior Marks: Female Genital Mutilation and Sexual Blinding of Women.* New York: Harcourt Brace Jovanovich, 1993.

Weld, T. D. *American Slavery as It Is: Testimony of a Thousand Witnesses.* New York: Arno Press and *The New York Times*, 1968.

Wallace, Michele. *Black Macho and the Myth of the Superwoman.* New York: Chapman & Hall, 1990.

White, Deborah. *Arn't I a Woman?* New York: W. W. Norton & Co., 1985.

Wyatt, G. E. "Changing Influences." In Bancroft, John. *Adolescence and Puberty.* New York: Oxford University Press, 1990.

———. "Ethnic and Cultural Differences in Women's Sexual Behavior." In S. Blumenthal, A. Eichler, and G. Weissman. *Women and AIDS: Promoting Healthy Behavior.* DHHS Publications, 174–182, 1991.

Wyatt, G. E., M. Newcomb, and M. Reiderle. *Sexual Abuse and Consensual Sex: Women's Developmental Patterns and Outcomes.* Newberry Park: Sage Publications, 1993.

Wyatt, G. E., and G. J. Powell, eds. *The Lasting Effects of Child Sexual Abuse.* Newbury Park: Sage Publication, 1988.

Articles

Barker-Benfield, Ben. "Sexual Surgery in Late Nineteenth-Century America." *International Journal of Health Sciences* 5 (2): 279–298 (1975).

Boyer, Debra. "Adolescent Pregnancy: The Role of Sexual Abuse." *National Resource Center on Child Sexual Abuse of the National Center on Child Abuse and Neglect* 4 (16): November/December 1995).

Brace, C. Loring. "Race and Political Correctness." *American Psychologist* 50 (8): 725–728 (August 1995).

Campbell, Bebe Moore. "Myth: About Black Female Sexuality." *Essence* 71 (3): 71, 108, 113 (April 1989).

Elmer-Dewitt, Philip. "Now for the Truth about Americans and Sex: The First Comprehensive Survey Since Kinsey Smashes Some of Our Most Intimate Myths." *Time* 144 (16) (October 17, 1994).

Freeman, Ellen et al., "Urban Black Adolescents Who Obtain Contraceptive Services before and after Their First Pregnancy: Psychosocial Factors & Contraceptive Use." *Journal of Adolescent Health Care* 5: 183–190 (1984).

Friedreich, W., P. Grambsch, D. Broughton, B. S. Kupier, and R. L. Beilke. "Normative Sexual Behavior in Children." *Pediatrics* 88 (3): 456–464 (September 1991).

Gebhard, Paul, W. B. Pomeroy, and G. E. Martin. *Pregnancy, Birth and Abortion. The Institute for Sex Research.* New York: Wiley (1958).

Giobbe, Evelina, ed. "Black Women and Porn." *Women Hurt in Systems of Prostitution Engaged in Revolt* (spring 1993).

Haller, J. "The Physician versus the Negro: Medical and Anthropological Concepts of Race in the Late Nineteenth Century." *Bulletin of the History of Medicine* 44: 154–167 (1970).

Kanter, John F., and Marvin Zelnick. "The National Survey of Adolescent Female Sexual Behavior." *Inter-Consortium for Political and Social Science* (1980).

Leitenberg, H., E. Greenwald, and M. Tarran. "The Relation between Sexual Activity among Children during Pre-adolescence and/or Early Adolescence and Sexual Behavior and Sexual Adjustment in Young Adulthood." *Archives of Sexual Behavior* 18 (4): 299–313 (1989).

Morgan, Joan. "The Bad Girls of Hip-Hop, Featuring Little Kim, Foxy Brown & Da' Brat." *Essence* (March 1997), pgs. 76–77, 132, 134.

Morrison, J., et al. "Mother-Daughter Correlation of Obesity and Cardiovascular Disorders in Black and White Households: NHLBI Growth and Health Study." National Heart, Lung and Blood Institute. *American Journal of Public Health* 84 (11): 1761–1768.

Muhammad, Aminyah, and Melodye Berry. Power News. *A Publication for the Healthy Babies Coalition's Perinatal Outreach Worker Empowerment Resources* 1 (2): 1–4 (spring 1995).

Mulholland, Lisa. "Off Our Backs: An Interview with a Wika Sudanese about Female Circumcision." *Herstory.* Santa Barbara: A. S. Women's Commission 24–26 (December 1992).

Nobles, Wade. "Reclaiming Our Traditions: An Explanation of the

Esoteric and Symbolic Meanings of the ABPsi Installation Ceremony." *Psych Discourse* 25 (10) (October 1994).

Poussaint, Alvin. "Blaxploitation Movies: Cheap Thrills That Degrade Blacks." *Psychology Today* 7 (9): 22–32 (February 1987).

Post, May Thein Hto. "Female Genital Mutilation and the Risk of HIV." *Support for Analysis and Research in Africa (SARA) Issues Paper.* The U.S. Agency for International Development (May 1995).

Staples, Robert. "Sex Behavior of Low-Income Negroes." *Sexology* 34: 52–55 (October 1967).

Steele, Claude M., and Joshua Aronson. "Stereotype Threat and the Intellectual Test Performance of African Americans." *Journal of Personality and Social Psychology* 69 (5): 797–811.

Tharinger, Deborah. "Impact of Child Abuse on Developing Sexuality." *Professional Psychology, Research, and Practice.* 21 (5): 331–337.

Toubia, Nahid. "Female Circumcision as a Public Health Issue." *The New England Journal of Medicine* 331: 712–716 (September 15, 1994).

U.S. Department of Commerce, Bureau of the Census (1990).

U.S. Department of Commerce, Bureau of the Census. *The Hispanic Population in the United States: Current Population Reports.* Prepared by the Economics & Statistics Administration. Series P20-475 (March 1993).

Vontress, C. "The Black Male Personality." *Black Scholar* 2 (10): 16 (1971).

West, Carolyn. "Mammy, Sapphire, and Jezebel: Historical Images of Black Women and Their Implications for Psychotherapy." *Psychotherapy* 32 (3): 458–466 (fall 1995).

Wriggins, J. "Rape, Racism and the Law." *The Harvard Women's Law Journal.* Massachusetts: Harvard University Press (spring 1993).

Wyatt, G. E. "The Sexual Abuse of Afro-American and White American Women in Childhood." *Child Abuse & Neglect: The International Journal* 9: 507–519 (1985).

———. "Re-examining Factors Predicting Afro-American and White Women's Age of First Coitus." *Archives of Sexual Behavior* 18 (4): 269–296 (1988).

———. "The Relationship between Child Sexual Abuse and the Adolescent Sexual Functioning in Afro-American and White American Women." *The Annuals of the New York Academy of Science* 528: 111–122 (August 1989).

———. "Sexual Abuse of Ethnic Minority Children: Identifying Dimensions of Victimization." *Professional Psychology* 21: 338–343 (1990).

———. "The Aftermath of Child Sexual Abuse in African American and White American Women: The Victims' Experience." *Journal of Family Violence.* 5 (1): 61–81 (1990).

———. "Child Sexual Abuse and Its Effects on Sexual Functioning." *Annual Review of Sex Research,* vol. 3. The Society for the Scientific Study of Sex (1991).

———. "The Socio-Cultural Context of African American and White American Women's Rape." *The Journal of Social Issues.* 48 (1): 77–91 (spring 1992).

———. "The Sociocultural Relevance of Sex Research: Challenges for the 1990s and Beyond." *American Psychologist* 49 (8): 748–752 (1994).

———. "Changes in HIV Related Sexual Practices and Condom Use of African American and White Women over a Decade." Under review. 1997.

Wyatt, G. E., K. Desmond, P. Ganz, J. Rowland, K. Ashing-Giwa, and B. Meyerowitz. "The Impact of Breast Cancer on the Sexual Behavior of African American Women." Under review. 1997.

Wyatt, G. E., and Kristi M. Dunn. "Examining Predictors of Sex Guilt in Multiethnic Samples of Women." *Archives of Sexual Behavior.* 20 (5): 471–486 (October 1991).

Wyatt, G. E., and S. Lyons-Rowe. "African American Women's Sexual Satisfaction as a Dimension of Their Sex Roles." *Sex Roles* 22 (7–8): 509–515 (April 1990).

Wyatt, G. E., and M. Newcomb. "Internal and External Mediators of Women's Sexual Abuse in Childhood." *Journal of Consulting and Clinical Psychology.* 58 (6): 758–767 (1990).

Wyatt, G. E., M. Newcomb and C. M. Notgrass. "Internal and External Mediators of Women's Rape Experience." *Psychology of Women Quarterly* 14: 153–176 (1990).

Wyatt, G. E., C. M. Notgrass, and G. Gordon. "The Effects of African American Women's Sexual Revictimization: Strategies for Prevention." *Prevention in Human Services* 12 (2): 111–134 (1995).

Wyatt, G. E., S. D. Peters, and D. Gutherie. "Kinsey Revisited, Part I: Comparisons of the Sexual Socialization and Sexual Behavior of Black Women over 33 Years." *Archives of Sexual Behavior* 17 (4): 201–239 (1988).

———. "Kinsey Revisited, Part II: Comparisons of the Sexual Socialization and Sexual Behavior of Black Women over 33 Years." *Archives of Sexual Behavior* 14 (4): 289–332 (1988).

Wyatt, G. E., and M. Reiderle. "The Prevalence and Context of Sexual Harassment among African American and White American Women." *Journal of Interpersonal Violence* 10 (3): 309–321 (1995).

———. "Reconceptualizing Issues That Affect Women's Sexual Decision Making and Sexual Functioning." *Psychology of Women Quarterly* 18 (4): 611–625 (December 1994).

———. "Sexual Harassment and Prior Sexual Trauma among African American and White Women." *Violence and Victims* 9 (3) (1994).

Wyatt, G. E., M. B. Tucker, et al., "Re-examining Predictors of African American Women's HIV Risk Taking: Traumatic Experiences, Sexual History and Psychological Well-Being. Under review. 1997.

Wyatt, G. E., M. B. Tucker, et al., "Sexual Risk Taking and Sexual Health Protection among African American Women." Under review. 1996.

Yee, A. H., H. H. Fairchild, F. Weizmann, and G. E. Wyatt. "Addressing Psychology's Problems with Race." *American Psychologist* 48 (11): 1132–1140 (November 1993).

Movies

Independence Day. Centropolis Film Productions, 20th Century Fox Films, 1996.

Set It Off. Miramax Films, 1996.

Colors. Orion Entertainment, 1988.

Gone with the Wind. Selnick International Pictures, 1939.

Index

A

Abortion
  age, statistics, 132–33, 249
  deciding to have, 177–78,
    259–60
  race differences, statistics,
    151
Abuse, physical, coping with
  history of, 183–84
Abuse, sexual. *See also*
    Harassement, sexual; Rape
  children, 48, 56–61, 73
  coping with trauma, 58–61,
    180–83, 238
  first sexual experience,
    impact on timing of, 136–
    40
  protection from, 226
  risk taking and, 143
  self-blame, 60–61
  warnings from parents on,
    78–79, 240
Adolescent development, 89–
    119, 241–46. *See also* First
    sexual experience; Puberty
  abortions, 132–33, 249
  Africa, sixteenth century, 116
  appearance, standards for,
    106–7, 244
  behavior, standards for, 104–
    5

  church attendance, 117, 246
  churches and religious
    sources, messages from,
    112–14, 246
  confidants, choice of, 94–95,
    242–43
  control of own body,
    learning, 121–47
  expectations regarding sex,
    95–97, 243–44
  friends, learning from, 114,
    246
  goals, personal, 97–98, 244
  homosexuality, messages on,
    91
  lack of information on sex,
    107–10
  "ladylike" behavior, teachings,
    90–91, 104–5, 244
  length of relationship with
    partner, 125, 133, 250
  makeup, 90, 106–7, 244
  masturbation and self-
    touching, 91, 128–29, 249
  music, sexual values and
    morality, 115–16
  nudity, messages on, 91
  parents, guidance by, 89–92,
    94–95, 98–107, 110–11
  petting, 111

Adolescent development
  (continued)
  premarital sex, messages on,
    91
  pride and respect, standards
    for, 107
  reputation, protection of, 90,
    98, 101, 119
  schools, sex education, 89–
    90, 112
  self-awareness, teenage sex
    and, 145
  self image, 95, 118, 243
  sexual practices, 128–34
  sexual protocol, standards
    for, 105–6
  sexual responsibility,
    learning, 227
  siblings, information from,
    111–12
  standards, setting of, 103–7
  warnings from parents, 110–
    11, 245–46
Adult sexuality, role of
  relationships. See
  Relationships, role in
  adult sexuality
Africa, sixteenth century
  adolescent development, 116
  childhood sex play, 5, 6, 62–
    64
  circumcision, female, 7–8
  family life, 9
  group solidarity, 6–7
  human body, view of, 5–6
  marriage, 9
  misinformation on sex, 6–7
  missionaries, 10, 97
  nonmarital sex, 5
  privacy and modesty, 5–6
  rites of passage, 7–9
  sex education, 84
  sexual boundaries, 9–10

Against Pornography: The
  Evidence of Harm
  (Russell), 34
AIDS or HIV virus
  contraceptives, decision to
    use, 174
  prevention of, 123
  race differences in
    contracting, 151
  research prior to epidemic,
    52
  sex education and, 69
  symptoms of, 180
Arn't I a Woman (White), 13
Ali, Shahrazad, 41
Allie (case study), 89–90
Amaduime, Ifi, 6–7
The American Negro: What He
  Is and What He Has
  Become (Thomas), 23
Amos 'n' Andy (telecast), 30, 35
Anal sex
  diseases and, 160–61
  race differences in practice
    of, 168–69, 257
  statistics on, 254
Angela (case study), 183–84
Appearance
  early pregnancy, effect on,
    242
  importance of,
    questionnaire, 213–14,
    219–20
  standards for, adolescent
    development, 106–7, 244
Aronson, Joshua, 42
Attitudes about sex, children
  and love
  questionnaire, 208–10, 217–
    18
Attractiveness, sexual
  questionnaire, 211–13, 218–
    19

B

Basic Instinct (film), 104

Battered wives, 183–84

Behavior, standards for in adolescent development, 104–5

Beloved (Morrison), 13

Birth control. *See* Contraceptives

Black Entertainment Television, 41

The Black Family from Slavery to Freedom—1750 to 1925, 17

Black Rage (Cobbs and Grier), 94

Black Women in America: A Historical Encyclopedia (Hine), 11–12

Blassingame, John, 18

Blaxploitation era (1970s), 41

Body weight
  breast development and, 93
  menstruation and, 242
  obesity, adolescence, 93–94

Boyer, Debra, 137

Breast cancer survivors, 169, 236

Breasts, development, 51, 93–94, 242

Brown, Divine, 29–30

C

California, University of Institute of Social Science Research, 234, 235

California Youth Authority, 184

Campbell, Bebe Moore, 32–33

Celia (slave), 11–12

Celina (case study), 159

Cherie (case study), 56, 58–59, 137–39

Cheryl (case study), 78

Childhood, knowledge of sex, 67–87
  affection between parents, effect of, 79–81, 87, 240–41
  Africa, sixteenth century, 84
  churches and religious sources, messages from, 81–82
  friends, learning from, 83–84, 241
  homosexuality, 74–76, 238, 239
  masturbation and self-touching, 63, 74, 75, 82–83, 238, 239
  nudity, messages on, 74, 238, 239
  parents, learning from, 68–81, 85
  premarital sex, messages on, 74, 76–78, 238, 239–40
  schools, sex education, 82–83, 241
  sexual abuse, 78–79, 240
  sexual hype, 83–84, 241
  sources of knowledge, 71–72
  warnings from parents, 240

Children. *See* Abuse, sexual; Childhood, knowledge of sex; Children, sex play

Children, sex play, 47–66
  Africa, sixteenth century, 5, 6, 62–64
  crushes, 52–56
  environment, influence of, 62
  folktales and, 63
  games (doctor-nurse), 49–50, 62
  masturbation and self-touching, 48, 50–52, 64, 237

Children, sex play *(continued)*
  mutual exploratory
    experiences, 53, 55–56,
    238
  nonconsensual childhood
    exploration, 48, 56–61
  sexual arousal, 52–56, 237–
    38
Children's Hospital Medical
  Center (Cincinnati), 93
Choices in relationships. *See*
  Love, choices
Churches and religious sources
  church attendance,
    adolescent girls, 117, 246
  sexual decisions of adults,
    influences on, 154–55
  sexual information and, 81–
    82, 112–14, 246
Circumcision, female
  Africa, sixteenth century, 7–8
Cobbs, Price, 94
Cochran, Rita, 34
Colors (film), 40
Contraceptives
  decision to use, 174–76,
    258–59
  first sexual experience and,
    122, 125–26, 248, 249, 251
  race differences in use of,
    175–76, 258–59
  statistics on use of, 129, 145,
    249, 251
Control of own body, learning,
    121–47
  delayed sexual activities,
    factors, 134–41
  first sexual experience, 122–
    27
  impulsivity myth, 122–23,
    158
  slavery, impact of, 143–44

Coping
  negative expectations about
    relationships, coping with,
    188–94
  physical abuse, victims of,
    180–83
  puberty, 92–94, 242
  sexual abuse, victims of, 58–
    61, 180–83, 238
  slaves, 22
Cora (case study), 113–14
Counseling, resources, 220–22
Crushes, children, 52–56
Cunnilingus
  lesbian relationships, 164, 255
  race differences in practice
    of, 168–69, 257,
    258
  reasons for, 160
  statistics on, 254
Cynthia (slave), 11

D
DaBrat, 41–42
Decision-making. *See also*
  Love, choices;
  Relationships, role in
  adult sexuality
  abortions, 177–78, 259–60
  contraceptives, use of, 174–
    76, 258–59
  control of, importance, 226–
    27
  study on sexual decision-
    making, 235–36
Delayed sexual activities,
  factors
  family background, 135–36
  profile, 140–41
  sexual abuse, protection
    from, 136–40
  wealth and education, 134–35

Devil in a Blue Dress (Mosley), 32

Dianne (case study), 55

Diseases, sexually transmitted. *See also* AIDS or HIV virus
  contracting, race differences, 151, 168

Douching, 121

Duvall, Robert, 40

E

Eboni (case study), 72–75, 78, 79, 82–83

Education
  delayed sexual activities, factor, 134–35, 141

Emancipation of slaves, 22–25

Erin (case study), 47–48, 58, 63–64

Essence magazine, 32–33, 41–42

Ethnic differences. *See* Race differences

Expectations
  negative expectations about relationships, coping with, 188–94
  sex, adolescents, 95–97, 243–44

Exploitation. *See* Abuse, sexual; Sexual harassment

Extramarital affairs
  race differences in practice of, 168, 257, 258
  statistics on, 162, 255

F

Family life. *See also* Marriage; Parents
  adolescent development, 89–92, 94–95, 98–107, 110–12, 117–18

Africa, sixteenth century, 9

African-Americans, 1920s to 1970s, media portrayal, 41
  children's knowledge of sex and, 68–81, 85, 87
  first sexual experience, impact on time of, 135–36
  "ladylike" behavior, teachings, 90–91, 104–5, 244
  race differences, 117
  sexual information and, 68–81, 85
  sexual responsibility, values and, 225
  slaves, 18–19

Faye (case study), 87

Fear of sex, 96, 243

Fellatio
  frequency of practice, 160
  race differences in practice of, 168–69, 257, 258
  statistics on, 254

Female partners. *See* Lesbian relationships

Fire Eyes (film), 8

First sexual experience
  age of, 123–24, 246–47
  contraceptives, use of, 125–26, 248, 249, 251
  critical questions, 123–26
  curiosity, 124, 247
  event-oriented incidents, 135
  family background, impact on, 135–36
  impulsivity myth, 122–23, 158
  length of relationship with partner, 125, 250
  lesbian relationships, 127–28, 248–49
  love, 124, 247

First sexual experience
    (continued)
    lust or sexual excitement,
        124, 134, 247
    partner, pressure, 124, 247
    peers, pressure from, 141–42
    place of occurrence, 125,
        247
    race differences, 126–27, 248
    reasons for, 124, 134, 247
    sex for sex alone, 134, 250
    who partner was, 125, 247–
        48
Fleiss, Heidi, 167
Francine (case study), 186
Friedrich, William, 52
Friends. *See also* Peer pressure
    puberty, discussions on, 94
    sexual decisions of adults,
        influences on, 152–54, 251
    sexual information and, 83–
        84, 114, 241, 246

G
Gagnon, John, 231
Ganz, Patricia, 236
Gertrude (case study), 128
Giovanni, Nikki, 223
Gloria (case study), 159
Goals, adolescent girls, 97–98,
    244
Gone with the Wind (film), 32
Grant, Hugh, 29
Grier, William, 94
Group sex
    frequency of practice, 161
    race differences in practice
        of, 168, 257, 258
    statistics on, 254–55
Group solidarity
    Africa, sixteenth century, 6–7
    slaves, of, 15–16
Gutman, Herbert, 17, 24

H
Harassment, sexual, 184–88,
    260–61
Hausa, 5
Healing, 228–29
    resources, 220–22
Heather (case study), 181–82
Hill, Anita, 153, 186–87
Hine, Darlene, 11–12
HIV virus. *See* AIDS or HIV
    virus
Homosexuality, messages from
    family on, 74–76, 91, 238,
    239
Human body, view of
    Africa, sixteenth century, 5–6
Hurston, Zora Neale, 35

I
Illiteracy, emancipated slaves,
    24
Impulsivity myth, 122–23, 158
Incest. *See* Abuse, sexual
Income, delayed sexual
    activities and, 135
Independence Day (film), 30
Information, resources, 220–22
Information on sex
    adolescents, 107–10
    Africa, sixteenth century,
        misinformation, 6–7
    churches and religious
        sources, 81–82, 112–14,
        246
    family life and, 68–81, 85
    friends, from, 83–84, 114,
        246
    siblings, information from,
        111–12
Institute of Social Science
    Research, 234, 235
Interracial relationships, 188–
    94

Irma (case study), 53–54
ISSR. *See* Institute of Social
    Science Research

J
Jessica (case study), 51–52,
    127
Johns Hopkins University, 136
Johnson, Virginia, 55
Jo-Jo (case study), 121–22, 125
June (case study), 145–47

K
Kanter, John, 136, 142
Kinsey, Alfred Charles
    comparison study, 169
    funding of studies, 231
    masturbation, reports on, 52
    parents, teaching children
        about sex, 68
    peer pressure, studies on,
        141–42
Kinsey Institute, 68
Knowledge of sex. *See*
    Childhood, knowledge of
    sex; Sexual knowledge
Kolodny, William, 55
Krobo society (Ghana), 7

L
"Ladylike" behavior, teachings,
    90–91, 104–5, 244
Laumann, Ed, 231
Learning about sex. *See*
    Adolescent development;
    Childhood, knowledge of
    sex
Lee, Spike, 152
Leitenberg, Harold, 54
Lesbian relationships, 163–66,
    255–56
    first sexual experience, 127–
        28, 248–49

Los Angeles Structured
    Interview, 235
Love, choices, 171–96, 258–61.
    See also Relationships,
    role in adult sexuality
    abortion, decision, 177–78,
        259–60
    African-American men,
        negative expectations
        regarding, 190–94
    contraceptives, decision to
        use, 174–76, 258–59
    decision-making process,
        173–74
    interracial relationships,
        188–94
    negative expectations about
        relationships, coping with,
        188–94
    physical abuse, coping with
        history of, 180–83
    sexual abuse, coping with
        history of, 180–83
    sexual knowledge, expansion
        of, 194–96
    sexual problems with
        primary partner, 178–80,
        260
    white men, negative
        expectations regarding,
        188–90
Lyons-Rowe, Sandra, 163

M
Madison, President James, 13
Madonna, 104, 111
Makeup, 90, 106–7, 244
Mammy stereotype, 31–32, 33,
    37
Maria (slave), 15
Marriage. *See also* Family life;
    Parents
    Africa, sixteenth century, 9

Marriage. *(continued)*
  age of, statistics, 142
  emancipated slaves, 24–25
  slaves, 19–20
Marte (case study), 164–66
Marva (case study), 185
Masai tribe, 9
Masters, William, 55
Masturbation and self-
    touching, 155–57
  Africa, sixteenth century, 5
  childhood, 48, 50–52, 64, 237
  guilt about, 252–53, 256
  messages from family on,
    63, 74, 75, 91, 238, 239
  methods of, 51, 237, 249,
    252
  race differences, 166, 256
  religious schools,
    condemnation of, 82–83
  statistics on, 128–29
Maya (case study), 194–96
Mayflower Madam, 167
McDaniels, Hattie, 32
McMillan, Terry, 152
Media
  families, African American,
    41
  goals of adolescents,
    television representations,
    98
  stereotypes of African-
    American women, 30, 35,
    40–42
Menstruation
  age of onset, 94, 242–43
  discussions on, choice of
    confidants, 94–95
Meyerowitz, Beth, 236
Michael, Robert, 231
Mickey (case study), 107–10
Middle age, sexual
    experiences, 65–66

Middle-class women
  abortion, decision to have,
    178
  delayed sexual activities, 135
Mire, Soroya, 8
Missionaries
  Africa, sixteenth century, 10,
    97
Missouri, slavery, 11–12
Mitchell-Kernan, Claudia, 235
Mo' Better Blues (film), 152
Mona (case study), 154–55
Monroe, Marilyn, 104
Morgan, Joan, 41–42
Morrison, John, 93
Morrison, Toni, 13
Mosley, Walter, 32
Multiple partners
  race differences, 250
  statistics, 133, 158, 253
Music, sexual values and
    morality, 115–16
Mutual exploratory
    experiences, children, 53,
    55–56, 238
The Myth of the Superwoman
    (Wallace), 31

N
Nakedness. *See* Nudity
Nancy (case study), 179–80
Nandi tribe, 7
National Center for Health
    Statistics, 242
National Institute of Mental
    Health, 231, 235
Newcomb, Michael, 183
Newsome, Robert, 12
"New World." *See* Slavery
NIMH. *See* National Institute
    of Mental Health
Nonconsensual sex. *See* Abuse,
    sexual; Rape

Nonmarital sex. *See*
    Extramarital affairs;
    Premarital sex
Nudity
    Africa, sixteenth century, 5–6
    messages from family on,
        74, 91, 238, 239
    slaves, 14
Nupe (Nigeria), 5
Nyakyusa society, 6

O
Oral sex
    frequency of practice, 160
    lesbian relationships, 164,
        255
    race differences in practice
        of, 168–69, 257, 258
    statistics on, 254
Orgasms
    race differences in
        achieving, 168
    statistics, 253
Our Voices, 41

P
Parents. *See also* Family life
    active role of, sexual
        responsibility and, 225
    adolescents, guidance of, 89–
        92, 94–95, 98–107, 110–11,
        245–46
    affection between, influence
        on children, 79–81, 87,
        240–41
    childhood knowledge and,
        68–81, 85, 87
    sexual decisions of adults,
        influences on, 154, 251–52
    warnings from regarding
        sex, 110–11, 245–46
Park, Peggy (case study), 99–
    103

Parmer, Pratibha, 8
Peer pressure, 83–84
    first sexual experience, 141–
        42
Penises, size of, 97
Penn, Sean, 40
Petting, 111
Possessing the Secret of Joy
    (Walker), 8
Poussaint, Alvin, 41
Pregnancy. *See also* Unwed
    mothers
    appearance, effect on, 242
    race differences, statistics,
        151
Premarital sex
    Africa, sixteenth century, 5
    messages from family on,
        74, 76–78, 91, 238, 239–40
Pride and respect, standards
    for, 107
Privacy and modesty
    Africa, sixteenth century, 5–6
    sexual experience and, 67, 72
    slaves, disrespect for, 14–15
Problems, sexual, with
    primary partner, 178–80,
        260
Promiscuous black woman,
    stereotype of, 29–31, 37,
        39–41
Prostitution, 159, 253
    race differences, 167
Puberty
    breasts, development, 51, 93,
        94, 242
    coping with, 92–94, 242
    menstruation, 94–95, 242–43
    sexuality and, 91

R
Race differences
    abortions, 151, 177, 259–60

Race differences *(continued)*
  adolescents, choice of
    confidants, 94–95
  AIDS or HIV virus,
    contracting, 151
  breast development, 93
  contraceptives, use of, 175–
    76, 251, 258–59
  diseases, sexually
    transmitted, 151, 168
  expectations regarding sex,
    96, 243
  family structure, 117
  first sexual experience,
    teenagers, 126–27, 134,
    248
  group sex, 258
  length of relationship with
    partner, 133, 250
  makeup, age allowed to
    wear, 107, 244
  masturbation, 166, 256
  menstruation, facts
    regarding, 95
  multiple partners, 250
  number of partners in
    lifetime, 166–67, 169, 256–
    57
  orgasms, achievement, 168
  pregnancy, statistics, 151
  prostitution, 167
  risk taking behavior, 167–69,
    257, 258
  stereotypes, view of, 38
Rape. *See also* Abuse, sexual
  emancipated slaves, 24
  slaves, of, 11–13, 16, 23
Rap music, 41–42
Relationships, role in adult
    sexuality, 149–70, 251–58.
    See also Love, choices
  church and religious
    sources, influence on
  ⸙ sexual decisions, 154–55

  friends, influence on sexual
    decisions, 152–54, 251
  influences on sexual
    decisions, 152–55, 251–52
  lesbian relationships, 163–66
  number of partners in
    lifetime, 166–67, 169, 256–
    57
  parents, influence on sexual
    decisions, 154, 251–52
  partners, influence on sexual
    decisions, 155
  questionnaire, 211, 218
  risky behavior, 157–62, 253–55
  role as woman, defining,
    150–52
  satisfaction, 155–57, 162–63,
    252
  sexual responsibility and,
    227–28
Religious sources. *See*
    Churches and religious
    sources
Reputation of adolescents,
    protection of, 98, 101, 119
  adolescents, 90
Residence, location
  delayed sexual activities, as
    factor in, 141
Respect, standards for, 107
Responsibility, sexual. *See*
    Sexual responsibility
Riederle, Monika, 183, 185, 187
"Right" thing, importance of
    doing
  questionnaire, 210, 218
Risk taking behaviors, 157–62,
    170, 253–55
  anal sex, 160–61, 168–69,
    254, 257
  cunnilingus, 160, 164, 168–
    69, 254, 255, 257, 258
  extramarital affairs, 162,
    168, 255, 257, 258

fellatio, 160, 168–69, 254, 257, 258

group sex, 161, 168, 254–55, 257, 258

multiple partners, 133, 158, 250, 253

oral sex, 160, 164, 168–69, 254, 255, 257, 258

prostitution, 159, 167, 253

questionnaire, 206–8, 216–17

race differences, 167–69, 257, 258

sexual abuse, influences on, 143

swapping partners, 161–62, 168, 255, 257

Rites of passage

Africa, sixteenth century, 7–9

Roberts, James, 13

Roe vs. Wade, 177

Role as woman, defining, 150–52

Romance, 146–47

Romero, Gloria, 235

Rowland, Julia, 236

Roxanne (case study), 57–61

Russell, Diana, 34

S

Sally (case study), 184

Sandra (case study), 129–32

"Sapphire" character (*Amos 'n' Andy*), 30, 35

Satisfaction, sexual, 155–57, 162–63, 252

Schools, sex education, 82–83, 89–90, 112, 241

Secrecy, childhood sexual abuse, 60

Self-esteem, sexual abuse and, 137, 238

Self image, adolescent development, 95, 118, 243

Self-touching. *See* Masturbation and self-touching

Semi (case study), 149–50, 171–73

Set It Off (film), 107

The Seven Year Itch (film), 104

Sexual abuse. *See* Abuse, sexual

Sexual arousal

children, sex play, 52–56, 237–38

Sexual behavior, study on, 231–35

Sexual development. *See specific topic*

Sexual experiences. *See also* First sexual experience

questionnaire, 204–6, 216

Sexual harassment, 184–88, 260–61

Sexual hype, 83–84, 241

Sexual knowledge. *See also* Childhood, knowledge of sex

obtaining of, and sexual responsibility, 224–25

questionnaire, 200–204, 215–16

Sexual protocol, standards for adolescent development, 105–6

Sexual responsibility

help in changing, resources, 220–22

principles of, 224–28

questionnaire, 199–220

Shana (case study), 139–40

Shannon (case study), 167

She-devil stereotype, 32–34, 37, 39–41, 80, 123

Shirley (case study), 70–71

Siblings, information on sex from, 111–12

Simpson, O. J., 153

Slavery
    beatings, 14, 15, 21
    breeding of slaves, 13
    childbearing, 12–13
    control of body, influence of
        distant past, 143–44
    coping, 22
    courtship, 17–18
    dignity and, 22
    emancipation, lack of
        change and, 22–25
    experiments on by
        physicians, 15
    family members, sexual
        contact between, 18–19
    first sexual experience, 122
    group solidarity and, 15–16
    house slaves, 16
    marriage and protection, 19–
        20
    privacy and modesty,
        disrespect for, 14–15
    psychological burden, 20–22
    rapes, 11–13, 16, 23
    role of women, preparation
        of girls for, 17–18
    secrecy regarding abuse, 21–
        22
    seventeenth century, 2
    sex as negative experience,
        11–13
Slave Testimony: Two Centuries
    of Letters, Speeches,
    Interviews and
    Autobiographies
    (Blassingame), 18
Smith, Will, 30
Sonia (case study), 67–68, 74–
    79, 82
Soul Slave (Cochran), 34
Spirituals, Negro, 15
Standards, setting of, 103–7
Steele, Claude, 42

Stereotypes of African-
    American men
    penises, size of, 97
    stud, as, 40, 180
Stereotypes of African-
    American women, 27–44
    adolescents, understanding
        of, 117
    belief in by African-
        Americans, 38, 43–44
    early sexual activity, 48
    hypersexuality, 23, 98, 101
    The Mammy, 31–32, 33, 37
    media, in, 30, 35, 40–42
    permissive stereotype, 29–31
    she-devil, 32–34, 37, 39–41,
        80, 123
    threat, 42
    virginity and, 48
    white women, views of, 38
    workhorse, 35, 36–37, 80
Stone, Sharon, 104
Support, resources, 220–22
Swapping partners
    race differences in practice
        of, 168, 257
    reasons for not risking, 161–
        62
    statistics on, 255

T
Television
    adolescent goals,
        representations of, 98
    Amos 'n' Andy (telecast), 30,
        35
    Black Entertainment
        Television, 41
    family life, 1920s to 1970s,
        41
Thomas, Clarence, 153, 187
Thomas, William, 23
Threat, stereotyped, 42

Trauma
  sexual abuse, coping with,
    58–61, 180–83, 238
Tubman, Harriet, 44
Tucker, Belinda, 235

U
Underground railroad, 15
Unwed mothers
  adolescents, 129–32
  religion and, 113–14
  sexually abused adolescents,
    137–39

V
Values and sexual
    responsibility, 225
Virginia (case study), 159
Virginity. *See also* First sexual
    experience
  stereotyping and, 48

W
Waiting to Exhale (film), 152
Walker, Alice, 8
Wallace, Michelle, 31
Wanda (case study), 65–66

Warnings from parents
  sex, regarding, 110–11, 245–
    46
  sexual abuse, 78–79, 240
Warrior Marks (Parmer and
    Walker), 8
Washington, University of, 137
Wealth, factor in delayed
    sexual activities, 134–35
West, Carolyn, 31
White, Deborah, 13, 14
White men, relationships with.
    See Interracial
    relationships
White women. *See also* Race
    differences
  sexual practices of, 166–68,
    256–57
  stereotypes, view of, 38
Williams, Isaac D., 18
Workhorse stereotype, 35, 36–
    37, 80
Wyatt Sexual History
    Questionnaire, 235, 236

Z
Zelnick, 136, 142

About the Author

Dr. Gail Elizabeth Wyatt, the first African-American woman to be licensed as a psychologist in California, is a professor of psychiatry and biobehavioral sciences at the University of California, Los Angeles, and Associate Director of Behavioral Science Research, Education and Training for the UCLA AIDS Institute.

Dr. Wyatt is a trained sex therapist and a diplomate and a founding fellow of the American Board of Sexologists. She has a private practice that focuses on sex-related and relationship issues. She has consulted with world-renowned sex researchers and scholars in the fields of anthropology, sociology, child abuse, sexual assault, domestic violence, adolescent pregnancy, and HIV and AIDS. She has been recognized for distinguished contributions in research on public policy by the American Psychological Association (APA), received an honorary doctorate of letters from the California School of Professional Psychology, and the Carolyn Sherif Award from the Division of the Psychology of Women of the American Psychological Association, was recognized for distinguished contributions to research by the Society for the Study of Ethnicity and Culture of the APA, and the Association of Black Psychologists has recognized her scholarship.

Dr. Wyatt has published more than 80 journal articles and book chapters on research conducted in the United States and in Jamaica. She is co-author of the book *Sexual Abuse and Consensual Sex* and has co-edited two books, *The Afro-American Family: Assessment, Treatment and Research Issues* and *The Lasting Effects of Child Sexual Abuse*. She volunteers her services in the community, has given hundreds of lectures around the world, and is a frequent guest on radio and television.

Dr. Wyatt, and avid skier and tennis player, has been married for 32 years to Lewis Wyatt, Jr., an obstetrician/gynecologist. They have two children, Lance and Lacey, and a son-in-law, Gavin Henriques. The family shares a commitment to health care, to the community, and to each other.